Amped

Amped

How Big Air, Big Dollars, and a
New Generation Took Sports to the Extreme

David Browne

BLOOMSBURY

06 Mays
3+T
2495(1385)

Published by Bloomsbury, New York and London
Distributed to the trade by Holtzbrinck Publishers

All papers used by Bloomsbury are natural, recyclable
products made from wood grown in well-managed
forests. The manufacturing processes conform to
the environmental regulations of the country of origin.

Library of Congress Cataloging-in-Publication Data

Browne, David, 1960–
Amped : how big air, big dollars, and a new generation took sports to the
extreme / David Browne.
p. cm.
Includes bibliographical references.
ISBN 1–58234–317–9 (hc)
1. Extreme sports—Economic aspects—United States. I. Title.
GV749.7.B76 2004
796.04'6—dc22
2004004822

First U.S. Edition 2004

1 3 5 7 9 10 8 6 4 2

Typeset by Hewer Text Ltd, Edinburgh
Printed in the United States of America
by Quebecor World Fairfield

For Maeve Rose,
who will not be allowed to attempt any of these activities
without express written permission (and a helmet)

contents

preface

O n   o n e   o f my first research trips for this book, I ventured to a newly
opened skatepark in Greenport, a town of winter-lashed homes
and waterfront businesses on Long Island's North Fork. On this late-
winter afternoon, roughly two dozen skateboarders, BMX bikers, and
in-liners were practicing grinds, kickturns, box-jumps, and drop-ins;
from a distance, the sight resembled a jumping-bean convention. Taking
it in while huddled on aluminum bleachers and sipping warm beverages
were the riders' parents, and I joined two of them, Bob and Phyllis, who
were keeping watch on their ten-year-old son Timothy. The couple ran
an auto-body repair shop an hour and a half's drive away and, in a
startling indication of the newfound acceptance of these sports, were
completely supportive of their son's seemingly risky pastime. At Timothy's request, they had bought him a skateboard for a Christmas
present; for Easter, he received a new pair of skate shoes.

"I don't see a lot of the kids he knows joining teams," Bob said.
Behind him, the baseball diamond of the local high school sat vacant.

"It's much more sophisticated now, isn't it?" Phyllis added, checking out the other, older riders in the park. "The kids seem nice.
Look—they're giving each other tips." She observed Timothy, who
wore knee and elbow pads and a helmet. "That was pretty good, the
way he was going back and forth a few times," she said. Bob, who
wore a Mets jacket, nodded.

After an hour, Timothy skated over to them. He had short, light-brown hair and an open, outgoing manner, and his red sweatshirt bore a snowboarding logo. "My wrist hurts," he said, a little surprised. Pulling off his gear, he said, "I can't feel my shins. Or my butt."

His friend Dylan, who was smaller and wore glasses, critiqued the park. "This is all vert," he squeaked confidently. "But where I live, we have street skating."

"What does that *mean?*" Phyllis said, dumbfounded.

"I can't feel my wrist," Timothy muttered.

I asked what they preferred to call these sports—extreme, action, alternative?

"Wiping-out sports," Timothy said, grinning.

Then I asked why they pursued these activities if they were so bruised. "It's more action," Dylan said. "You get more hurt playing football." He said he had wrecked his first board while attempting a kickflip down the stairs at his school. "I put my foot through it and broke it," he explained.

"They *let* you do that?" Phyllis gasped.

"Yeah, at high school," Dylan said. "But not at elementary school."

"We can go down the stairs at our school," Timothy said.

"After it's closed, right?" Phyllis asked, concerned.

"Yeah, but they don't see us," her son explained.

"I don't wanna *know*," Phyllis said, shaking her head. "It's a whole other language."

She was right, of course: It was another language, not to mention another world—a parallel sports universe with its own stars, history, language, culture, and sensibility. It was a world, it turned out, with which I had had a few brushes over the years. As a scrawny preteen in New Jersey who had little interest in joining teams (especially after having dealt with the humiliation of being chosen last for one basketball squad), I eventually tried my hand at skateboarding—which ended when winter arrived and, housebound, I accidentally rammed my board into one of my sister's feet as she stepped into the hallway. During the same period, I practiced wheelies on my banana-seat bike; many years later, I took a brief, doomed stab at in-line skating. As much as I tried, though, I was not especially adept at these activities, perhaps because I am not a particularly fearless person. I have a vivid childhood memory of trying to dive into a friend's backyard pool. Afraid of belly flopping or injuring myself, I stood paralyzed on the board for what felt like hours until finally my friend's father threw up his hands and walked away. I never did learn.

I wasn't meant for a life of such experiences, but others clearly were. As the decades rolled on, I watched, fascinated, as skateboarding and similar anti-team sports grew in scope and popularity. Evidently, a sizable portion of the public was rejecting traditional sports—and the values they entailed—and replacing them with physical activities that stressed the individualistic and the idiosyncratic. I saw and heard about the increased levels of participation in skateboarding, snowboarding, and bicycle motocross; I noticed the stream of movies, TV shows, and commercials that utilized their imagery. I watched as snowboarding was featured in the Olympics. I read about skate-shoe companies posting gains of $50 million. As a pop-music writer by day, I observed action-sport exhibitions on the sidelines at rock festivals. By the nineties, the so-called "extreme" sports world—which also came to include freestyle motocross riders, wakeboarders, mountain boarders, downhill skateboarders, snowmobile racers, street lugers, downhill mountain bikers, wall climbers, and any number of other, more questionable activities—was not only thriving but had become a vast, valid, and significant community and industry. It comprised millions of participants and raked in millions of dollars, and like the punk rock with which it identified, it was an irascible, unconventional subculture continually grappling with issues of integrity and identity, especially in the wake of its increasing acceptance.

Eventually, my own anxieties eased somewhat, and I learned how to kayak and pilot a mountain bike off-road. Still, my victories were nothing compared to the continuing numbers who plunged down ramps or slopes or flew into the air on their bikes and motorcycles. If only for myself, I wanted to know why anyone would willingly do such things. I wanted to learn about the iconoclastic spirit that fostered this world and what it said about the culture and the generation behind it. This, I felt, was a story as much about the riders and their worldview as the sports themselves. Who were these people, and why did they take to half-pipes and isolated mountain trails over football fields and basketball courts? How much more ubiquitous would it all become? Questions such as those eventually led to this book.

In search of this world, I immersed myself in the community as much as an admitted outsider could. My journey stretched out to nearly three years and took in cross-country trips and interviews with over a hundred athletes, business executives, sports journalists, and pioneers. I tagged along on a bus tour with preeminent skateboarders and spent time at an extreme summer camp. I sunburned myself at BMX events and was coated with dust and exhaust fumes at motocross contests. I attended winter and summer editions of ESPN's X Games. I hiked up mountain trails in twenty-degree weather to watch snowboarders and found myself unable to take notes when my pens froze. I stood alongside moshers at skate-and-music festivals. I climbed atop massive motocross dirt mounds. I ventured to the offices of the companies that make equipment and beverages aimed at this market and then sampled "extreme" deodorants, soft drinks, and razor blades, some of which did the trick and some of which were too harsh in taste or aroma. I tried on many different brands and styles of BMX and skateboard shoes before realizing my preferences (less technical and padded, more streamlined and lighter). I watched hundreds of videos and DVDs. I spent hours at skateparks, observing and talking to amateurs and weekend riders. I refrained from using the word *extreme,* which, I quickly learned, was verboten. Along the way, I decided to exclude any of what could be called adventure sports—rock and wall climbing, skydiving, and other activities lumped in with the board sports—and stick to skateboarding, snowboarding, BMX, and freestyle motocross in order to give each the space and depth it merited. The chapters were then arranged in roughly chronological order to give readers a sense of what a fairly typical year in the life of this universe was like.

Finally, to complete my education and inform the book as much as possible, I took to the boards myself. At a Quiksilver store in Park City, Utah, I bought $95 waterproof pants, which hung so loose on me that I felt I should be rapping. When the blond saleswoman learned I would be receiving my first lesson the next day, she just smiled and said, "You're going to be so sore." Later, at another store where I bought wrist guards, hip pads, and goggles, I heard the same comment. Neither remark soothed my nerves; nor did the moment when, at a local resort, I signed away my life—literally—by putting my signature on a form that didn't hold anyone liable in case I died trying. Finally, I found myself jamming on two, bulky space-suit boots and trudging into the snow, a fifty-four-inch snowboard under my arm. I felt ready for a trip to Mars.

I was part of a class—and, to be kind, the slow-learning part of one. My respect for snowboarders tripled as soon as I pushed off and took my first slow ride down the snowy hill—and involuntarily kept putting my untethered foot in the wrong position on the board. I felt awkward and horribly uncoordinated, especially compared to the riders whooshing past me. I fell numerous times, thanking the inventors of wrist guards and hip pads each time. The instructor told me I needed to relax and let go, which, like coming to a stop on the board by using one's toes, was proving to be more difficult than I thought. After several attempts, though, I was finally able to glide down the slope, bending slightly forward to turn; to stop, I discovered the heel side was more comfortable for me. For a few moments I felt some of the rush, the sense of unencumbered freedom, to be gained from snowboarding. And yes, the store clerks were right: About twenty-four hours later, the ache—in my upper arms, shoulders, and thighs—set in.

Because I had done it before, skateboarding proved to be somewhat easier. I began with the laborious process of buying a board—selecting the proper one by standing on a wheel-less deck for the right feel and good action and, just as important, the best sick artwork—before choosing from one of many styles of wheels and ball bearings. (I opted for conservative cruising wheels as opposed to ones for half-pipe drop-ins.) Wearing skate shoes, cargo shorts, a rock-and-roll T-shirt, and an old bike helmet, I then ventured to New York's Chelsea Piers. With the help of a patient instructor named Gustavo, I learned to push off with the correct foot, place the other foot on the board at the right moment, and shift my body weight while continuing to stare straight ahead. Right away, I felt the advancement in skate technology that had taken place since my childhood. My old board had metal wheels, no grip tape, and no kicktail; in essence, it was a death trap. My new one was bigger and made for a smoother ride. Although the idea of falling on pavement wasn't at all appealing, I rolled back and forth across a lot, relishing the gently bobbing sensation and the raw, strangely intoxicating sound of polyurethane connecting with asphalt. After determining how to attain the right balance, I even managed a kick-turn (jamming down on the tail in order to move in another direction). I was beginning to learn to ride and curve my body with the board, but reality always returned, either when I fell off the board or when a kid walked by, looked at me, and said to Gustavo, "Learning how to skateboard?"

The following day, I practiced on my own at an empty basketball court near Riverside Park in upper Manhattan. I wasn't sure if I was allowed there—would my riding scuff up the surface?—so I kept on the lookout for police. As I shoved off, carefully crouched on the board, and rolled from one basketball hoop to the other, I felt vaguely renegade. I was experiencing another sensation associated with this world—the illicit thrill of being somewhere you're not supposed to be, doing something you're not supposed to be doing. I also tasted the focus and clarity that come with the sports. I didn't care how silly I must have looked to the Hispanic kids hanging out nearby. I knew I might never completely master this language; I would never be a Timothy or Dylan, much less a Tony Hawk. But it was a start, both for the book and my own understanding. For those already immersed in this world, I hope *Amped* adds to their intimate knowledge of it. For aliens like me, I hope it helps illuminate something about the men and women who rolled into this community—who they are, and why they stayed.

1 . PROLOGUE
the awards show

As the car services and stretch limousines began picking them up at their hotels and motoring them to a sprawling compound north of Hollywood, they knew this much: Everything was the same, and yet everything was different.

On one hand, they were still doing what they had always done, indoors or outdoors, on glorious, sun-baked mornings or brisk, jacket-required evenings sprinkled with rain or snow. They would step onto a skateboard with scratched wheels and chewed-up edges and willingly tip over into the curved plywood of a half-pipe, where they would weave back and forth until they flew back up the wall and into the air. Or they would tighten the bindings on a snowboard, shove off, and speedily glide along powder until they reached a ramp and soared up its side. Or they might straddle a stunt bicycle and, with every muscle in their calves, pedal toward a pyramid-shaped box with the hope of soaring over it and, while in the sky, spin their handlebars completely around. Even though some of them were professionals who took home six-figure salaries unimaginable when these sports were conceived, many still practiced in the same places they always had: in drained pools and alleyways, on snow-covered bluffs, in backyards, or in parks that had been specially designed for them.

When they were teenagers, they had started doing these sports— and "sports" they were, in their minds, not cheap stunts—because they were pleasurable and exhilarating. If they completed their moves correctly, they would attain a rush equivalent to an entire game of touchdowns or basketball dunks condensed into less than a minute. They were not unilaterally opposed to team sports and could kick a soccer ball or skid into home plate about as well as the next person. Ultimately, though, something about that traditional world—its game and practice schedules, its coaches, its uniformity, its *uniforms*—did not speak to them. So, at one point or another, they took a stab at these alternative sports. Without a moment's hesitation, they could remember the precise moment at which they first pushed off on a skateboard or snowboard or hopped onto a stunt (BMX) bicycle or motorcycle.

Then as now, the decision to partake in these sports was theirs alone; rarely did their parents push them into it. If they stumbled and weren't able to complete a move, it was up to them to get up and try again until they nailed it. If at the end of their session they were bruised and bloodied—or if they had inflicted injury upon their bones, heads, backs, wrists, ankles, or spleens—they only had themselves to blame. No matter which of the sports they practiced, it was down to them and their bike, board, or motorcycle—no tryouts, no team on which to rely, no instructor staring down their every move. They would not have had it any other way. Through their choice of maneuvers, routines, clothing, even the stickers slapped onto their gear, they had defined themselves and found their voice.

Yet for all the constants, something had changed, which they glimpsed as soon as the limos arrived at their destination, the Universal Amphitheater in Universal City. Given a choice, many of the athletes would not have been here. They were not averse to parties; letting off steam came as naturally to them as breathing. But they didn't have a choice, not really, not when a division of the Walt Disney Company and its cable sports network, ESPN, was presenting an awards ceremony to honor them and had flown many of them out to Los Angeles for the occasion. Had someone once told them they would be vying for statuettes for what they'd once done for kicks and a few hundred dollars, they would have laughed, incredulous. The evening would serve as both a wrap-up of the preceding year of professional action sports and an unofficial kickoff to the one that lay ahead.

Squinting in the late afternoon sun, they stepped out of the limos and onto the green AstroTurf—"a hip spin on the traditional preshow ceremony," announced the organizers—that had been rented for the occasion. They had just enough time to soak up the football-field brightness of the carpet when they saw the gauntlet that awaited them—the line of everyday people staring at them from behind sagging velvet ropes, and the even longer line of reporters and cameramen grasping microphones and clipboards and jockeying for position.

The amphitheater was part of City Walk, the sprawling, neon-rung outdoor shopping mall. Had they strolled through it beforehand, the athletes would have glimpsed other signs that something in the universe had shifted in their direction. They would have witnessed groups of boys gathered around a vendor selling miniature motorized skateboards for $19.99. In a storefront window, they would have spied a large poster of Danny Kass, who just months before had won a silver medal in men's half-pipe snowboarding at the Olympics. That one of their sports was part of such an august global athletic competition was itself hard to grasp. After walking past the film-memorabilia store, the Chinese restaurant, and the franchise restaurant, they would have arrived at a movie theater showing an oversize-screen IMAX movie about them. One eatery advertised "extreme dining," but given their disdain for the first of those words, there was little chance any of them would have stepped inside.

The previous year, at the first of these so-called ESPN Action Sports and Music Awards, the media largely stayed away. But in another sign of changing times, such was not the case tonight. As soon as the athletes began strolling up the carpet, with expressions that ranged from bemused to startled, they were pulled aside for interviews with television reporters. The phalanx, which included CNN, all the syndicated entertainment shows, and at least one crew from Japan, extended to the last threads of the carpet. Some reporters had few clues as to whom they were about to interview or what they looked like, so a slew of publicists, gripping clipboards and constantly speaking to one another by way of combat-ready headsets, distributed a four-page, double-sided pamphlet listing the names and photos of each athlete. The reporters clutched these sheets as if they were rare scrolls; no one wanted to confuse one of the nominees for BMX Rider of the Year with the Feat of the Year finalist who had qualified by doing a skateboard move they could not even envision.

Across from the media, on the other side of the carpet, were club kids in flower-print blouses and leather jackets, and older men and women in plaid shirts, recruited by Seatfiller.com as a way to make sure all the amphitheater seats were occupied. Once they had taken their positions, the fillers weren't always sure whom they were supposed to be cheering. "Who's that?" one asked, referring to Dave Mirra, the king of freestyle BMX and tonight a chiseled figure in brown leather jacket and short, gelled hair. But it was a night out, and they would cheer when they were told. (They had also been told they would be arrested if they attempted to jump onstage during the ceremony, so they would only get so excited.) Behind them, a DJ discharged bass-heavy hip-hop and announced each athlete's name as he or she arrived—like tall, telephone-pole-lean Brazilian skateboarder Bob Burnquist, who wore baggy blue jeans, sneakers, and a short-sleeve gray T-shirt, topped by a backward baseball cap. In another indication that this telecast would be unlike most others, the seatfillers were better dressed than Burnquist, and unlike him, none were clutching a skateboard with dried blood on their knuckles.

The scene had been much calmer during rehearsals the day before. Technicians had scurried about testing the sound system and lights; banners trumpeting Mountain Dew, the evening's major sponsor, were being hung. The time came to run through the part of the show in which the Bones Brigade, the innovative skateboard team of the eighties, would be reunited. If these sports had a Beatles, the Bones Brigade were it; everyone seemed to own a battered VHS cassette of one of the long-form Bones videos that, in the early days of VCRs, had introduced new tricks, attitudes, and fashion to a generation of skaters. The tapes were cherished artifacts, and the more worn, the prouder the owner. In the years since, the team's best-known members—Tony Hawk, Steve Caballero, Lance Mountain, Tommy Guerrero, Mike McGill, Rodney Mullen, and former skater Stacy Peralta, who had directed the videos—had become icons to one degree or another. Now weathered, crow's-feet-eyed men in their thirties in wrinkled T-shirts and jeans, they ambled onto the stage in the empty hall to practice reading their cue cards for the Skateboarder of the Year award. "We'd like to present the award for goatherder of the year," cracked Guerrero, whose horn-rimmed glasses, goatee, and black, curly hair gave him the look of a street-corner mad scientist. The others yucked it up beside him. They were doing their best to take it seriously, but sometimes it was hard. Another veteran of another sport, a small, hard-faced BMX rider named Rick Thorne, had been scampering around like a hyperactive eight-year-old. Grabbing a script out of the hands of a peer who would be introducing the Red Hot Chili Peppers, he began reading it out loud, mocking its attempts at hip lingo: "Through all the *funk* and all the *love* . . ." He laughed, as if wondering how much someone had been paid to write this material.

By showtime, though, the mood was undeniably more intense as the skaters, snowboarders, and bikers, along with their predecessors and successors, began making their way down the carpet. When word filtered down that Hawk had arrived, the reporters jumped to attention. Although he carried himself without airs—his face retained a deadpan, seen-it-all expression even during the most stressful situations—Hawk unofficially ruled this community. Not fifteen or so years before, he had been a string-beany blond pip-squeak from Southern California shooting up half-pipes alongside older, more experienced pros. Hawk had had his good times and bad since then, but he was now a million-dollar industry unto himself—his name and image plastered on video games and skateboard decks and cropping up in snack-food commercials. If the public associated any face with these sports, it was Hawk's, complete with his now brown, conservatively cut hair. Reporters scrambled to talk to him, and Hawk, ever the accommodating ambassador, stopped to chat with anyone who asked.

The situation was manageable until the arrival of Carmen Electra, the cheese-TV starlet, and her beau, goateed guitar stud Dave Navarro. "Carmen! Right here!" yelled the photographers. With that, any sense of orderliness and informality vanished. More and more rock stars and B-level actresses—even the little person from the *Austin Powers* movies—began popping out of limos and exciting the press contingent. Lime-green-carpet gridlock took over, making it nearly impossible to turn around, much less greet anyone.

Into this increasingly buzzing swarm entered Danny Kass and his fellow snowboard medalists, Ross Powers and J.J. Thomas, who had won the gold and bronze, respectively. Few in their sports could top the strange year they had had. The three had won the men's half-pipe competition at the Olympics, marking the first time the United States had swept a Winter Games category since 1956, for figure skating. "And they said snowboarding was a fad—*ha ha!*" barked the DJ. Kass, the most audacious and punk rock of the three, had donned a blue pinstripe suit with black sneakers—one lace united—and a gray

T-shirt bedecked with a tan tie. On his face was the bemused smirk he seemed to carry around at all times.

At first, Kass looked calm, cool, and relatively collected for someone who had rushed over to the event after a quick shower at his hotel. But when he was next spotted, a half hour of carpet time later, he didn't look the same. "Hey—you guys having another fame moment?" someone yelled at him and his fellow snowboarders.

"Yeah, this is *crazy*," Kass muttered. By now, his tie was over his head, his cap was crooked to the side. The smirk had been wiped away, and he looked overwhelmed.

Inside the amphitheater, with its ushers, security force, and five thousand red plastic seats, the invitees were again confronted with a new world order about which they had only fantasized. Awards shows in Los Angeles seemed to take place weekly, but tonight, the front rows were reserved not for movie stars, directors, and producers but for Hawk; Tony Alva, who had virtually invented aerial skateboarding in the seventies and was one of its first rock-style stars; Kelly Clark, who had won a gold medal at the Olympics in the women's half-pipe snowboarding division; and braided, part-Hawaiian motorcycle stunt rider Clifford Adoptante, who sat in the same section as model Rachel Hunter. The sight amounted to a parallel universe in which these athletes were celebrated, not shunned or derided.

Granted, certain aspects of their work had remained intact. Skateboards still had the same inherent structure conceived decades before: a pressed-wood deck with a metal truck beneath that held four polyurethane wheels. (The steel wheels of the sport's early days had thankfully been relegated to the dustbins.) The boards cost ten times more than they did when they were first introduced in the sixties; the manufacturing and parts had become sturdier and more intricate; and the tricks were off the hook compared with the early days of handstands and similarly genteel moves. At one time, it would have been impossible to conceive of a kickflip, in which the skater not only ollied (jettisoned into the air by slamming on the tail of the board) but flipped the board 360 degrees beneath him in midair. These were moves the rock-and-roll riders of the Santa Monica seventies known as the Z-Boys had only imagined in their wildest dreams. But at its core, skating, whether done on suburban blocks, on a half-pipe, or down a handrail in front of the nearest school, was fundamentally the same: It still came down to skater, board, chosen terrain, and a seemingly endless array of tricks.

The miniature bicycles used for BMX, or bicycle motocross, had improved much in the way skateboards had. When the bikes were first manufactured in the seventies, they had fewer spokes, and the brake wiring at the time (since streamlined) made it hard to spin the handlebar around in a full circle. They were less rugged and also less expensive then; these days, it was possible to spend over a thousand dollars for a top-of-the-line model. But BMX was still BMX: one bike, one rider, two pedals, a series of ramps or wedges, and the rider's eternal challenge of staying on that bike as it flew up and over those obstacles. (Another factor remained the same as well: Certain skate-park owners still banned them or chased them away.) Freestyle motocross—the art of jumping on a motorcycle, ripping up a ramp and skyward, and attempting such tricks as throwing one leg or another over the side of the bike and back again—was a relatively new addition to the alternative-sports ranks, having emerged from the racing scene. For such a young sport, though, motocross was already challenging the others in terms of crowd attendance; some were referring to it as the new NASCAR. But despite the sudden attention being paid to it, its appeal to the riders remained the same: one motorcycle, one rider, one engine making a beeline for a ramp or a sand dune before thrusting into the sky, then one full-on, raging party afterward.

Starting with its design, the snowboard had endured the most radical permutations. It had begun as a kid's toy, but gradually, thanks to a raft of innovators, the board had been transformed into a hefty slab the size of a giant's tongue depressor. Inspired, as were the BMX boys, by the original skateboarders, who in turn owed their moves to the California surfers of the Kennedy years, snowboarders were going bigger than ever; the phrase *big air* took on an entirely different definition when one watched a rider on a snowy half-pipe shoot a dozen or more feet into a crisp winter gust and then turn himself into a human pretzel. Snowboarding had ripened into the most mainstream and respectable of these sports: Both the Olympics and most of the ski resorts that had once banned the activity were now openly welcoming its riders.

Of course, the riders preferred to think of themselves as slopeside mavericks, and so did the disgruntled skiers with whom they would come into close contact on those same hills. This proud air of disrepute was another aspect of the collective action-sport universe unaffected by the passage of time. The punk rock of the sports world, skateboarding, snowboarding, motocross, and BMX were not quite respectable and would perhaps never be. No matter how many corporate tie-ins were struck, no matter how interested future Olympics became in other aspects of their universe, the skaters, bikers, and boarders were still accustomed to being greeted by the sneers of pedestrians, the suspicious looks of the local police, the shouts of security guards followed by the barking of guard dogs, the disdainful glances of the men and women in business suits who saw these overgrown boys ride by on the street and could not understand what they were doing. Those perceptions never seemed to fluctuate, and the new-style athletes had grown accustomed to being seen as pariahs.

Yet the changes around all the riders were manifold. Their activities were now dubbed "action sports" (or, to others, "extreme" sports), they were now *called* "athletes," and they had "seasons" much like mainstream ball-and-stick sports. The ones who had stuck with skating, biking, or boarding long after their childhood friends had taken day jobs found that, if they were lucky and had enough talent and made the right connections, corporate sponsors would help them earn a decent living. From their sponsors and agents, they had also heard the statistics that were both pleasing and hard to grasp. For instance, either ten or twelve million people (depending on the source) had skateboarded at least once, up 73 percent in just three years. That figure, it was said, was precisely one million more than for participation in baseball. Add in about six million professional, amateur, and weekend snowboarders and a couple million BMXers, and the days when they would know everyone in the skatepark or on the slopes were distant memories. It was also said that 25 percent fewer kids were tossing baseballs around the diamonds than they had years before, and that participation in team sports, while still formidable, had dropped to 54 percent. Even standard, on-road bicycling was slowing down, for which they were responsible, too. Every time they turned on their TVs, they stumbled upon yet another ad featuring a skateboarder or snowboarder. Whenever they dropped by their local supermarket, they saw another product with the word *extreme* plastered on it. Each passing month, they heard about another new movie in the works that would attempt to depict their world on the big screen.

Such statistics were gratifying to hear, but they signified something larger and more important. To the riders, the numbers proved they had been onto something all along; they weren't the freaks, losers, stoners, or slackers so many locals or classmates had thought they were. A ringing cell phone or a new batch of e-mail could bring news of another offer from another major company to endorse anything from food to gear to deodorant. ("Sweet," many of them would say, one of numerous examples of the specialized lingo that had developed in their community.) At times it was difficult to keep their priorities straight, especially when they were approached to promote a product

they might not normally use. The money wasn't the problem—
everyone, they agreed, had to make a living—as was the issue of
integrity and credibility. The advertisements had to be executed
correctly, based on certain standards, or else the riders could easily
tumble into laughingstocks. In that regard, they were now dealing
with a dark side some had not expected. They saw themselves on
television, but not merely on ESPN: Footage of their tricks was
popping up on sensationalistic, believe-it-or-not TV shows that
normally aired segments on cutesy animal tricks and people who
covered their bodies in checkerboard-style tattoos. They cringed at
the thought of seeing their own accomplishments reduced to cartoonish caricatures, and they resented being lumped in with stunt acts and
freaks, not to mention skydivers, bungee jumpers, or rock climbers. In
their own eyes, they were as much athletes as the ballplayers in the
nearest baseball stadium. All they could do was keep reminding
themselves why they had been drawn to these sports in the first
place—the rush they felt when they combined several tricks into one
routine, the sense of creative opportunities, or the simple thrill of
doing something no one else had done before. As long as they
continued to balance their outer adult with their inner child, they
assumed everything would stay on track.

At precisely seven-thirty P.M., the houselights dimmed, the spotlights
began to oscillate frenetically, the kids from Seatfiller.com were
herded into a mosh pit in front of the stage, and the second annual
ESPN Action Sports and Music Awards commenced. From his seat in
the middle of the theater, Chad DiNenna glanced around and took in
his surroundings. Tall and chunky, with a head of curly, brown hair
that could have made him pass for actor John C. Reilly's more
traditionally handsome brother, DiNenna had been part of this
community for many years. He had worked for *Transworld Skateboarding,* one of the many slablike, advertising-crammed magazines

that catered to this audience, and was now the co-owner and cofounder of Nixon, the watch company of choice for those in what Madison Avenue would call the extreme-sports market. Regardless of the outgoing message on his cell phone ("Leave a message, mother-*fucker!*"), he was well-liked and respected within the community. Tonight, he had dressed for the occasion with black slacks and a long-sleeved, black dress shirt, topped with a pair of black skate sneakers. "None of us get dressed up like this very often, so we have to take advantage of it," he said, shrugging down at his sneakers.

The show started with a literal bang: the decidedly unsubtle metallic throb of Static-X, whose guitarist was so stringy and pale it looked as if his guitar were propping *him* up. At one time, the music they made—a relentless, harsh, amelodic rivet-gun of sound— would have been relegated to fringe status, but this new style of metal, which took some of its rhythmic accents from hip-hop, was now the standard-bearer in mainstream rock. Then, from the back of the theater, out marched Xzibit, the short, strapping rapper with braids and rippling-biceps arms. "Come on, y'all, welcome to the *future!*" he screamed as he began stalking down the aisle toward the stage. Xzibit had a blunt, choppy way with rhymes, which perfectly suited the musical clobber Static-X ground out behind him. This fusion of rap and metal had taken over the pop charts at the same time the sports had reached a new level of mass popularity, and it was not uncommon to enter a skatepark and hear Static-X, or one of the dozens of bands who sounded like them, shredding the PA system.

The host for the evening, smirky blond actor and comedian Jay Mohr, appeared onstage to welcome everyone to the ceremony— "fueled by Mountain Dew!" he added, thrusting a devil's-horn hand gesture into the air. Over the past decade, Dew's parent company, Pepsi, had invested millions to convert the blossoming audience for these sports into fans of its product. The evening's other corporate overseer, ESPN, had also successfully tapped into this demographic. Around the time of the first Mountain Dew "extreme" ad, the country's leading sports network had discovered that skateboarding, BMX, even bungee jumping, would enable it to attract a youth market craved by advertisers. The athletes knew well how important ESPN was to them and how televised events such as the network's now established X Games had broadcast their names, images, and tricks to the masses, leading to varying degrees of fame and fortune. If they wanted to make a career of this, they had little choice but to see where companies like ESPN took them. Yet they still griped about the kind of money they were making compared to the millions they presumed the network was raking in from advertisers, and even the idea of competition irked them: Some of them did not want to feel as if they were playing baseball or basketball, two of ESPN's biggest franchises.

From his seat, DiNenna looked on, curious to see how his community and its activities would be portrayed. "It's cool to see it get respect, but it's hard to see it get compromised," he said, taking in the unfolding spectacle. "When you become like rock stars, it changes your focus. It changes why you do what you do. I mean, I still wear my skate sneakers, but . . ." He shrugged, and his voice trailed off. "You need to compromise if you want to go on the ride."

In 1989, DiNenna, then a teenager from Westlake Village, California, was chosen as one of Sunkist's "top five trendsetting teens in America." Even then his candor was refreshing. "We're not trendy— there is nothing outrageous about us," he told a reporter at a press conference announcing the contest winners. Eventually, he had gone to work for a surf shop before ending up in the advertising department of *Transworld Skateboarding*, where his affable, easygoing manner fit in well. Along with his partner Andy Laats, a graduate of Stanford Business School and a former employee of Burton, the dominant snowboard manufacturer, DiNenna had started Nixon in

1998. Between them, DiNenna and Laats had only five grand, but with the help of private, adventurous backers—"angel investors"—they managed to cobble together enough to secure office space and start-up fees. When it came to choosing a company name, they preferred a moniker that did not conjure images of surfing or skating; they needed one, DiNenna said, that was "pretty much meaningless that we could build the meaning into. We thought Nixon did a good job of just being a name that didn't have a lot of connotations to it." For the new, emerging teen generation, called Gen Y or the Millennial Generation, the name of the thirty-seventh president of the United States, who had resigned in disgrace over three decades before, was about as insignificant as it got.

Numerous well-known action-sport professionals, such as Hawk and Burnquist, were among those who wore the watches and appeared in ads as part of the Nixon team. "Skaters make good money, but they don't have a good watch to wear," DiNenna explained as the stage was prepared for the presentation of the first award. "It's like a little community, and I just make watches for my community." He added that the jewelry was not intended simply for skate sessions. "They have to be able to wear them when they go out at night, and it has to have style. They want kids to look at their watch and say, 'Oh, you skate?'" The watches were also designed for durability: According to Nixon ad copy, the Super Rover featured "a high-end chronograph that you can get down and dirty with."

"You can beat the hell out of them," DiNenna said. "If a guy throws down a watch once and it breaks, he'll drop it." Neither the watch nor the image came cheap, though. Nixon products were priced as high as $300, with the more expensive models including barometers for snowboarding. "It's an industry built on kids," DiNenna, who was thirty-one, continued. "We haven't grown up. I mean, we've grown up in a sense, but it's still an industry built on kids. Other people dropped skateboarding years ago, but we just kept doing it."

His was just one of many grassroots companies that had organically emerged from these sports. There were now dozens upon dozens of homegrown businesses that made sneakers, snowboard boots, boards, bikes, and long-form videos of footage of the athletes at work and play. The trick was staying core—retaining their connection to the kids and the street—while growing as a business. Those like DiNenna worked hard at having it both ways, having seen too many endemic businesses overshoot their goals by, for instance, selling their products in shopping malls. In so doing, they had alienated the core market and watched, helplessly, as their sales and status took a slam. No company wanted to experience the same stumble, and every day brought a new challenge in maintaining that eternal balancing act.

Nixon had begun with a mere four watch models; now, a few years later, the company had over forty, and DiNenna was the boss of thirty-one people in their offices in Encinitas, near the beach. Employees were allowed to surf or skate during lunch hours, but DiNenna also knew he had a large company (including a seven-person satellite office in France) to run. "It's weird," he said. "There are days when I tell everyone, 'Let's take a break and all go down to the beach.' But there are other times . . ." His voice trailed off again. Then it was time to turn his attention back to the stage and see what an action-sports awards ceremony would bring.

The trophies would be handed out in seventeen categories in skateboarding, BMX, snowboarding, freestyle motocross, and in tribute to the founding extreme sport, surfing. As with the Oscars, each category included five nominees, representing a mere fraction of the professionals in each sport, and each nominee was selected by committees composed of media, former pros, and marketing executives; the winners would be voted on by other athletes. As the presentation began, the name of each nominee was followed by footage of the rider doing a trick, accompanied by piercingly loud music and eye-damaging spotlights. As the amphitheater audience watched, snowboarders vaulted off cliffs, skateboarders ground down handrails of stairs with kinks in them, or BMX bicyclists pedaled up the sides of near vertical ramps and spun around in full circles.

As anyone attempting to learn these sports quickly discovered, the maneuvers involved a deft mix of coordination, physics, and bravado. A fledgling skateboarder, for example, had to first make sure his or her toes were touching the bolts near the nose (front) of the board before pushing off with the other foot. Then, as he put his back foot on the board near the kicktail, he had to pivot the front foot so that both feet were side by side, in the direction of the side of the board. The synchronization did not end there. Even though the body moved with the feet, the rider's head had to face straight forward—an awkward position at best. Basic moves, like a front turn, involved leaning forward with one's toes just slightly over the side, the key being to crouch down with bent knees and to apportion one's body weight. The gentlest twist or turn of the body could affect the board, and standing up straight could lead to a quick end to a ride. The same with snowboarding, where a rider had to keep his or her shoulders square with the board, rigid yet loose, looking forward and not to the side. The subtle coordination between knees, feet, and shoulders came naturally to some, not at all to others. To stop, one had to lean forward ever so carefully and dig his toes into snow.

As the nominees continued to be announced and their filmed tricks broadcast, the parade of celebrity presenters began. Supermodel Hunter stepped out of the wings in a swath of miniskirt to introduce footage of a rider nominated for Feat of the Year—in particular, pulling a backflip on a snowmobile. As a clip was shown in slow motion, the precision of the trick, the way in which the rider yanked at the handlebar at the right moment and pulled a five-hundred-pound machine over his head up in the air, resembled something between lunacy and skill. The crowd applauded but was equally fixated on Hunter's wardrobe. Quickly, she was barraged with strip-club hooting and hollering. Somehow, she managed to retain her smile and composure and read from the teleprompter. Right behind DiNenna, two young men, clear-cut descendants of the lead characters from the *Bill and Ted* movies, shouted, "Take it off!" again and again. Hunter beat a fast retreat, although the same scenario played out again moments later when another model was nearly shouted down by the crowd as she introduced another list of nominees.

Although those who lived and worked in the sports knew a certain amount of raging male hormones was standard, they wondered how much there should be. From the earliest days, their world was one of shy, creative types—latchkey kids or the victims of broken homes—who had always been too small, too skinny, or too disinterested to try out for their school teams. As adults, they weren't disinclined toward pleasure and sin: At various times, they were all guilty of drooling over women, drinking and toking up too much, and battling feelings of professional jealousy. They could easily make boors of themselves at the local watering hole after a skate, bike, or snow session. But they liked to think of themselves as vastly different from the knuckleheads of their old high-school football teams, the jocks who made cutting remarks about their sports, their slouches, and their shaggy, uneven haircuts. Their idea of humor did not necessarily amount to the type of laddie-magazine jokes Mohr was spouting this evening: Introducing a female surfer, he gulped that she was "the woman who gives *me* a half-pipe!"

Still, the tenor of the evening was set. Celebrities reputable and otherwise emerged to present awards to young men and women dressed in cargo pants, T-shirts, and sweatshirts who ambled to the stage and made brief, self-deprecating speeches. The trophy for BMX Rider of the Year was given to tall, lanky, twenty-one-year-old Van

Homan, who accepted his award with "All this is great, but the best days are spent on the road." Mat Hoffman, the groundbreaking BMX rider with dark, curly hair and a self-effacing manner, took his Action Sports Achievement Award with a tight, crinkly smile and gently thanked his friends for continually bringing him to the hospital. He then told the crowd that nothing, not even his biggest action-sport feat, compared to having a child; his first, a daughter, had arrived eighteen months before. To those in the audience who were expecting flamboyant characters, Hoffman's gentle, unassuming manner must have been a shock; it contrasted with the media-derived image of these athletes as psychotic wild men.

In his seat, DiNenna nodded approvingly. "That's great," he said. "They're giving awards to the right people."

When awards were not being handed out, the stage shook to the music favored by action-sport athletes and spectators alike. Jay-Z was backed symbolically by members of Static-X and another band, Korn, that had similarly revived hard rock with more nihilistic elements and vocal or rhythmic touches lifted from rap. One of the newest of these bands, 3rd Strike, was fronted by a burly leader with gang membership in his background and a roar so emphatic it appeared blood vessels would jettison out of his shaved head. Shortly after ten P.M., the evening's featured band, the Red Hot Chili Peppers, were presented with an Artistic Contribution Award. The band's mix of punk, funk, crowd-surfing rock, and speed-freak rapping had been a long-time favorite of the athletes'. "Death might be really, really great, so don't worry about it," Flea, their bass player, told the crowd. Awards were also handed out for perfect musical accompaniment: Jay-Z for skateboarding, speed metallists Slayer for BMX, veteran punkers Pennywise for motocross, and Radiohead for snowboarding. Some choices made sense and some didn't, but the bond between music and these sports was authentic. Surfing's Musical Artist of the Year went to Jack Johnson, who had graduated from making surf movies to becoming a laid-back folk-reggae troubadour for both his crowd and jam-band fans everywhere.

The reunion of the Bones Brigade rehearsed the previous day proved to be a low-key but emotional highlight. The applause was enthusiastic and respectful, with no interruptions save a few squeals when Hawk stepped up to the microphone for his part of the presentation. Tellingly, Guerrero refrained from his "goatherder" joke. The Feat of the Year Award went to Jim Rippey's snowmobile backflip, which beat out Hoffman's drop-in on a ramp from twenty-five feet up, with the help of a tow; Burnquist for a loop switch, or skating a continuous 360-degree loop in which he was upside down part of the time; and Seth Morrison for a Lincoln Loop, a free-skiing trick that was in essence a cartwheel in the air. "*So* gnarly," said the guys behind DiNenna; DiNenna himself sat watching with an expression that ranged from enthusiastic to passive.

"It's cool to see this stuff, but you have to keep your integrity," he finally said. "It's not a true representation of our sport, but it scratches the surface." Then the Chili Peppers returned, this time with their instruments, and the pit came alive one more time, the kids from Seatfiller.com leaping up and down and cheering for the cameras. With that, the official part of the evening was over.

Those lucky enough to score an invitation to the VIP Post Party at the nearby Hollywood Globe Theater arrived at their destination by walking back through the mall and past the Danny Kass poster, miniature skateboards, and "extreme dining" nightspot. Inside the theater, tables of burgers and hot dogs were being laid out, and an open bar or three began serving; a DJ spun club music and disco oldies in the cavernous, high-ceilinged room. "This is *not* representative of our world," said DiNenna, standing amidst the bustle with a smile of slight discomfort. While high-octane good times were not alien to the athletes, he did not want outsiders to get the impression that such high-roller events were a regular occurrence.

Then DiNenna continued on his way, touching base with friends and business acquaintances. They were all around, clasping palms and exchanging knowing smiles: the athletes both veteran and up-and-coming, the sports managers and agents who negotiated their deals, the representatives of the sneaker companies and advertising agencies. For all the glitz and the bring-the-noise tumult, an undeniable sense of history also wafted through the room: Bony fortysomething skateboarders strolled past their descendants, the two camps exchanging mutual compliments. The envy and rivalry that occasionally seeped in were checked at the door as those in attendance commemorated the year that had just finished and the one to come. A new round of BMX competitions and demos would be under way the same month; spring and summertime skateboard tours were in the planning stages. The X Games were scheduled to take place four months away, in Philadelphia. Summer camps that would instruct a new generation on how to ollie, tailwhip, and barspin would open for the season. The night before the awards, Vans, the oldest of the action-sport shoemakers, had held a press conference at a Sunset Strip club to announce the lineup of the Warped Tour, the annual traveling festival of punk rock and action sports. For all the free-form, freewheeling ethos of the community, little about its behind-the-scenes planning and scheduling was casual; there were careers to make and further, corporations to please, contests to arrange.

Although the ESPN party would carry on for many hours, it would do so without one of the people partly responsible for the community it celebrated. His young son by his side, former Zephyr team skater Stacy Peralta darted out immediately after the last award was presented. At the organizers' suggestion, he had shown up to reunite with his former Bones Brigade boys—which he called "really sweet and emotional"—and, in so doing, to promote *Dogtown and Z-Boys,* the enthralling, if somewhat self-promotional, documentary about the groundbreaking seventies skateboard unit of which he was part and which he had directed. "We went all over the world and infected kids with this virus," he said with a smooth, confident smile, shortly after the event was over. Dressed in baggy pants and T-shirt, his receding mane of blond hair tucked under a porkpie hat, Peralta at forty-four looked more like a goateed, aging bohemian artist than the flaxen-haired skate hero of his youth. In the years since the Dogtown days, he had helped grow the action-sport industry in many ways: He co-owned a skateboard company and spearheaded the skate videos now sold in malls and department stores the globe over.

Peralta had enjoyed his onstage reunion with the Bones Brigade, the team he had organized after the Dogtown days; he hadn't seen some of his protégés in years. Then he chuckled and said, "They were looking around at just the *decadence* of the whole thing and were looking at me and going, 'You started this whole thing, you know.' And I said, 'I had nothing to do with this whatsoever.' It was too much of a spectacle. What happens is that these big corporations like ESPN, they hear this thumping beat coming out of skateboarding, and all they're doing is turning up the volume as high as they can. And they end up sucking the style and life out of it. It was like, I don't want to be a *part* of this.

"A thousand percent testosterone with no peaks or valleys," he continued, recalling the evening. "There's no beauty in it. It's every-one trying to top everyone. Everyone's up there swearing on camera." He paused. "I gotta be careful. I'm not trying to sound puritanical, but it's very easy to play along with marketing the whole bad-boy image. I just feel like they're taking the bone marrow out of these sports. They're making everything look like pro wrestling. I know they provide a service; they do distribute the sports to millions of kids, which is cool. But the thumping beat of the way they present it is horrible." For that reason, Peralta said, he would most likely not attend future awards shows.

Back at the ESPN party, the beat carried on for many hours after Peralta fled. Many would continue to throw down drinks and stay out much later than the party's announced closing time. When they eventually arose, there would be business calls to make, meetings to attend, video parts to be filmed, and photos to be taken for an advertisement or one of the core magazines. Finally, when those tasks were completed, they would again do what they had always done— roll on down to a park or empty space and attempt to pull off a new trick or take another shot at an old maneuver, but better, smoother, higher, or in combination with another move. At some point, as they stood atop a ramp or stared ahead at the park obstacles or dirt hills before them, they would think back to their night out in Hollywood and ponder the enormity of it all. No one would have imagined their activities would become so popular, so prevalent, so businesslike, so *upstanding*. Still, it beat whatever part-time jobs they had held, and it was better than wearing a jacket and tie. Tugging at their extra-large shorts and T-shirts, they pushed off on their board or bike, went back to work, and prepared for the year ahead.

2. PUMP IT UP
UNTIL YOU CAN FEEL IT
riding high and low with bmx

The bicycles started crashing early, during practice, and no amount of skill seemed to prevent them from doing so. An experienced rider who had traveled from Canberra, Australia, to this western part of North Carolina was the first to go down. Like the others, he started his run by dragging his small-framed bike up a steep, battered wooden incline until he arrived at a platform about one story up. When his name was called and it was his turn to compete in the dirt-jumping contest, he pedaled furiously back down the ramp and up and over one of the half dozen mounds of clay that dotted the course and jutted six feet into the air. Then he tried to pull a trick—some thought it was a barspin, in which a rider whipped his handlebar around 360 degrees while in midair—and something went very wrong. The next thing he knew, he was lying on the ground, the medic hired for the weekend at his side; the doctor took one look at the kid's swollen ankle and guessed a dislocation fracture. No matter what it was, surgery would clearly be required, maybe a pin to secure his foot to his ankle. To compound matters, the sky, which had threatened to crack open all morning, finally did, and the kid found himself screaming in agony as layers of goopy mud rose around him. His run was over, and so was his entire weekend in Charlotte.

Not long after, it was Joey Marks's turn to go down early. Marks—

or Whitesnake, as he was known—didn't look like the type who
would slam; with his brick-shack build, it was easy to imagine him as
a high-school linebacker in his hometown of Fort Wayne, Indiana,
albeit one with a blond-rooster spike. Whitesnake's practice run had
started well, with a no-handed backflip, in which he went into the air
and flipped upside down while extending his hands off the handlebars. Then came a tailwhip, wherein he swung the bike counterclockwise beneath him as he more or less stayed in the same upright
position. Finally, he tempted the fates and took a shot at a Superman,
one of his sport's many notoriously difficult tricks. After pedaling
straight for one of the dirt mounds, he zoomed up it, soared into the
sky, and once there, took his feet off the pedals, lifted his butt up off
the seat, and extended both legs horizontally behind him, as if he were
flying like the superhero after whom the trick had been named. The
move was hard enough, but just as crucial was jumping back *onto* the
seat as the bike descended. This, Whitesnake failed to do properly,
and as a few dozen locals gathered in the green bleachers watched, he
lost his balance. His face plowed into his handlebars, and the whole
mess of intertangled flesh and aluminum hit the dirt before anyone
had time to react. Once more, the vigilant medic scrambled over to
assess the damage and saw the blood running down Whitesnake's
nose and streaming from a slash on his right cheek; his right knee did
not look in glorious shape, either. Whitesnake's dreams of conquest,
of grabbing part of the contest's $10,000 purse, were effectively over.

Staring both riders in the face, very hard, was the agonizing fact
that this year's BMX season had just begun. Another thirty or forty
contests lay before them—some in arenas, complete with television
cameras and network exposure, and some in harsher, less exotic
locales with only a few hundred spectators watching. This weekend's
contest lay somewhere in between: It was the first leg of the presti-
gious Vans Triple Crown competitions, but in keeping with BMX's
role in the action-sport universe, the locale—Cedar Yards, a complex

of empty or renovated industrial buildings in the northwest part of the city—still felt remote. Traditional BMX, short for "bicycle moto-cross," was a tense, highly competitive racing sport, a foot-powered, all-American NASCAR. This weekend's riders were practicing free-style BMX, which abandoned racing in favor of pulling jumps and tricks on ramps and half-pipes. In the eyes of the mass audience, freestyle BMX was a fringe sport: It didn't yet have the cachet or high profile of skateboarding or snowboarding, and no one seemed to speculate, as they always did with skating, whether freestyle would eventually be incorporated into the Olympics. When the International Olympics Committee announced in 2003 that BMX would be part of the 2008 summer games, few were surprised that it was the racing contingent, not the freestylers, who were invited.

But freestyle was *not* racing, which was both the point and the allure. It was one thing to climb onto an eighteen-speed mountain bike, pedal uphill, and then hurtle down, the wind smacking your face as you doggedly gripped the handlebar to avoid cracks and potholes in the road. For many, that experience defined two-wheel thrills, but not for the freestyle BMX crowd. Real freedom, and real expression, came only when their bike was not simply a piece of lightweight aluminum beneath them but was part of their body, and together man and bike twisted, turned, and leapt over mounds of earth or plunged down the ramps normally reserved for skateboarders. The bikes had no shocks or gears, and pegs jutted out from the front and back wheels so the riders could grind on copings of decks or anyplace else they desired. It was more like riding a horse than a bike; if the horse occasionally threw them, it was the price they expected to pay.

By the time Whitesnake hit the dirt, his fellow competitors had all arrived at the site. In workmanlike fashion, they began unloading their bikes from their dust-covered station wagons and vans and pedaled over to a covered, roped-off wooden deck that would serve as their de facto private lounge. They were a battalion of young men in faded T-shirts and low-rider jeans that dropped down to reveal their underwear tags and bunched up at their ankles like overlong curtains. They joked, slapped palms, and exhibited the camaraderie of co-workers getting reacquainted after lengthy vacations. Given their clothing and that their bikes were smaller than traditional models, with twenty-inch rather than twenty-six-inch wheels, they resembled neighborhood bullies riding off with your little brother's bike. (It was as if the kids had grown up but their bikes had stayed the same size.) They forked over their $75 entry fee, signed a liability waiver that would hold their own insurance company (and not the event organizers) responsible in case of accidents, then signed up to compete in any of the specific freestyle disciplines.

The event had never been held in Charlotte before, so no one knew what the venue (or the bars and strip clubs) would look like. As it turned out, the three courses—the dirt track, the vert ramp, and the street layout—looked passable, even workable. Far more worrisome was the oncoming weekend heat that could easily soften the tires on the bikes. By late morning, a dusty haze had begun settling over the entire grounds, and the thermometers began inching toward ninety degrees. Killing time, the riders chowed down on tacos they slopped together themselves. The food didn't look especially appetizing, and more than a few rolled their eyes at it, but they ate it anyway; it was free, and besides, there were no other immediate options in this frontier part of town.

When the first burst of rain arrived, it happened so fast that everybody immediately stopped eating, leapt to their feet, and dashed down the steps of the deck to grab their bikes, which had been strewn around the parking lot, and drag them out of the rain. The pizzazz of events like the X Games felt more than a few thousand miles away.

It was possible to make a decent living from BMX: Dave Mirra, one of the sport's biggest stars, was said to be pulling in seven figures thanks to lucrative deals with AT&T, a video game, and a toy company that manufactured a Mirra action figure. Mirra, the defending champion, had driven to Charlotte directly from Pennsylvania, where he had been filming his AT&T spots. Yet most of the riders made nowhere near the kind of money he did. Only a few earned six or seven figures a year, while the remainder of these fifteen-to-thirty-year-old men took home only about $30,000 annually. Contest winnings could range from the low five figures to a few hundred bucks to quite possibly nothing, and some would sleep in their cars or share dingy motel rooms with other riders for the privilege of participating. But for the next five months, the height of the freestyle season, they would attend as many of these competitions as possible. And if all went reasonably well, they would place well enough to make a little cash and emerge at the end of the season without any of the serious injuries that had sidelined some of their peers. It didn't matter how experienced they were, either: Dennis McCoy, one of the pioneers of the sport, was walking the grounds of Charlotte with a huge white cast from his right elbow to his hand, fresh off surgery for a broken wrist.

Injuries were integral to any sport, and it irked them and their peers in skateboarding and snowboarding to be asked repeatedly about bruises, breaks, and hospital visits. They would either brush aside the queries or crack that athletes in other sports were injured far more often. Surprisingly, they were right: A study by the appropriately named *Journal of Trauma* revealed that, in one sample year, basketball injuries outnumbered skateboard wounds ten to one. The riders preferred to think about which tricks they would attempt, in what order, and on which course.

Soon, the time came to do just that. By midday, the rain had trickled to a halt and the sun muscled its way through the clouds. Particularly hard hit by the weather was the street course, an area the size of a strip-mall parking lot and featuring what looked like massive building blocks dropped haphazardly from the heavens. Thanks to

workers wielding snow-shovel-size mops, the course had been dried
out by late afternoon, and when the word spread to the athletes' deck
that it was ready to go, everyone, including Koji Kraft, hurriedly
grabbed a bike and rode over to get a feel for the course.

At nineteen, Kraft was part of BMX's new school. The son of a
German father and Japanese mother, he had a far more multicultural
look than many of his fellow riders, and his short, dark hair and
black, horn-rimmed glasses lent him a more studious visage as well.
On his bike, though, he was anything but reserved. He didn't just
drop into the vert ramp; hunched over his handlebar, he *pounced* into
it, with no hesitation and no noticeable tentativeness. If anything, he
never really thought much about it; as he would say, he just *did* it.
"The more you think about it, the less you'll probably do it," he said
with a chuckle.

He had stumbled into the sport almost by accident. Raised in
Addison, Illinois, he came from a family steeped in the military; his
father had served in World War II, and his brother and sister had also
done time in the armed forces. In high school, young Koji had
competed in track and field and gymnastics, but when he discovered
a skatepark not far from his home, complete with BMX riders, team
sports were no longer part of the plan. "It's like meditation," he
would say of riding. "You think about things in life. It helps you get
cleared up." Soon after, he began participating in stunt shows held in
parking lots and at state fairs, where he would earn a few bucks with
tailwhips and can-cans (taking one foot off the pedal and moving it to
the other side of the bike, which, like other moves, was harder than it
sounded) to tiny but enthusiastic crowds. In 1999, still in his teens, he
had entered an ESPN-sponsored competition in Nashville and sufficiently impressed everyone in attendance. With that, college was no
longer considered. By the time of the Charlotte competition, he had a
group of sponsors, including one, Yoo-Hoo, that paid him $30,000 a
year just to stick a company decal on his helmet and be a part of Team

Yoo-Hoo. He had signed up for the army years before, thinking he would follow in the family's uniformed steps, but any thoughts about such a career had also been vanquished—even if, much to his amusement, the army did still call him from time to time.

As Kraft knew well, warming up was crucial when preparing to ride a street course. Ramps and boxes, and their accompanying angles and transitions, could be radically different from city to city, as could the ways in which they were arranged on a course. The riders had to start determining what they could pull off in the sixty seconds they would be allotted during the contest, so the course quickly sprang to life, bikes flying perilously close to each other. Wearing black, baggy pants and black sneakers, Kraft piloted his Schwinn—courtesy of another of his sponsors—onto the grounds. He did a few basic moves, then a smooth backflip. But then he attempted to grind the peg of his tires on a rail along the side of the course and suddenly lost his balance, and he and the Schwinn slammed to the ground, the bike flying away from him and spinning into asphalt.

When action-sports athletes took a spill, some bounced back immediately; others lay motionless in the dirt, or in the half-pipe, for what seemed like endless minutes as everyone waited for a flicker of movement. The silence of collective held breath was hard to miss. As a few riders rushed over, Kraft was holding his left wrist and twisting and squirming on the ground, his face contorted with pain. With his other hand, he managed to yank the watch off his injured wrist and violently throw it away. A fellow rider bent down and touched the wrist, and what emerged from Kraft's mouth was far from the sound of joy. Not knowing what else to do, the others stood by watching; eventually, a few wandered off as other riders pedaled right past Kraft as part of their own practice runs.

After several prolonged minutes, Kraft finally stood up, but he was in no mood to communicate with anyone. Walking over to a chain-link fence, he kicked it, then kicked it again. He couldn't believe he'd done something like this so early, and he was livid with himself. At that point, no one, especially Kraft, knew if it was all over and if he would spend the rest of the weekend on the sidelines with White-snake, watching dolefully as others had all the fun and a shot at the prize.

It had commenced at night, in the darkness, after everyone else had gone home for the day.

As long as he could remember, Bob Haro had to have wheels, and to push those wheels to their limits: As a kid in San Diego in the mid-sixties, he had done wheelies and other tricks on his Sears banana-seat bike. There was plenty of time to practice, since his parents were conservative, blue-collar people who worked long hours at the local supermarket—dad as the manager, mom as the accountant—and sometimes didn't return home until nine at night. That schedule left their children plenty of time after school to ride bikes, but that wasn't enough, and soon Haro had graduated to motorcycles. He had been on the swim team and ran cross-country in high school, part of his competitive streak, but racing was something else; the speed, exhil-aration, and jumping were thrills he hadn't experienced before. His parents tolerated his new passion—"As long as you don't get in trouble, it's okay," he remembered them saying—and his father even encouraged him to buy a motorcycle as long as it was first and foremost for transportation. Before long, at fifteen, young Bob had a Honda 100cc dirt bike, and within a month he'd stripped it down, removed the lights, cut the exhaust pipe, and added plastic fenders, all with racing in mind. Needless to say, his father was less than enthused: "Basically, he said, 'You wrecked a perfectly good motor-cycle,'" Haro recalled.

Motorcycle racing had been all the rage in his part of the country, and like many his age in his area, he had watched *On Any Sunday*, director Bruce Brown's 1971 documentary about the booming subculture of motocross road racing, complete with cameos by dedicated amateur Steve McQueen, who lent a rugged, Hollywood-cool image to the new sport. Mythology had it that the children of the moto men would kill time at the track by racing and doing wheelies on their bikes, all in attempts to imitate their parents' motorcycle moves. The story was confirmed by footage in *On Any Sunday* of kids pulling their wheels up into the air and careening down streets as they raced other tykes. At that point, the original BMX racing came into its own, with multiple riders competing against each other on dirt tracks an eighth of a mile long and jumping over dirt mounds as high as six feet. Whoever finished while still on his bike more or less won. There were rules, like wearing full-face helmets, but the scene was also vaguely lawless—the children of roughnecks trying to be roughnecks themselves, as early in their lives as possible.

Like many of his buddies, Haro—who was lean and wiry, with the long, curly hairdo sported by many of his generation—had watched those pedal-fever scenes in *On Any Sunday,* and in them he saw his destiny. Motorcycles were fun, but the damn things cost too much to keep up; when he took his Honda apart and promptly ran out of money to put it back together, that was the end of that. By chance, his older brother Scott had a BMX bicycle, and before long, Bob had borrowed it and begun using it for the same high-speed riding and jumping he had done on a motorcycle. Not surprisingly, he soon wrecked the frame, and the bike became his property by default when he had to pay to repair it himself.

Despite the mishap, he was intrigued by the idea of doing more with a BMX bike than mere racing, and adapting his motorcycle moves to a less costly, less dangerous pedal bike. He began riding all the time—after school, over dirt hills in the neighborhood, after dinner, into the night—as his parents toiled away. Soon he came across a skatepark in nearby Spring Valley. By the mid-seventies, skateboarding was in its second wave of popularity, and Haro gazed at the park's concrete pool and surfaces and small half-pipe and saw infinite possibilities. There was only one problem: The park was for skaters exclusively, with no bikes allowed. So, with John Swangeun, his sister's boyfriend and a fellow rider, at his side, Haro waited until nightfall arrived and the park closed, then threw his bicycle over the chain-link fence and slipped in.

In the darkness, Haro took his bike places it wasn't intended to go, made it do things its manufacturer didn't intend for it to do. Instead of cornball moves like making the bike bounce up and down like a pogo stick, he adapted skate tricks like kickturns and fakies (riding backward) to a bike. Reflecting his show-off tendencies as well as his years on motorcycles and at BMX races, the moves were fearless. Eventually, he and his buddy John talked the skatepark owner into letting them ride during the day. The skaters were, to be kind, not happy; this was their park, and seeing big kids pedaling around on little bikes did not please them. Then they began to notice what Haro and his friends were doing. "At the time, it was so novel and the stuff we were doing was so different that they were curious just to watch us pull it off," Haro remembered. He and his fellow riders would stand atop a bowl and drop in straight, with only their coaster brakes to prevent major accidents, and carve the bowl on their bike and do 360s (whip the bike around in a full circle), among many maneuvers.

At this point, fate and family coincided to further his cause. Haro's parents broke up in 1976, and their eldest son, then a teenager, was forced to find a job. Haro found one as a cartoonist and artist with *BMX Action,* a then new magazine that covered the bike-racing world. It was, he said, like "running away to the circus." R. L. Osborn, the son of magazine founder Bob Osborn, was a BMX racer himself. During lunch breaks, he and Haro worked on their freestyle bike moves on plywood ramps set up on the side of the building. As legend had it, Bob Osborn glanced out his office window one day and saw the two at play and decided they were worthy of an article. When it ran not long after, the piece was titled "Trick Riding—a Whole New Thing," since no one was yet using the term *freestyle*.

Like a pioneer in the Old West, Haro took his show on the road. He couldn't actually *compete* against anyone, since hardly anyone else was freestyling, but he could perform. During intermission at bicycle races sanctioned by the two leading bodies, the National Bicycle League (NBL) and the American Bicycle Association (ABA), he jumped through hoops and launched himself into half-pipes. "The early days, we were a freak show," he recalled. "I remember sitting on airplanes and people would say, 'What do you guys do?' And we would say, 'Well, we ride ramps and do tricks.' '*What* do you do?' And we'd say, 'Well, ever see skateboarders?' And they'd go, 'Well . . . I don't *know*.'" Haro and his handful of fellow riders weren't doing it for the fame or God knows the fortune, since there was literally no money in it. They were young and bold, and they wanted to do something no one else had done before. "It was a bit of novelty," he said. "I don't think I had a long-term vision. I just thought, 'It's something I do and it's fun.'" Cash was important, though, and by 1977, Haro began making number plates for racing bikes to sell at the events; to him, it was a better way of making a few bucks than bagging groceries back home. A fledgling entrepreneur, Haro then designed his own freestyle bike frame—one intended to take more abuse by way of steeper head angles and a thicker head tube—and began selling it at races. By 1978, he had incorporated the company, which he named after himself.

With a few other riders who composed his company's team, a van, a trailer for the bikes, and one of his brothers along as an announcer, Haro hit the circuit, performing and selling his gear at racetracks, bike shops, malls, state armories, wherever there was a crowd to watch. "We were a small band of bicycle gypsies," he recalled. "We'd roll into town and set stuff up and do a show and then go on to the next town." By the end of the seventies, at least six professional freestyle teams, including Haro's, roamed the land, and the purses at competitions rose to as much as $5,000. Then, in what seemed like no time at all, freestyle BMX went mainstream. Suddenly kids just entering their teen years were attempting tricks in their driveways—balancing their bikes on one wheel (an endo) or doing tabletops, in which they would somehow twist the bike in midair so it became parallel to the ground. Entire magazines with names like *Freestylin'* were devoted to the new sport; an organization, the American Freestyle Association, rose up to organize contests. By the early eighties, nearly half of all bikes being sold—about five million—were freestyle models, and corporate America took an avowed interest as well: Levi's, Mountain Dew, Coke, and McDonald's recruited a young rider named Eddie Fiola, who was also hired to do the bike stunt tricks in the Kevin Bacon messenger-boy movie *Quicksilver*. BMX racers looked down on the freestylers, seeing them as a novelty act, but the sport progressed nonetheless.

Haro's riding career ended not long after, in the middle of the eighties, when he kept blowing out his knee and shoulder. With the younger riders he would recruit for his team—like Mike Dominguez, who could hit a ramp without even warming up and sail up eight or nine feet—Haro saw a new breed of BMX athlete who were approaching the sport with an intensity and daredevil attitude he had never imagined, and he figured it was best to quit while he was ahead. By 1985, when he stopped riding freestyle professionally, Haro Design had a factory full of employees and was making $7 million annually, 70 percent of that from the forty thousand bikes a year the company manufactured and sold for everywhere between $180 and $600. He left the riding to the Haro team, which included Dominguez, a young Oklahoma City hotshot named Mat Hoffman, who was on his way to becoming a major force in the sport, and a Kansas City kid named Dennis McCoy. Eventually a thirteen-year-old from upstate New York named Dave Mirra, who had entered his first race when he was ten, came aboard as well.

The McCoy kid was typical of the young, hyperactive riders Haro recruited. At a contest at a mall in Kansas City, the locals kept telling Haro he should check out a new local talent. McCoy, then about seventeen and a scrappy kid with a brown shag, had snuck into the competition with his other buddies in the BMX Brigade, a ragtag local group that reveled in various types of mischief, such as jumping on their bikes after school and being chased by older kids or cops. McCoy had started racing BMX bikes in 1980, but had a change of heart once he saw the article on Haro in *BMX Action*. "It was totally refreshing because it didn't revolve around that whole start-to-finish, who-gets-to-the-finish-line-first mentality of racing," McCoy said. "It was like, take your time, invent your own stuff." Soon after, he started the Brigade—what he called a "club-slash-gang"—with his brother and some friends. Numbering as many as thirty, they all wore black-and-white baseball shirts with BMX BRIGADE on the back, and they were loathed by jocks and stoners alike.

"Bike riding was not accepted when I grew up," McCoy recalled. "All we had to do was leap on our bike and the cops would give you crap for trespassing. Part of what made us close as a group was the fact that it was us against the world." Being chased by security guards who patrolled the shopping centers or by the seniors in high school who would yell "It's past your bedtime!" was, for the BMX Brigade, an opportunity to work on their skills: They'd make getaways down narrow streets and jump down a set of stairs, which guaranteed they wouldn't be followed. They knew the dangers of possible arrests or tickets, but they didn't care; as McCoy said, "You didn't want your life to suck, so you kept doing it anyway." McCoy was serious enough about this new sport to build a wooden ramp in his backyard. His parents were a bit reluctant. "But I had my ways of saying, 'It's gonna kind of look like this.' You ever see that *Spinal Tap* movie where they design the Stonehenge thing? I'd show my parents what the ramp looked like, but they had no idea what the scale was. And then I'd build this massive half-pipe in the back."

At the time, the prevalent nonracing form of BMX was flatland, the art of doing bike tricks on just that, with no ramps or half-pipes. The rider climbed on and spun around on the bike, essentially turning it into monkey bars. McCoy learned many of its tricks, like a bunnyhop 360 (yanking the entire bike off the ground by pulling up the front wheel first and then popping up the rear end, then spinning around in a full rotation). But along with friends and riders like Hoffman, he wanted to take it to another, more intense level. He remembered a steep drop-off without stairs at a nearby shopping center and decided to jump his bike off it. "Then the next extension was to take it to two or three steps, and then it just became a mental challenge—'Man, if I get the nerve up and pedal full speed, I could do it over this *massive* set of stairs.'" One day he did a 360-degree spin on the bike down that set of stairs, fifteen in all. "I remember the first time I ever went for that," he recalled, "and thinking, 'Wow, this is something cool.'" By then he could go up twelve feet on a quarter-pipe, and in 1984 he quit racing for good and went with freestyle.

At this point, McCoy met Haro in the mall; in the parking lot afterward, McCoy impressed the master by besting him at one of his own tricks. Next thing McCoy knew, Haro gave him a card, and McCoy was part of the team. He took a semester off college, intending to return one day, but instead became one of the sport's first professionals, earning the nicknames The Real McCoy and then DMC, which symbolized both his initials and that he sometimes rode to Run-D.M.C. songs during events. He came up with classic moves like the fufanu, in which a rider would ride up a ramp, touch the coping with his back tire, rotate 180 degrees, and come back down the ramp. One of his personal favorite inventions—although he hated the word *invent*, since it was too presumptuous—was the truckdriver, when he would spin both the bike and the handlebars 360 degrees. The phrase *doing a McCoy* came to mean going to any lengths to pull off a trick. By age nineteen, he owned his own house, with ramps in the backyard. "All of a sudden I'm making a living at a bike," he recalled, "and I thought, 'You know, I might not have to do this whole *work* thing.' "

With early stars like McCoy leading the way, freestyle BMX kicked into first gear by the end of the eighties: Teams traveled nationwide, money was rolling in, and bikes were exclusively made for the sport by manufacturers. In their massive helmets and pads derived from the BMX racing world that still required them, the freestylers looked, as one newspaper account at the time put it, like "miniature Road Warriors." Then, catching everyone by surprise, it was over. Companies were churning out so many bikes that the market became oversaturated—BMX bikes, it turned out, didn't have to be replaced as often as skateboards—and a natural correction of the market was inevitable. Overnight, sales of Haro models were cut in half, and Haro eventually sold the company to another. The slump in the teenage population, the rising popularity of mountain bikes, and a recession were other factors no one had anticipated. The fifty or so pro freestylers who lived large in 1987 dwindled to a handful by 1990, with purses dropping to a hundred dollars and sponsorships drying up. Before anyone could adjust, freestyle BMX went back from whence it came, into the darkness and the night.

What had once been an underutilized Charlotte parking lot had been transformed into a visible confirmation of BMX's dramatic turnaround since those dark times. The comeback began with ESPN's incorporation of stunt biking into its first Extreme (later shortened to X) Games, at which the power of the media bore fruit. By then, riders like Hoffman had started their own bike companies, taking their futures into their hands rather than riding for other people's outfits.

The bikes were better now, too—sturdier and stronger, sometimes lighter, with stronger wheels and forty-eight spokes rather than thirty-eight. Along with skateboarding and snowboarding, BMX was swept up in the new interest in so-called extreme sports; even Mountain Dew returned to the fold, using bike images in a new series of ads in the mid-nineties. The Triple Crown series was one such beneficiary of this renewal. The long, narrow lot was now a sponsors' carnival: Mountain Dew, Right Guard Xtreme Sport deodorant, Ford Ranger, and Xbox each had booths, tents, and trailers that were helping to underwrite the costs for the event in exchange for exposure to a desirable young-male demographic. When the event was broadcast on NBC a few months later, it was officially billed as the "Right Guard Xtreme Sport Championships of BMX Presented by Vans and Mountain Dew." At the Xbox tent, a dunking contest featuring bikini-clad girls was under way, while a Dew employee handed out free paper-cup samples to anyone entering the grounds. Techno and hip-hop shook the grounds.

The riders had not made the trip to Charlotte to partake in any of these festivities, though; they had a job to do, and it began in earnest on Saturday afternoon. The rain had stopped, and the eight hundred cubic yards of red-clay dirt that been hauled over from a local motocross track were dry now and caked with what looked like veins; the only remnants of the previous day's downpour were the reddish mud puddles alongside the course. Twenty-four hours after his crash, Joey Marks sat by the side of the dirt-jump course in a wheelchair, a vertical scar extending from below his right eye to his cheekbone, another over the bridge of his nose. Worst of all, his knee was blown and would require surgery, although he had decided to wait until his trip home to California to have his doctor inspect it. The injured knee was wrapped in bandages, the shoeless leg propped up on a metal folding chair. His face crisscrossed with gauze, Marks sat, glum and dispirited, as his fellow riders walked by and slapped his palm or shoulder as a show of support. They had seen that expression many times before on their own faces, and they knew there was only so much they could say or do.

One by one, the riders competing in the dirt jump lugged their bikes up the ramp, this time for the finals. This was the grimiest and grittiest of BMX courses, and it showed in the patches of brown clay caked on the riders' jeans—clear evidence of who had already taken spills. One by one, their names and sponsors were announced. ("It's like NAS-CAR but on a smaller scale," cracked a Vans employee, referring to the confluence of logos on the riders' helmets and shirts.) They pedaled hard down the ramp, building momentum, and when they arrived at the first mound seconds later, they straightened their legs, lifted their butt off their seat, and flew up the dirt and toward the clouds. Once there, they tried any number of initial tricks—a tailwhip or a turndown, in which the rider would turn the handlebars 180 degrees while holding on to them, like rassling a bronco, or maybe a no-footed can-can no-hander, pulling one's legs apart from the pedals, hurling one leg over to the other side, then taking one's hands off the handlebar so that, for a second or two, only one's butt seemed to have any physical contact with the bike. To control the bike when they took their hands off it, they'd grasp the seat with their kneecaps. Assuming they landed without crashing, they tackled the next mound, did another trick, then hit the dirt again before rounding the curve at the end of the course and starting into the final three hills. The rain had made the jumps soft, which slowed down some of the riders, but they had to take what was handed to them.

Each run only lasted fifteen to thirty seconds, but within that short time, a rider would attempt at least three or four difficult tricks. BMX was advancing wildly; the basic moves of Bob Haro's days were over, and no one back then could have imagined some of the tricks being attempted today, like a backflip or the difficult double tailwhip. (A relatively new bicycle mechanism, a gyro, allowed riders to spin their

handlebars without getting them tangled in brake wires.) Routines
became a series of trick combinations, such as Superman seat grabs—
a Superman but with one of the two hands holding on to the seat
instead. Stephen Murray, an audacious young rider from Newcastle,
England, who has recently relocated to Southern California, did a
huge turndown 360—to which even the announcer said "Wow!"—
followed by not one but two backflips to the accompaniment of the
Scorpions' "Rock You Like a Hurricane." Mike Aitken, a rider from
Salt Lake City with the toothy looks of a ragged Tom Cruise, did an
astounding turndown 180. Occasionally a pant leg would get caught
in a bike chain, and bike and rider would go separate ways during a
landing, but for the most part, there were no repeats of the previous
day's nasty spills.

Murray and Aitken were superb, skilled riders, but the person
everyone was watching was the kid with the ruddy face, stocky torso,
close-to-the-skull blond fuzz, and small, silver triangle pin just below
his lip. Like his competitors, Ryan Nyquist wore the unofficial
nonuniform of freestyle—baggy jeans with a hole in the back pocket
and a long-sleeve T-shirt. But once he put on his blue helmet and
black goggles, he took on a very different air, one immediately far
more serious than his scraggly-haired peers, an image in keeping with
the career he had fashioned for himself.

He was twenty-three now and, only in the world of action sports,
already a wise old veteran of freestyle BMX. A child of the sport, he
was born in Los Gatos, California, in 1979, shortly after the sport had
been hatched. After first learning to ride a bike at age three, he kept
crashing and destroying his training wheels "to where they couldn't
be fixed," he recalled in a voice flat and affectless. He was never
opposed to team sports—he had even played soccer and baseball and
in some ways missed the locker-room chumminess of it all—but he
loved the sense of accomplishment with BMX even more. "When you
learned a new trick, you did it yourself, there wasn't a coach out

there," he said. "You walked away going, 'Damn, that was awesome.' " Since there were no ramps in his immediate area, he took to jumping dirt at a dried-out creek behind a local park.

Few BMXers attended his high school, though, so Nyquist had to ride with kids from other towns, and before he knew it, he was leading two separate lives. His fellow students didn't mock him; they just didn't understand why anyone would do what he was doing. He figured out how to do a barspin early on; near a baseball field, he began learning 360s and other moves, all of them new and thrilling. By senior year, he had already lined up his first sponsor, a small local bike company that gave him T-shirts and nothing else, but it led to another, bigger backer. Before long, he was traveling to New York and Chicago and staying in first-class hotels, all in exchange for appearing at BMX contests. "It was pretty crazy," he said. "It made me grow up and mature a lot faster than a lot of the guys in high school."

His parents weren't pleased at first, since neither had gone to college and therefore wanted more for their son ("I was supposed to right all their wrongs, that kind of thing"). He did eventually go—for about three fourths of a semester, at California Polytechnic State University, San Luis Obispo—but took "bullshit classes," as he called them, like bowling. Most weekends he was at contests and demos instead of his own dorm room. "Eventually it got to where I was getting Ds and Fs, and I wasn't there mentally," he said. "And I had to tell my mom, 'I don't think I wanna go there anymore.' And she was like, 'Where do you want to go?' And I was like, 'No, I don't think I want to go to *school*.' She was bummed. In her eyes, I was throwing something away." She was right, in a way, since at that point BMX was more a hobby than a living, and he only earned about ten grand a year. But in 1996 he won his first contest, and turning professional was relatively easy since there weren't many top-level jumpers at the time. Nyquist's climb was slow but steady; with each X Games and

Gravity Games, he seemed to move up a notch, finishing third, second, and finally, in 2000, first in dirt at the X Games. He had won contests as far away as France and Germany, and he was the American Bicycle Association's King of Dirt between 1997 and 1999. In his sport, he was among the most well-rounded, competent in all three disciplines of street, dirt, and vert. "He's the guy," said Mark Losey, the editor of *Ride BMX* magazine, "the guy who does every trick every time."

By this point, Nyquist had seen it all: the hard life traveling to the contests, the jealous backstabbing of other riders who coveted his sponsors and fame, and the injuries, from the torn thumb ligaments to the time he jammed his handlebars into his kidney and pissed blood for a while ("more of a scare than an injury, but it definitely sucked"). Once the season began, he settled into a routine: riding contests on weekends, then returning home to Greenville, North Carolina (where he'd moved in 1999), on Monday, where he would rest and let his body heal and ride very little. Then Thursday would inevitably roll around, and he would leave town for another chance to pull tricks, make money, and please his sponsors. "I think it takes a certain kind of person," he said of whatever it was inside of him that led him to freestyle. "It definitely takes different qualities for sure to want to go out and try the crazy stuff." Asked if he agreed with the scientific and medical theories about these athletes, he smiled politely and shook his head: "That's just a different language to me." He agreed there was a rush associated with his job, but any implications that it was akin to a narcotic addiction offended him. "When you go out there and pull something hard, it's definitely a blast," he said. "Makes you feel good. But it's not like a fix or a drug where we need it to function daily."

This was the side of Nyquist—earnest, clean-cut, antismoking, antidrinking, antidrugging—that his manager of four years, Steve Astephen, called, with a big, pleased smile, "American pie." In addition to his X Games medals, Nyquist had a slew of sponsors and corporate tie-ins, from phone companies to candy bars, that added up to a six-figure income; Adidas was about to introduce an upgraded version of his signature shoe, which would retail for $80 and include the extra padding he demanded. "He's very corporate friendly," Astephen said. "Butterfingers couldn't be happier." Nyquist and Astephen even jointly owned a real-estate business. Other riders cultivated images as hard-living, scuzzy wild boys on two wheels. Nyquist knew them all, even liked many of them, but that image was not for him; he was and remained a dedicated professional BMX rider. At times, he could still be that goofball kid from Los Gatos, throwing orange peels at fellow riders between runs and fooling around. But on the course, he was—like his friend and former roommate Mirra, who like him lived in the BMX-central burg of Greenville—all business. His fantasy, he said, was for the twenty top riders to make the kind of living golfers did.

It was now Nyquist's turn for the dirt finals, but the less than satisfactory condition of the course was not his ally. He noticed that many of his competitors were attempting hard tricks, so he decided to change his routine as he went along in order to keep up with them, especially on his second and last run. During the first run of his finals, he pulled a 720; on the second, he did a switch-handed backflip but fell, his bike shooting out from under him. Then, for his final run, with nothing and everything to lose, he decided to try something he had only attempted twice before. He pedaled fiercely down the ramp and began with a backflip no-handed tailwhip, meaning he removed his hands from the handlebar when he was upside down in the air. Then he aimed himself directly at the last mound, pedaling ferociously and stopping just as he hit the minihill; at that point, momentum took over and skyward he went, up the side of the hill and into the air. As his fellow riders watched, he did a no-handed, no-footed can-can on the way up, and then, in midair, spun the bars around. No one had ever seen that combination before, and with good reason: It looked vaguely suicidal. It had taken him a short lifetime to learn and all of five seconds to do, but everyone knew he'd done something special, and so did he. He looked up, smiled, and stuck his finger in the air triumphantly. Afterward, he stood on the dirt he had just jumped and was presented with his trophy; the $7,500 first-place check would be awaiting him in a caboose that had been turned into a Vans office. For Nyquist, if not for the others, the season was off to a solid start.

Reflecting a lifetime spent riding and spilling off many bikes, his knees felt like crap, especially tonight. Most kneecaps are either smooth or slightly hilly, but Rick Thorne's were lumpy and craggy, like a small mountain range that jutted out halfway down his legs. It was after midnight, the end of a long first day, and Thorne lay on the bed in his hotel room still in his traditional riding outfit of black T-shirt, black shorts, and ankle-high black sweat socks. It was easy to see the tattoos that spiraled around his body, like the one of a flame that shot up his left leg. In his hand was his massage instrument of choice, a blue rubber ball stuck onto a metal stick, and he lay there gently bouncing the blue ball off one knee—*tap tap tap tap*—and then the other. The ball's steady, hollow thump was like the beat of a disco remix underscoring his conversation, and to him there was no better sound at the end of a day of contest riding.

He was there when his sport rose to national prominence two decades before, and he was still there, at age thirty-two. At times, he looked older than that number, thanks to a chiseled face hardened by experience and injury and a patch of short, receding dark hair. The life was not always a placid one: He was on the road two thirds of the year, which took him away from his wife more than he wanted. "I have [former BMX riders] come up to me and say, 'I had to grow up and get a real job,'" he said. "I *hate* that. This is the hardest job I've ever had. I've worked normal jobs, and it's a lot easier, let me tell you, than this." Still, when he jammed on his black baseball cap—backward, generally—and straddled his bike, the years disappeared, and once again he was that scrappy kid from Kansas City. When he spoke, it was with the motormouthed enthusiasm of a hyperactive teenager; more than just a rider, he was BMX's court jester.

The smiles and jokes temporarily evaporated when Thorne rode, though, as they had the previous night during the vert contest. The riders began assembling by the side of the ramp early, plopping themselves, and their bikes and duffel bags, in the gravel. When their turns were announced, many began their suiting-up ritual: leg brace, kneepads, elbow pads, gloves, and finally an oversize helmet that made their heads appear too big for their bodies. (It was one thing to hit dirt hard, another entirely to slam your head into wood.) Then they climbed a metal ladder up to the deck and dropped into the twelve-foot half-pipe. The riders flew down, then up the other side of the ramp and went aerial, sometimes four or five feet up, then came back down, rode back and forth a few times from wall to wall to gain momentum—in the so-called pumping zone—and then tried another trick. Each had two sixty-second runs to prove themselves, with an extra fifteen seconds if they so desired, and only the best of the two counted. The small crowd in the bleachers bobbed their heads back and forth as if watching a tennis match.

Koji Kraft was among the competitors, his wrist wrapped in a smaller bandage than the day before; as it turned out, he'd merely sprained it. Undaunted, he did a high flatspin 540 (spinning one and a half rotations and landing backward) and a huge no-hander (taking his fingers off the handlebar while trying to keep the bike straight without them), but finished his run early when his wrist pain returned. Mirra, a brilliant technician who caught bigger air than anyone and was so fluid he almost seemed to stop in freeze-frame in midair, attempted a huge tailwhip and fell, effectively ending his chance at first place. Thorne, who looked like a black-garbed pit bull on two wheels, hadn't performed well either.

Twice he tried a corkscrew flair—a backflip with a 180-degree spin, a move he hadn't attempted in some time—and twice he didn't make it and hit the bottom of the ramp. When the points were tallied, he hadn't made the top ranks, but what mattered was his relentlessness, especially when competing against BMXers nearly half his age. By his own admission, he wasn't the world's greatest rider, but he may have been its most persistent.

The vert finals finished at dusk—just in time, it turned out, since only one overhead light was available and the riders were close to riding in darkness. Dinner consisted of a couple of pizzas ordered at the last minute; like raptors, the riders descended on them and devoured them in what felt like seconds. It may not have been the ideal work setting for a thirtysomething man, but Thorne was nevertheless glad to be anywhere but in his hometown. When Thorny, as his mates called him, was six, his father had up and left. Eventually, his mother remarried, and both she and his stepfather worked the night shifts at a Wonder Bread factory. But Thorne didn't take to his stepdad and, like many children of divorce, grew angry and resentful and went in search of alternative outlets. "Dude, I tried traditional sports like *soccer*"—the word dripped with sarcasm—"and basketball, and to be quite honest with you, I never had the confidence for it. Just because . . ." He paused. "Just because I didn't have much confidence growing up. Team sports just seemed too competitive for me. When you're from a broken home and there's a lot of alcohol involved and your parents aren't around and are divorced, and you can't go somewhere for soccer meetings or basketball and you're from a lower-middle-class family, you don't have much ambition unless you can learn it somewhere. My parents weren't pushing me to be in sports or anything. We just existed." He and his friends preferred to shoot bottle rockets at the school football players. To this day, his interest in televised basketball or football games amounted to watching the highlights and nothing more.

In search of himself, he discovered a BMX bike. Racing didn't interest him—"too jocky," he said—but wheelies and half-turn spins off curbs, as well as then-dominant flatland tricks, suited his manic energy. When his parents periodically confiscated his bike as a way of punishing him, he lashed back at them. "I've done a lot of things when my parents took my bike away from me," he said. "I went *nuts,* dude. I've done everything from breaking into stores, stealing cars. I was on my way to nowhere." He refused to elaborate on this part of his past—"Dude, it was gnarly" was all he would say. Later there were drugs: "Not supergnarly, but enough to where I don't want to do them again." He ran away from home, shoplifted, stole denim jackets, and resold them at his high school for twenty bucks.

Salvation of a sort arrived when he fell in with the BMX Brigade. "I saw something in him I didn't see in a lot of the other guys," recalled McCoy, his fellow Brigade rider and still one of his best friends. "There were a number of better riders than him in the Brigade. But I saw he was gonna stick with it." From riding, Thorne found the self-esteem, self-confidence, and motivation he hadn't encountered any-where else in his life. "We got something from bike riding," he said. "We knew it was something that made us feel cool and good about ourselves. We were the outcasts—but instead of us giving in and saying, 'Yeah, you're right,' we rebelled." In his autobiography, *The Ride of My Life,* Mat Hoffman wrote about the first time he met Thorne, after the kid had been beaten up by "a group of skinhead U.S. Marines who'd taken an instant disliking to Rick's smart mouth, his passion for hard-core music, and riding bikes."

Thorne didn't make it to the end of high school, choosing instead to ride and bus tables at local restaurants, which earned him just enough money to lug his bike to state fairs, car conventions, and anywhere that would have him. The gigs rarely paid much—some-times fifty bucks for an entire weekend—but people watching him ride quarter-pipes and wedge ramps constituted a new type of high.

"I thought, 'Wow, I'm expressing myself with my bike and people are watching.' It felt good." When the sport crashed in the early nineties, he did what he could to survive, becoming part of the Sprocket Jockeys, a group of touring riders founded by Hoffman and McCoy and, later, Mirra. Times were hard: They would share rooms, wake up in the morning, and eat the leftover pizza from the night before, sometimes getting food poisoning. The tours would last for weeks, up to six riders crammed in the same room, and if they were lucky, they made $100 a day collectively; Thorne and his first wife survived on $5,000 to $8,000 a year. Later, it would amaze him to think he could make that amount of cash in one day, at competitions like the Triple Crown.

For his lifelong devotion to the sport, Thorne had paid a physical price. Contemporary riders practiced by jumping onto foam, but in the eighties, "you had to cross your fingers," he said with a grin, and hope you didn't land too hard. His knees, which had been operated on six times, had had screws inserted into them; screws in his ankles had only recently been removed. Another time, the peg of his bike shot up and into his crotch. "My testicle swelled up the size of a grapefruit." He laughed at the memory. "But who cares? There's doctors out there who'll fix you. People say you'll regret it when you're older, but I think I'd regret it if I was a guy who went to work in a factory and didn't get out of Kansas City." In one year alone, 1993, he had surgery on a shoulder, knee, and hip, broke a rib, cut his chin, and tore his urethra so bad that, to pee, he had to wear a catheter. Several times he quit altogether, but after a few months clearing tables at an Olive Garden, he would invariably ride again.

The night that should have cost him his career came in 1996 in St. Louis, where he and his first wife had moved for a while. Fresh off a fight with her, angry and looking to take out his aggression, he grabbed his bike and jumped onto a loading dock, but came up short and hit the dock—with his face. "I got a hairline crack along my eyes," he said, pushing his hair back to reveal a thin scar along his forehead. "And it came down and broke my palate, deviated my septum, and destroyed my sinuses. So they cut my head from ear to ear and pulled my skin down, took some fat from my stomach, put some fat in my skull, stopped a leak because fluid was going down the back of my throat. I had double vision for two weeks after. Right now I've got about twenty-six little screws in place in my face and my eye, and I had a tracheotomy during surgery. It was pretty nuts."

He was now at an age where he had to be more careful about his body, and when he did ride, he had to focus and concentrate more than ever. "If I wake up tomorrow and don't feel like riding, then I'm not gonna go out there and kill myself," he said, referring to the last day of the Triple Crown. *Tap tap tap tap.* "If my body's physically thrashed, then I'm not gonna go thrash it more." His current financial status was secure: He had sponsorship deals with companies that made sneakers, soda, calling cards, sunglasses, clothing, and tires. Still, he had to start thinking ahead. He knew the day would come when competing with kids half his age would no longer be an option, and he saw his future in Hollywood, near his current home of Santa Ana. He loved being on camera—he had a freelance career as a television commentator for events in these sports—and he saw acting as his next step. He already had an agent to move that process along, and he had six lines—*six lines!*—in *XXX*, an "extreme" action flick that would premiere shortly.

For all his success and that of his sport, he admitted that something had been lost: "When you grow up riding bikes and people don't like you, but now they come and watch you, it's weird." The night was growing late, and his face grew more serious, the tapping less frequent. "I catch myself sometimes. You get so fucked-up with which shoe, tour, TV show, and all these things, and you have to detach yourself and just go ride. In our sport, it's a fine line between keeping your dignity and selling yourself. You want to stay in the magazines, the videos, the contests, and keep your sponsors happy to maybe get *more* sponsors, but you have to catch yourself and put it in perspective. It's a weird balance, you know."

But this was his job, and he could not think of any better way to make a living. "Too stubborn to quit," he said, "because I thought if I quit, I'd go back to being that kid who doesn't like himself. If you give up again and again and again, you just lose more and more aggression. You might as well just go for it, dude. I could have a perfect body and never do anything, you know? I've been to Australia six times. I didn't pay for *one trip.*"

He smiled. "It's *sweet,* dude." Then it was time, finally, to rest up for whatever tomorrow might bring.

Early the following afternoon, Koji Kraft was slumped on the bike, trying not to glance too much at the sun above. For once, riding had nothing to do with it. The previous night, he and a group of his peers had partaken in a nightly custom—the bar visit after the session— and Kraft was dealing with the aftermath. "I stayed out late" was about all the words he could muster. Afterward, some had taken the party to an area strip club, another part of the routine; it was their way of easing their nerves regarding the contests that awaited them the next day. The life did have its share of headaches: If they blew a tire or encountered a problem with a gear or a fork during a contest run, they had to repair their equipment on their own with their own tools, and insurance was a constant source of irritation. Kraft, for instance, had to fork over $200 a month for a $500 deductible and always seemed to be in debt. But if they were lucky enough to hook up with a few solid sponsors, and if they had no immediate aspirations to go to college and instead wanted to see the country and perhaps the world, the life was a relatively good one for those in their late teens or early twenties: hotel rooms and bikes paid for, admiring kids at each event demanding autographs, even more admiring women at the local watering holes who were drawn to their bad-boy images.

On the topic of injuries, their attitude was akin to Thorne's: The pain was worth it, and they did their best not to think about it. But the reminders were always present, always on display. By the last day of the Triple Crown and the start of the third and last contest, in street riding, the number of riders walking around with bandages or blocks of ice taped to their hands grew by the hour. All one had to do was walk past the blue-striped medic tent to see one rider lying on a table with a massive, goiterlike bandage completely swallowing an arm or knee, or another on his stomach as the medic jammed two large bags of ice under the biker's T-shirt or hurriedly taped up a shoulder. Whitesnake was now on crutches; even the seemingly indestructible Dave Mirra, nicknamed Miracle Boy, required stitches near his elbow for his vert spill and was now stalking the grounds with a cast. There was as much an art to learning how to crash as to pulling a trick, but it was, at best, an imperfect art form.

The local paramedics hired to supplement the official medic just shook their heads in admiration and amazement. "I've never seen a bunch of younger guys more beat up," said Ed Ramsdell, a mustached local EMS worker leaning against the chain-link fence and keeping an eye out for spills. "They're walking like they're old men. I'd like to see them when they're fifty. See how some of these guys walk?" he said, jerking a thumb in the direction of a biker hobbling by. "You don't expect to see twenty-two-year-olds limping along." Thorne, as he himself had predicted, had opted out of today's competition because of his knee aches; instead, he could be spotted scurrying around on the deck, offering encouragement or a smart-ass joke to the other riders or exchanging his trademark knuckle-to-knuckle greeting with them.

When it came to the potential for bodily harm, it did not help that street riding—which tried to duplicate the feel of biking down city or suburban blocks, onto rails, down steps, and up walls—was back in vogue, and that some of the riders, unlike those on the vert ramp, opted out of wearing helmets or pads; they didn't want to bog themselves down or, perhaps, look dorky. (BMX racing, by comparison, had clear-cut rules: The handbook for the NBL made it clear that mandatory equipment included a helmet "in good condition," mouth guards, "long-sleeved shirt," pads, and gloves. Riders could be disqualified if they didn't conform.) During the preliminaries leading up to the finals, five riders went down, some so hard that they lay on the asphalt for minutes without moving. The crowd hushed, the music on the PA stopped, and the medic ran over and bent over them, asking how they were doing and hoping for a nod of recognition. The other riders stood by, hoping their buddy would be able to stand. The biker eventually did, to scattered applause from the crowd, and would then be helped off the course and over to the medical tent.

An outsider could look at the street course and see a bewildering, playgroundlike collection of scuffed walls, ramps, quarter-pipes, pyramids, and oversize boxes. But to a freestyle BMXer, the course was an artist's canvas—a blank piece of paper upon which he could craft a series of moves, one after another, into a distinctive run that reflected his strengths and downplayed his weaknesses. Just as artists could begin by scribbling in one corner and then working their way across the blank page, the riders began their routines anywhere they wanted, since there was no officially designated starting point. From there, they could do whatever they wanted, whenever they wanted; for approval, they only looked to the three judges staring down at them from the balcony of the empty warehouse next door. When it was their turn, a buzzer would sound, a song—generally punk rock or an MTV oldie like "Video Killed the Radio Star"—would begin rattling the PA and the bleachers, and they would start.

More competitions than ever took place every year, which had led to concern within the industry. In the old days, riders had more time between contests to practice new tricks. Now, with so many events each season, some held back from trying anything expressly daring and experimental for fear that an injury could derail their chances of entering *other* contests. No one knew the solution, since the more competitions, the better the chances of making a living; it was simply another sacrifice to be paid for progress.

At the Triple Crown, some riders began atop the deck of one of the wall ramps, others on a box in the middle. Dropping in, they tasted some of the chicken sloppy joes they'd been given for lunch as it came back up their throat. Some had their routines mapped out in their heads. Others opted to improvise: dropping in, doing one trick, stopping, quickly glancing around to see where they were on the course, and using whatever was around them—a box, a ramp—for their next move. Sometimes one trick easily flowed into another; other times the runs had a herky-jerky, stop-start rhythm. Either way, they had between sixty and seventy-five seconds for each of their two runs, and each crammed in as many as fifteen tricks per run. There were downside tailwhips followed by tabletops or turndown 180s (in which they did a turndown, a 180-degree turn, and a backward landing). There were ice picks, keeping the front tire up while grinding the back peg on the coping of the deck; there were huge transfers followed by barspins followed by backflips; there were fast runs up a quarter-pipe to gain speed for a jump off a box; there were tailwhip backflips, a move Hoffman had pioneered a decade before and which had made a comeback. Many times over a long afternoon, the riders looked less like bikers and more like baggy-jeaned, no-shirted jazzmen improvising as they went along. When they finished, they pedaled back up to their starting point and were greeted with a series of backslaps and palm slaps from their fellow riders.

Until the very end, the street portion had not gone well for Nyquist. He was most comfortable jumping dirt, which he had been doing longer; the street course, which required more nuance and adjustments, was always a little trickier. To his initial dismay, it showed. During the preliminaries, he had blown a tire just as he had finished an impressive run that had ended with a huge no-handed transfer. Then, on the first of his two final runs, he had tried a big 360—going completely around in the air, keeping his head turned at the same time to prevent the body from stopping—and fallen off his bike, albeit without hurting himself. Frowning with self-criticism, yet remaining calm, he sat on his Haro in the middle of the course, checked his gear, started again, pulled a backflip, and again had to stop afterward, this time to adjust his chain and seat. As with traditional sports, at times all the hard work and practice bit the dust and one simply, excruciatingly *sucked,* and one could do little about it.

For his last run and final chance to redeem himself against the eleven other finalists (winnowed down from sixty-eight in the prelims), Nyquist knew he had to amp it up. Aitken had already given him a run for his contest money with a dazzling run, including a 180 in reverse. Pedaling onto the course with a straight-backed determination, Nyquist kicked off his run with a huge no-handed transfer and a backflip. Suddenly, he was back on top—focused, in control. Should they want it, the riders had fifteen optional seconds they could use at the end of their run. Sometimes they took it, although just as often they were physically and emotionally spent from the half dozen tricks they had tried. Nyquist rolled onto the top of the middle box and stopped as the clock began ticking down—*fifteen seconds, fourteen seconds* . . . He looked left, then around, surveying the options and the course in his head, then looked over his shoulder, in the direction of the judges, and squinted in the sun. *Thirteen, twelve, eleven.* The other riders began yelling "Go! Go!" in support, as if they wanted to see him succeed, wanted to see what he could pull out. For what felt like a small lifetime, he sat on his bike and thought.

And then, with only a few seconds left, he jammed his foot onto the pedal and plunged down the ramp. Just as he hit the wall, the buzzer went off, but he kept going and pulled off a 720 over the spine—two full rotations in midair, which people hadn't seen done by anyone in several years. He had taken a few extra seconds to do it, but no one seemed to care. The other riders were screaming and cheering and rushing onto the course toward him, amazed that he had been able to complete such a difficult trick so under the wire. The judges—who were basing their ratings on a combination of originality, degree of difficulty, and flow—almost had no choice but to award him first place; his 94 points beat Aitken's 90.25. With that, the weekend's events were officially over.

After he was given his trophy, at a brief ceremony in the middle of the course, Nyquist walked his bike over to the side. What happened next was what always happened next. Bashful little boys, all teenaged or younger, converged around him, holding out pens and asking him to sign anything available—baseball caps, posters, T-shirts. He exchanged a few polite words with each, but his mind already seemed to be somewhere else, perhaps on the next competition. Or, perhaps, on leaving. As soon as the fans thinned, he grabbed his bike and ran it over to a small caboose-office and collected his two checks of $7,500 each for finishing first in dirt and street. Nearly a quarter of the BMXers who had shown up a few days earlier would be heading home with one injury or another. But for Nyquist, at least, the weekend had not been a total wash, and he now advanced to the next round in the Triple Crown series with a considerable advantage over his peers.

He was not alone in his hasty departure. The other riders also grabbed their bikes and duffel bags and beat the quickest of retreats, as if they couldn't wait to leave Charlotte. Left behind were empty bottles of water that emitted squishing sounds as bike tires rode over them. The athletes all made a beeline for the parking lot, and with their ragged, dirt-caked pants, bare, bandage-covered torsos, and occasional hobble, they resembled young Civil War soldiers after a particularly hard-fought battle. They stashed their bikes into the trunks of old trucks, SUVs, and station wagons and gunned the engines, and gravel-dust clouds began to form in their wake. They would celebrate, as they always did, then return home to heal up and prepare for the next weekend. There was always another contest somewhere, and they would not want to miss it.

3. THE BOYS ON THE SKATE BUS
going big with tony hawk's
gigantic skatepark tour

The ritual began before they arrived at each skatepark, and it would be no different today. In fact, there would be two rituals, one mandatory and the other not. In the first, Ian Votteri, an ESPN coordinator who kept a watchful eye on the proceedings for his corporate overseers, would wait until all the skateboarders had climbed aboard the jumbo blue-white-and-red bus with the TONY HAWK'S GIGANTIC SKATEPARK TOUR logo emblazoned on the side. Once everyone had hiked on, settled in, and tossed their boards and backpacks wherever there was space, and once they had wiped away some of the previous night's postsession festivities from their eyes, Votteri, who sported a goatee and dressed in cargo shorts and hiking sneakers, would call them to attention.

"Hey, everyone," he announced this morning in Denver, raising his voice just enough so that groggy heads turned, more or less, in his direction. "I have to announce that ESPN recommends you wear helmets." The reactions differed from day to day, the athletes either sniggering or ignoring him completely. This time, Colin McKay, the wiry Canadian veteran vert skater with the wrung-out eyes and tangle of hair, stepped up. *"Wellll,"* he shouted back, sarcastically, "tell ESPN *thanks* for the recommendation!" As he always did, Votteri smiled sheepishly; he had fulfilled his obligation, and there wasn't much more he could do to ensure their safety. With that, the bus lumbered out of the parking lot of the four-star hotel in which the skaters had been staying, and the final leg of Tony Hawk's Gigantic Skatepark Tour, starring many of those who had helped make the sport a new national pastime and million-dollar business, rolled out.

Once they cruised onto whatever new highway they were on, the second half of the daily ritual began, this one courtesy of the tour's certified athletic trainer. A crinkly-eyed, walrus-mustached oak of a man, Barry Zaritsky was a fifty-one-year-old health taskmaster who had worked for Hawk since the skater was twelve and who carried with him an MRI X-ray of Hawk's skull in the event the skateboarder cracked his head open. Zaritsky approached his job with unwavering, focused intensity, especially when it came to his main client, who soon emerged from the back of the bus. Hawk was a gangly thirty-four-year-old with praying-mantis legs, conservatively cut brown hair, and an expression of perpetual unflappability. At six foot three, he stood at least one shoulder above the shorter, stockier, more muscular skaters on the bus, and he had more creases around his eyes, more bruises on his bony limbs. He dominated them culturally as well; thanks to a hugely popular video game named after him, innumerable appearances on television and in commercials, and a career that was now two decades old, he was a star, the biggest the world of action sports had ever known. He was widely recognized as a superior, skilled athlete who had taken skateboarding to new heights, physically and financially. Watching Hawk zigzag effortlessly on a half-pipe before cruising up one of its walls and launching into the air, going eight or ten feet above the coping, was like watching a pelican hover over a body of water, swoop down for food, and continue on its way. The effect was fluid and seamless—the work of a seasoned craftsman doing his job extraordinarily well. Every day, he would stand on a seven-ply wood board roughly seven inches wide and about two and a half feet long, with four polyurethane wheels beneath it, and then blend, twist, turn, and spin on it, sometimes removing his feet from the board entirely before landing on it again. And he made it all seem as natural as walking.

As he hoisted himself onto the small marble table in the middle of the bus, he was now just another skater preparing for another session. His battered shins and ankles had to be protected, so Zaritsky attended to his regular routine of wrapping Hawk's feet tightly in brown, then white, adhesive tape. At the trainer's recommendation, Hawk had already soaked them in the hotel pool. Below his left kneecap was a considerable bruise the shape of South America.

Once he had finished with Hawk, Zaritsky moved on to the others. Hardly anyone on the bus—or in the sport, for that matter—warmed up in traditional ways; those wishing to see jumping jacks, push-ups, and chin-ups would need to head to the nearest high-school gym class. In this universe, stretching out amounted to stepping onto a board and pushing off. So, like Votteri, Zaritsky did what he could to prevent the most damage from occurring. "It ain't like football," Zaritsky said in a craggy voice that matched his looks. "These guys are not on steroids." He began by taping the ankles of Kris Markovich, the fearless big-gap skater with the haunted stare and long, scraggly mane he tucked under a painter's cap when he skated. Then Zaritsky threw open his blue cooler, grabbed one of its many bags of ice, and handed one to Bob Burnquist, the star Brazilian with the glasses and mellow smile, who pressed the bag onto his knee with a wince. Zaritsky made his way to Mike Vallely, the thirty-two-year-old veteran whose burly build, shaved head, small chin shrub, and severe demeanor lent him the look of a menacing skinhead. On the first demo of the tour, Vallely—or Mike V., as everyone called him—had missed a landing and pulled a groin muscle from his knee to his hip. At first he could barely walk, but the worst had passed, so Zaritsky came to his rescue by wrapping his knees and wrists. "It's brutal, man," Vallely said, shaking his head and smiling tightly. "I'm being held together by tape. Every guy on this bus has a serious ailment. Everyone has something." His statement was borne out by the many bruises—road rashes, they were called—in evidence, each a different shade of pink, crimson, or brown, each a mark of honor and a souvenir of the innumerable crashes and falls they had taken to get to this point in their careers. "Injuries help you to be focused," added Vallely, who, like Hawk, had been skating since the eighties and began as a member of the famed Bones Brigade team. "If you don't have that focus, you're just cruising."

For all their battered bodies, there was no place any of them would rather have been. They were rock stars now—ones with skate decks in place of guitars, but rock stars nonetheless—and they had the fully equipped bus with the two large-screen TVs and video-game consoles to prove it. The tour had begun in 2000 when Hawk signed with ESPN to serve as an on-air analyst at skate events and to develop programming; the Gigantic Skatepark expedition, filmed for a highly rated ESPN series, was one outcome of the deal. For about five weeks, starting in Houston before winding up in Carlsbad, California, the bus would cruise from one skatepark to another for autograph sessions and demos—spontaneous, free-form exhibitions as opposed to strict competitions with winners and second-placers. In the beginning, the tour was seen as a curiosity item by both spectators and the skate community; more than a few name athletes declined to participate during the first year, unsure if the pay was high enough or if they wanted to be part of an ESPN television series. The early demos attracted only a few hundred at most to each park. "Back then, who knew?" said Robert Earl Wells IV, aka Robert Earl, the tour mascot with the explosion of electric-shock hair who was, at various times, video director, author, consultant, and on-air personality for the ESPN series. "We were just a bunch of retards on a skatepark tour."

By the following year, though, the tour began to draw more spectators to the parks and more viewers to the series, which paralleled the rising popularity of the sport itself. Over four decades, skateboarding had witnessed countless highs and lows—it was the stock market of the sports world—but during the first two years of the new century, it was on a major high, thanks to competitions like ESPN's X Games, the use of skate imagery in too many advertisements to count, the anti-team-sport mentality that had been instilled in the two post-baby-boom generations, and the financial input of numerous corporations. A handful of those companies, including Wrangler, Nokia, Snapple, Best Buy, and Activision, had put up a collective $1.8 million for Hawk's latest skateboard expedition in exchange for having their logos displayed on the side of the bus. The influx of cash allowed Hawk and ESPN, who split the production costs, to walk away with a reasonable half-million-dollar profit and to put on a road trip complete with all the trappings of superstar musicians, from luxury buses (as opposed to the vans most skaters were used to) to top-rated hotels. The first time out, they barely had enough money for gas, Hawk said, but three tours later, he called it "very much like a rock-and-roll tour, with someone else footing the bill."

As the undertaking began to wind up its third season, Hawk's words had begun to haunt him. He sensed the tour had outgrown the skateparks, especially ones unaccustomed to handling the thousands of people who now routinely appeared out of nowhere to watch a bunch of young men in jeans, shorts, and long-sleeve T-shirts grind, ollie, and execute fakies and boardslides. Hawk was already finalizing plans for a far more ambitious project: a choreographed show of bikers, BMXers, and motocrossers called the Boom Boom HuckJam that would play arenas and, unlike the skatepark tour, charge admission. Once word went out that his third annual Gigantic Skatepark Tour might be the last, so many skaters wanted to be a part of it that an extra minivan had to be rented for the overflow. The result was an array of personalities, styles, and lifestyle preferences that amounted to a rainbow coalition of modern professional skateboarding, from vert, done in a half-pipe, to street, which involved grinding rails, benches, concrete, and anything in sight. The attendees included not just Hawk, Burnquist, Vallely, McKay, and Markovich but the red-haired, scruffy-mopped, fifteen-year-old snowboarder and part-time skater Shaun White, the Baltimore-based vert icon Bucky Lasek, *Jackass* star and video heartthrob Bam Margera, the taciturn and talented Philadelphian Kerry Getz, Liverpudlian Brian Summer, Canadian Alex Chalmers, and skater, ESPN commentator, and all-around Australian rogue Jason Ellis. A few BMXers, including Rick Thorne, the Midwesterner who had been doing it, like Hawk, for two decades, had also been invited along for variety. Even as Hawk mapped out more expansive plans for himself and his sport, the final Gigantic Skatepark Tour would be more than simply a last hurrah for this particular undertaking; it would be the culmination of skateboarding's fourth and largest wave.

Like most of the stops on the tour, the one scheduled for the Denver Skatepark had been announced and advertised beforehand, and as the bus chugged off Interstate 25 and made its way toward the venue, it became immediately clear that Hawk's fears of overcrowding were well-founded. From inside the bus, the skaters looked through the black-mesh-covered windows and saw hundreds of kids smiling and gesturing, or running alongside the bus and frantically waving their arms; others knelt down and flapped their limbs in "we're not worthy" salutes. Combined with the cars parked haphazardly along the way and the barren, industrial-wasteland feel of this isolated part of the city, it was as if the bus had entered a skating Woodstock. It crept along the gravel road slowly, gingerly, so as to not accidentally squash any of the overeager under its wheels. McKay, the tour's unofficial DJ thanks to his ever-ready case of downloaded CDs, punched up War's "Low Rider," the barrio-funk hit from the seventies.

"We're supposed to be *pissed!*" snapped Ellis, in his burly, half-mocking Aussie accent. McKay dutifully replaced the song with more aggressive rap-metal.

Finally, the bus rumbled to a halt, the door flew open, and the skaters grabbed their boards and walked into oppressive ninety-degree heat; to their surprise, they also stepped into the arms of the spectators. The park was supposed to have provided security, and it had—but apparently not enough. They were rock stars now, appearing before rock-star-size crowds, but right now, they were rock stars who had, to their dismay and irritation, been told to enter the concert hall by way of the front door, not the backstage entrance. Hawk stepped off the vehicle in jeans and blue T-shirt, flashed the quick, shy smile he often did in public, and began making his way toward the park's main bowl. Sooner than even he expected, though, hands were reaching out for him; mouths were beseeching "Tony, you rock!" and "Yeah, you fuckin' *rock!*" He pushed off on his board into the mob, and thankfully, the sea of bodies parted for him as he began skating toward the bowl.

Once the skaters finally saw the grounds, they had to gaze in a certain degree of wonder. According to the Skatepark Association USA and its head organizer, a self-described former "designer and manufacturer in the home furnishings industry" named Heidi Lemmon, at least one thousand skateparks dotted the American landscape, with hundreds more in development. Getting them built was not easy and involved schmoozing local politicians, circulating petitions, and making appearances at public hearings in the skaters' communities. (One of Lemmon's self-appointed tasks was advising kids on how to handle themselves during the latter: "We say get up there, state your name, say you want a skatepark and that you've been harassed. Say police are taking your boards and that you have all these petitions signed.") A decent park, with concrete bowls and rails, could be built for as little as $300,000, but the city of Denver had gone much further, spending $1.5 million for these sixty thousand square feet and the numerous pools, bowls, and street courses of varying shapes and sizes. It was as if the world's largest marble kitchen counter had been laid out and a series of massive sinks, one after another, had been inserted into it. The skaters lived for structures like it, and that a major American city had constructed such a park at no small expense validated both their sport and themselves.

As any park designer would tell them, however, no two facilities were alike, and today's challenge, as it would be nearly every day of this tour, was to get a feel for this particular park as soon as possible. A challenge under normal conditions, it was even trickier today thanks to the estimated five thousand people who had amassed around the bowl; others hung off the railing of a nearby highway bridge to get an aerial view. As soon as all the skaters began dropping into the bowl and trying basic ollies and kickflips, the feel became that of a massive pool party, with the skaters as entertainment.

One ride at a time, the skaters loosened up. The crowd oohed and aahed as it took in Burnquist's graceful carving, Vallely's low-crouched attack up one of the walls, or White's heel flips, wherein he flipped the board beneath him as he ollied. Everyone was trying to destroy the park (*destroy* meaning something far more positive in this world than in the outside one), but the flow, the uninterrupted groove, that they sought was not materializing. In this sport, it was not unusual to screw up a trick but to keep trying, over and over, until it was mastered. Doing it while fans reached out for a handshake, on a surface more slippery than expected, was another matter entirely. Boards began shooting into the air, skaters missing each other by inches. As usual, Zaritsky, towels and ice bags in hand, roamed the park vigilantly eyeing each rider; today, he also had to keep spectators from swiping some of the water bottles set aside for the athletes. The downside of being a surrogate rock star was that the people wanted a piece of you, and the downside of appearing in a million-unit-selling video game was that everyone wanted to see you perform perfectly, just like in the game. One could sense the crowd's disappointment when a skater didn't stay on his board. Sometimes it was also evident in the skaters' faces, in the exasperated, teeth-gritted *Fuck!* that came after a stumble. Even Hawk was having a few problems finding his footing, although he managed to pull off a few basic moves to the cheers of those around him.

Crowd-control matters did not improve much when the demo moved to a nearby, smaller pool that substituted for the half-pipe normally used for vert skating sessions. The athletes seemed relieved to drop into the pool, where they actually had room to move, but the crowd around the deck soon closed in on them. Sal Masekela, the affable, dreadlocked huggy bear of an ESPN commentator (and son of jazz-Afrobeat trumpeter Hugh Masekela), who was the tour's emcee, began beseeching the spectators to move back, move *back;* skateparks had liability insurance, but no one wanted to see anyone accidentally fall into the pool or get hit by a stray board.

Eventually, after Burnquist carved the bowl so elegantly that he seemed to be a human hovercraft, Hawk decided it was time to try to pull an indy 540, a move he had invented in 1986 but had not tried much since. It was difficult to master, since it involved spinning one and a half times backside (in the air and with one's back to the ramp) while grabbing the board "indy," a complex move in itself that required moving one's back hand around the back leg and to the middle of the board on the toe-edged side. "Grabbing indy is generally harder because it requires ollie-ing into the trick and catching the board later into the rotation," Hawk would say. "There's a better chance you won't complete the spin when you land or that your board will fly away before you get ahold of it." He wasn't completely sure he would be able to do it again, but for Hawk, such eternal challenge was part of the continual appeal of skateboarding. He dropped in, skated to the other side of the pool, went up the other wall and straight into the air, twisted, and then fell, skidding on his knees as his board shot the other way. The crowd fell silent. Again and again, for a half dozen times, the pattern repeated. He was pulling some of the maneuvers but not all at once, and each time he missed, he simply grabbed the board and hustled back onto the coping to start again. By now, Masekela was pumping up the crowd and everyone was staying put, their eyes on Hawk. Hawk was aware of the attention yet completely absorbed in his quest; the crowd melted away into a blur. At one point, he looked up, almost bashfully, and the audience emitted a huge belch to egg him on. He gave a thumbs-up, then dropped in again. And again, he pulled up short and came off the board.

Then, just as the demo was officially scheduled to conclude, he decided to go for it again. He dropped in, glided over to the opposite wall, and before anyone knew it, had twisted around one and a half times, grabbed the board, and landed. It was over in seconds, and when he came down into the belly of the bowl, the place erupted in home-run cheers. The timing could not have been more perfect, and it brought to mind a comment his sister Pat would make a few months later. "Even as a child," she recalled, "Tony would always be very strategic about when he'd pull out his big tricks. He'd make the cut in all the heats without pulling out his big trick. Then in those last couple of runs, he'd pull the stuff out that no one had ever seen him practice in the park. He had that *thing,* that strategic thing. He can say it's not about competition, but he's a great competitor. That doesn't mean he *likes* it; he's just good at it, like a great tennis player. He knows when to pull it out of the bag." In other words, her brother was and had always been a master showman.

His newly remastered indy 540 in hand and in his own personal record book, Hawk held up his board to accept the applause, then skated directly back to the bus; a line of preteen boys trailed after him as if he were a pied piper on wheels. Once ensconced in the vehicle, he rarely came out again; with this many in attendance, an autograph session could last hours, and a schedule was a schedule, even on a road trip that celebrated independence. "I know it might piss some people off," Hawk said inside the bus, peeling off a sticky T-shirt and stretching out on one of the up-front sofas, "but I don't want some kid sitting there for hours and then not getting an autograph." Some skaters took their cue from Hawk and stayed inside; others decided the throngs outside were worth a look. As John Rogan, the bus driver and part-time bodyguard who was built like a fire hydrant on steroids, looked on, two locals asked Bam Margera not to sign anything but to slap them, a tribute to Margera's costarring role in MTV's human-demolition-derby series *Jackass*. No sooner had Margera asked them if they were sure than his hand quickly zapped out and whipped across both their cheeks in a flash, to which the kids laughed happily. Another fan offered up his girlfriend as a way to get on the bus. "Shut *up!*" she snapped back. Finally, the skaters piled back inside, tossing battered old sneakers out the window as souvenirs for whoever wanted the hammered old shoes. Laughing at first, Ellis and McKay watched as a miniature mob scene erupted outside the window. As understaffed and overwhelmed guards in yellow shirts stood by and watched, kids began mauling anyone in their way in order to grab the shoes. With that unsightly scene, no one questioned that the time to leave the Denver Skatepark had finally arrived, and Rogan started backing up the bus, constantly checking the rearview mirrors so as not to flatten the fans still roaming around it. Even for a road warrior like Rogan, who had years under his belt as a rock-tour driver, the departure was like taking driver's-ed class all over again.

"Well, *that* was ridiculous," he growled, still shooting looks at the mirrors as the bus finally lurched away. "How many kids did we run over?"

Discussion turned to the park's security—or the lack of it—and how to avoid the problem in the future. "When you go to a basketball game, you don't expect to touch Michael Jordan," barked Morgan Stone, Hawk's hulking production partner, in his standard outfit of fisherman's cap, shorts, and white T-shirt. Vallely sat quietly up front, staring at the road ahead, absorbed in his headphones; others settled in, exhausted and overheated, on the couches. Finally, McKay punched in an AC/DC song, and he and Ellis leapt up and turned into an air-guitar karaoke duo. "We're an army of millions!" McKay shouted out the window to the remaining fans in the park to hear. Today, the army had reached out back at them. There were still a half dozen stops to go.

No one could pinpoint the precise moment at which the idea of standing on a piece of wood equipped with wheels seemed like the basis for a good time. In his history of skateboarding, *The Concrete Wave,* author Michael Brooke wrote that the origins of the sport dated back to the early twentieth century and that the first skateboard "was actually more like a scooter," complete with roller-skate wheels. The concept itself probably dated back even farther, as did the very idea of speed and the sensation of flying on the ground. As far as the actual scooters, little in the way of improvements took place over the next fifty years, but the postwar baby boom called for new toys for a new generation, and the skateboard as the world began to know it started developing in the late fifties. Its roots lie in scooters, roller skates, and a California surf community looking for ways to amuse itself when the waves weren't conducive to their hobby. In 1963, an L.A. County lifeguard named Larry Stevenson rolled out the first professionally manufactured line of skateboards, naming his company Makaha after the Hawaiian surf championships. "He noticed kids riding around on planks of wood that were really crude," recalled his son Curt, "and he thought to himself, 'Maybe I could make a sleeker, neater skateboard shaped like a surfboard.' " Makaha boards, made from standard hardwoods, were thinner than later models by several inches and sold only for about ten bucks apiece. The company's original market was surfers, but the new invention— by Makaha and other companies—soon spread, helping to make skateboarding (sidewalk surfing, it was often called) a dominant fad, a new leisure-time activity for the post-Kennedy, pre-Vietnam years. Before long, Makaha was receiving orders for ten thousand boards a day; overall, millions of decks were gobbled up.

As with many crashes, skateboarding's was unexpected and arrived only a few years after its ascent. Despite technical improvements such as the replacement of steel wheels with tan-colored clay ones, making for an easier ride, the boards were still treacherous to maneuver, resulting in numerous accidents and injuries. Skateboarders became a menace to polite society: "By August 1965," wrote Brooke, "20 cities had banned skateboarding from sidewalks and streets." The pastime began the first of many comebacks in the early seventies, starting with the introduction of polyurethane wheels, which helped prevent spills caused by pavement cracks and other skateboarding nemeses. Thanks to this innovation, it became possible to ride on all different kinds of terrains, including pools, with greater zip and control. The change was, in the fitting words of Jocko Weyland in his skateboarding memoir and history, *The Answer Is Never: A Skateboarder's History of the World,* "a shift akin to jet engines in aviation or the handheld camera in photography." The revival kicked in with the arrival of the Zephyr team, a group of Venice-area surfers and latchkey kids who began adapting more aggressive surf moves to skating. Unlike the almost gentlemanly skaters of the seventies, the Z-Boys, as they were called, treated their boards the way Jimi Hendrix treated a guitar, as a starting point for creative freedom. A concurrent California drought, which gave this new community an untold number of empty pools in which to practice their art form, furthered their cause. The Z-Boys from Dogtown (local slang for the rough part of Santa Monica and

Venice) weren't simply about revolutionary moves like aerials in pools but about image: Revered by the emergent skateboard press, Z-Boys like Jay Adams, Tony Alva, and Stacy Peralta looked like surly rock stars and were treated that way. The sport kept progressing during this period thanks to the introduction of the ollie—slamming one foot down on the tail of a board and popping into the air with it—by a Florida rider named Alan Gelfand (and nicknamed Ollie, according to legend). But once again, the skate revival didn't last. Encountering problems with insurance and attendant liabilities, skateparks closed and were summarily bulldozed, and other new alternative sports, such as BMX, grabbed the public's attention.

At this low point, Hawk, a hyperactive suburban urchin born in 1968 and raised in the San Diego area, entered the picture. In his autobiography, *Hawk—Occupation: Skateboarder,* he recalled having what he described as a "sugar buzz" as a child that was only cured when his older brother, Steve, lent his six-year-old sibling his blue fiberglass board. "It wasn't some sort of epiphany," Hawk recalled of his first attempt at riding at his family's house. "It was fun, and I was happy I could do it right away." Inordinately skinny at the time, he felt he had to compensate for his physique by tackling any and every physical challenge in his path, and skateboarding fit the bill; his parents allowed him greater leeway than his three older siblings partly because they were, by then, in their forties. Young Tony began practicing at a local park and trying to decipher particular tricks by reading skate magazines, and before long, he had found his calling. "I didn't *want* to be an outcast," he said. "I didn't care about going to social events or being cool in school. I felt it was more important to me to be accepted by the skaters than to worry about who's dating who. It felt more important to have this sort of all-welcoming community, and all you had to do was bring your skateboard." He eventually dropped out of Little League despite his father, an appliance salesman and former navy officer named Frank Hawk, being involved ("It was hard—I had to confront him," his son recalled), and Tony eventually entered his first competition at age twelve. Frank Hawk would ultimately form a California amateur league and then, in 1983, the National Skateboard Association, partly as ways to showcase his son's talent.

At the time, Hawk remembered, the freestyle skaters, with their quaint handstand moves derived from the sixties craze, were considered "nerds," so Hawk opted for pool skating, which in turn led to vert skating, done on U-shaped half-pipes and vert ramps. For such a small kid, he went awfully big in the air, which caught the attention of former Dogtown skater Peralta, then a partner in the Powell Peralta skateboard company and the manager of its team. In 1982, Peralta recruited the fourteen-year-old Hawk, although the kid's future was, at best, uncertain. "Tony at the start was the ugly duckling," said Peralta, "the kid no one ever thought was gonna be the one. He was super-duper thin, like noodle thin, and he was *weak*. Tony couldn't even make it up the side of a pool. But there was something really special about him. There were other kids who were a lot better than him. But he had something that was going to blow them all away someday—he had a will of iron. When he wanted something, he was going to get it." The Powell Peralta team, named the Bones Brigade after founding member Ray "Bones" Rodriguez, was an impressive collection of new-breed talent, from wiry, young San Franciscan Tommy Guerrero to the compact Steve Caballero. They were a tidier-looking, more youthful lot than the Dogtown crew, but their skills on vert ramps and on the street were undeniable. Thanks to skateboarding's eighties resurgence and a series of Peralta-directed videos, which spread the word and their moves from California to fledgling street skaters in New York City, the Bones Brigade became superstars, and Hawk rose with them. With his long, flaxen mane dropping over the left side of his face, Hawk had an everykid appeal—neither too raw nor tough, just the little crack-up down the block who was able to do 720s (two full rotations in midair) and 360 aerial inverts. The image was so marketable that by the time Hawk graduated from high school in 1986, he was taking home $100,000 a year in sponsorships and endorsements and had been hired to film skate stunt work in a *Police Academy* sequel. "Everything was direct deposit, so it was just ATM, ATM, ATM," Pat, his older sister by eighteen years, recalled. "It was crazy. Nobody in the family made money like that. Everyone was really concerned it wouldn't all be blown at The Sharper Image."

When skateboarding went through another down cycle at the beginning of the nineties, so did Hawk, who had to sell the house he had bought with his first wife to help pay the bills; a career as a video director was considered but soon abandoned. The vert skating with which he had been associated became outmoded and gave way to the grittier street style, in which anything in sight, from concrete plazas to garbage cans, became a canvas. With a partner, skater Per Welinder, Hawk scraped together enough money to start his first company, Birdhouse, a play on his last name and nickname (The Birdman), in 1992. He had a hunch skateboarding would eventually return—and it did, in the mid-nineties, thanks largely to the media exposure afforded it by ESPN and its annual X Games. When sister Pat, a former backup singer for Michael Bolton, took over as his manager in 1995, she brought with her a few lessons learned in the music business: In essence, she realized her brother had to be marketed as a pop star. "Very early on, we pitched him to companies as a celebrity, even maybe more so than as an athlete," she said. "The authenticity all these companies needed from him was as important as if he was a musician or actor." One of his sister's other suggestions was to start a clothing line for preteen boys, Hawk's major fan base.

With that, Hawk's second and bigger act began. Each year brought another new corporate tie-in as well as a new display of the technical skills he had displayed as a child. In 1999, the first of his stunningly successful Tony Hawk's Pro Skater video games was launched. The summer of that same year, in front of an X Games audience in San Francisco, he decided to nail a trick that had eluded him his entire life—a 900, or rotating two and a half times in midair. No one had pulled it, ever, and as the audience in the stands and fellow skaters on the deck of the vert ramp hooted him on, Hawk tackled the trick again and again and again—until, on the thirteenth try, he nailed it. "All I could think was, finally, *finally,* I got it over with," he said. "It was just such a relief." The overwhelming media attention that resulted made him a recognizable commodity and a name; from now on, whether he liked it or not, he was the global face of skateboarding. "It meant something to people worldwide, not just skateboarders," said Vallely. "They got to see, live on their TV, this guy just going for it and sticking it out and eventually making his trick that had never been done before." After the 900, he had officially retired from competition (but kept skating on tour and at demos), yet that did not stop the calls from corporations looking for him to appear in commercials. In an appropriate turn of phrase, *Advertising Age* would dub him "Tony Hawker."

By the time of the skatepark tour, Hawk had eluded many of the serious injuries that had derailed other athletes. True, his shins had been punishingly banged up, his front teeth had been knocked out, he had torn some knee cartilage, and he knew his right ankle would strain much easier than his left, but those were minor concerns. He was now the overseer of an empire, Tony Hawk Inc., that included not only his Birdhouse and Hawk Clothing companies but co-ownership of a board and clothing distribution company, a film and video production firm, an official shoe, and a role as an advertising spokesman for Doritos and H.J. Heinz's Bagel Bites minipizzas. His annual take was reported to be in the range of $10 million; one recent estimate, which his camp would neither confirm nor deny, was that three fourths of that income derived from royalties from his video game. The days when he would earn only a dollar for each signature skateboard sold were long gone; these days, he could make $20,000 for one day's work at a demo.

The days of simple tricks were also over. At first, there seemed to be a finite number of tricks one could perform on a piece of seven-ply wood, but that didn't turn out to be the case. The sport had progressed to the point where the number of tricks and combinations seemed infinite. An index in Hawk's autobiography listed 85 tricks alone he had invented or mastered. It was not unusual to encounter a skateboarding Web site that listed 150.

In at least one regard, Hawk was penalized for the sport's new-found repute: Members of the underground community tended to discount him, especially after they saw one of his television commercials or heard he was filming a cameo for a sitcom. "How much is too much?" cracked Jake Phelps, editor of the long-standing, core-geared skate magazine *Thrasher,* echoing a criticism common of Hawk and his peers. "Why don't they build skateparks? Why don't they go fucking quest for someplace that's never been skated? They're not trying. They're just short-terming it. Bottom line. They're not looking at the big picture." Hawk had endured the gibes for years and responded to them with only a hint of bruised feelings. "I've just learned that you get labeled a sellout when your stuff actually *sells,"* he said. "I've had a signature skateboard since I was fourteen. I've had products with my name on them for twenty years. And just *now* I'm a sellout?" The way he saw it, the issue was control. He had it when he skated, when he took charge of his board and his knees and feet and knew precisely what he was doing every second of the way. The matter was no less important when it came to his business. "When companies come in and say, 'We want to sponsor you,' and you don't have any control over it, they always screw it up—the representation, the integrity, the pictures," he said. "If I have control over it, that's the only way I can be sure it has the integrity it should have." To ensure that integrity, Tony Hawk Inc., with its staff of fourteen, had a department of approval for photos and the use of his image so that nothing looked, as Pat Hawk said, "too corny." Credibility consumed him in other ways as well. He required that certain Hawk products only be sold in skate shops as opposed to chains like Wal-Mart, and he had turned down offers over the years for Hawk-logo linens, scooters, pasta, and skateboard-shaped chocolate bars.

Now in his middle thirties, a divorcé with three children—one from his first marriage, two from his current one—he fully embraced the image that had served him so well. "There's part of our culture that's not . . . squeaky-clean," he admitted. "You've got guys with tattoos. But at the same time, it doesn't mean this type of person represents all of skateboarding. We have such a diverse crew. The outlaw aspect came because there was nowhere to skate. People saw skating office buildings as destructive and rebellious. But now it's not about being rebellious, it's about pushing limits. That's what people don't understand. That kid skating in front of your storefront is not there to pester you or to try to hassle people coming in. He wants to learn the noseblunt slide. And," he said with one of his short, abrupt chuckles, "your curb is perfect for it."

As he said this, Hawk was polishing off a quick chicken-sandwich lunch in his hotel's restaurant before the next demo was to begin. Eventually, one of the bus drivers appeared, complete with a newly blackened eye: In a semiplayful scuffle with one of the skaters the previous night, the driver had been punched in the face. Sure enough, the slugger had been one of the skaters with tattoos. Hawk knew there was only so much he could change, or should, so he simply chuckled again and shook his head.

The plan called for leaving Denver at ten the next morning, but no one factored in the Bam element, and once they heard the cops were on the way, they realized they should have. By shortly after nine, many of the skaters were still dragging themselves out of bed and into the lobby, hungover and hauling their huge duffel bags and scuffed boards toward the parked bus; others hadn't even made it that far, especially after a typical postdemo night out at a nearby bar. Bam Margera, though, was not only awake but had decided this would be the ideal time to film a new trick for his next video. There was only one very Bam-like catch: The location was inside the hotel. As startled waiters and vacationing families glanced up, Margera climbed onto a sloped wood roof that was part of the hotel restaurant's decor and, before anything could be done to stop him, ollied onto the indoor ceiling. He skated down it and onto an adjoining balcony, where he crashed and, in his usual post-tumble manner, cracked up at his own body-be-damned craziness. It was a remarkable sight, a definition of the *Jackass*-generation attitude of doing anything, anywhere, anytime. The only problem was that Margera, who was never known to ask for official permission to do much of anything, hadn't checked with hotel management. It was also just a matter of time before someone called someone else, and before the inevitable confrontation between Margera and the manager would erupt. Within minutes, both of them—along with two hotel security guards—were outside the hotel, the female manager angrily chastising Margera as he looked anywhere but in her direction.

Other than Hawk, Margera generated the most looks of recognition and awe at each tour stop, thanks to his roles in *Jackass* and his own popular videos, the *CKY* (*Camp Kill Yourself*) series, in which he interspersed his own skating footage with bits involving the tormenting of his long-suffering parents and anyone else in his vicinity. With his surf wave of brown hair, devious smile, and matinee-idol eyes, Margera was an underground star at twenty-two. He was also the tour's mystery man. Behind those eyes lay an impossibly mischievous streak that seemed capable of anything at any moment, a mellow tiger ready to pounce. (He was born Brandon but nicknamed Bam Bam by his parents for his reckless abandon, and half of the moniker stuck.) When the bus was in motion, though, he seemed the calmest and most relaxed of the bunch, sitting on a couch and smiling beatifically out the window. At moments like that, he hardly seemed capable of stirring up anything, much less aggravating someone to the point of legal threats.

Yet this morning, Margera had accomplished precisely that, especially after he snuck away from the manager and the guards. Normally, everyone would have laughed off the confrontation, but suddenly, cell phones and walkie-talkies were going off, and the air became thick with anxiety. "The cops will be here in ten minutes," Stone barked into his cell.

No one could believe it—the manager had called the *police?* "We've got to go before the cops get here," said tour manager Bruno Musso to another caller. "We're leaving in a minute."

That minute was about twenty-nine earlier than planned, so the word was passed down that those skaters still in bed would have to meet up with the bus somewhere out of town, most likely at a truck stop. Anyone already on the vehicle would have to leave, *now.* From inside the bus, the skaters, Stone, and Musso could see the manager and guards scanning the parking lot; "I think he's in one of these," she was saying. Before the manager was able to pinpoint the exact vehicle, the bus lurched out of its curbside spot and onto the closest road. "Yeah, they'll never catch us," McKay cracked sleepily. "A big blue Tony Hawk bus going five miles an hour down the highway." Nervous glances were exchanged, but after a few minutes, it was apparent no police were in pursuit. Hawk emerged from the back—he had awoken early and decided to catch a few extra hours sleep in the rear lounge—and so did Margera, flashing a sly getaway smile. "Everyone was telling her I was some random dude," he said, "but I was hiding back there." He tried the trick three times and fell each time. "It's probably funnier that I fell," he added.

"Bam can be a walking problem," said Musso, "but we love him." With his dark, wavy hair and curlicue mustache, Musso could have passed for a silent-movie villain a century earlier. Now he was Hawk's tour manager and producer and, as he dubbed himself with a wry smile, "chaos manager." His cell phone headset seemingly embedded in his ear, Musso was charged with keeping things on schedule, getting directions to the next skatepark, buying the athletes new shoelaces, and, in general, keeping tabs on the twenty-one riders, two cameramen, and crew of the skatepark tour. A skater himself, he knew there was only so much he could do to keep the boys in check. "The only rule," he said, "is to get on the bus."

By late morning, everyone finally had; at the designated truck stop, the skaters who'd been left behind reunited with the bus, and what now lay ahead was a five-hour afternoon drive—a relatively short one by the standards of this tour—to the next demo, Aspen. Unlike actual rock stars, who drove overnight to the next gig, the skaters were traveling in the daylight hours, and everyone attempted to make good use of the wake time. Ellis, who called the Denver park "a slippery death trap," was peeling off expert metal riffs on an electric guitar; Vallely sat quietly with his laptop and headphones, writing his online journal. ("The demo yesterday was mediocre . . . the park was outdoor, cement, and sprawling . . . I never really got started.") Margera decided it was time to preview his upcoming CKY video, and the skaters gathered around a TV monitor to watch footage of lesbians making love and young men vomiting wine and stepping out of cars to defecate on streets. During a graphic masturbation scene, Hawk looked up from his laptop and said dryly, "That is *disturbing*," then groaned and laughed along with everyone else.

The drives were grueling, but it was hard for them to complain. Up front were three leather couches, a marble table for card games, and a big-screen TV and stereo, followed by a midsection kitchenette (the refrigerator perennially stocked with cold cuts, salads, water, and cheese), and a back lounge—the designated chill-out and nap space—with another massive entertainment system and more couches. The athletes flipped through skate magazines, mocking particular riders, and fiddled with their digital cameras and video cams; electronic gear, including iPods, was everywhere, the symbol of this particularly lucrative period of skating. On previous tours, including those Hawk had undertaken in the early nineties with his Birdhouse team, six skaters would share a room. On this tour, the athletes crashed in pricey hotels and earned $1,350 per demo; ESPN covered their travel fees, salaries, insurance, and per diems. The income, the business, the *attention,* never failed to astonish them. As the bus chugged along, Markovich talked about encountering a fan in Australia who asked him to sign his leg—after which the kid had a tattoo artist turn the signature into a tattoo. Still flabbergasted, Markovich recounted the way in which fans would approach him and repeat, verbatim, insignificant phrases he had uttered in one of Hawk's instructional videos. "It was just something I *said,*" he muttered.

When the bus eventually arrived at the Rio Grande skatepark in Aspen, the signs of their sport's passage into the mainstream were once again in their faces: the newish cement park with the scenic mountains in the distance, the teenagers flashing devil's-horns hand gestures in salute, the overall air of crowd anticipation and expectation. Boards tucked under their arms, the skaters filed out to applause and gapes and began skating the various bowls. Markovich, who always aimed for the grandest trick each time, attempted to skate down a cement walkway and ollie over shrubs and onto a basketball court below. "We gotta see this—this guy's gonna *die,*" one adult smiled to another as Markovich shouted for everyone to get out of his way. He then roared down the path, jumped over shrubs and rocks, landed on the court below—but didn't stay on the board. He tried, over and over, until finally, after ten attempts, he pulled it, and the now large crowd let out a collective "Whoa!" when he landed right and applauded. By then Markovich had a huge bruise on his side, above his butt.

For Hawk, scenes like these—the crowds, the applause, the flurry of activity upon his arrival—had become routine but not always entirely pleasant, and the herds gathered around to watch him skate were, again, not leaving him much room. As soon as he dropped in, he heard the three words he most dreaded: "Do a 900!" No one watching seemed to realize exactly how difficult it was to pull such a trick, how many attempts it would involve, and how certain conditions, such as the size of the ramp, were important factors in pulling it. After a while, he returned to the bus, and once the others filed back on, talk turned to the quality of the park and how the crowds were once more too overwhelming. Burnquist noted how one local criticized him for not wearing wrist guards. "Those kids were bummin' me out," Hawk piped in. "I was in the middle of a transfer and I hear, 'Tony!' And I'm like, 'Can I finish first?' Then when I fell and crumpled, some kid said, 'That's why it's good to have pads.'" Hawk flashed a deadpan frown. "I could do without the sarcasm."

One of the last to get back on board was Jason Ellis. Again and again, he dropped into one of the bowls; by late afternoon, only a few fans were left to watch, but it didn't seem to matter. Ellis was thirty now, a legendary skate-tour party animal from Melbourne relocated to Southern California, who was trying to rein in some of his past excesses. With his two-hundred-pound frame and boisterous rasp, he could have been mistaken for a club doorman as much as a skater who had, the year before, set a new Guinness world record for highest skateboard drop (twenty-eight feet). "I wouldn't know what to do with myself if I didn't scare myself every day," he said, taking a breather on a bench next to the bowl, helmet in hand, sweat dotting his forehead. "Sooner or later, I'd have to find something else to scare myself. It's about having butterflies and being alive." He smiled ruefully. "It's cheesy, but that's why I do it." He dropped in again and again, finally pulling his trick on what he estimated as the fiftieth time. By then, hardly anyone was left to cheer, but his job was done.

In a development as common as the sight of a product sticker underneath a board, Ellis paid the price the following morning. Daylight never came easily to the tour or the skaters, barging in on them when they least welcomed it. As another early departure loomed, this time from their Aspen hotel, the skaters slunk out of their rooms, and none looked more uncomfortable with the concept of walking than Ellis, who was hobbling around with what he called "the heel bruise from hell" from his solo session the afternoon before. "That's the thing about getting older—it hurts the next day. But like I said yesterday," he added with a wince-smeared smile, "it's all worth it." He hoisted himself aboard the bus, where medic Barry Zaritsky taped an ice pack to his right wrist and began massaging Ellis's arm as the skater sat silently on a couch, head bowed in pain. The sensation of ice on bruised or sprained skin was one few of them relished, but they had grown as accustomed to it as they had to their lifestyles, which required them to be away from their recently purchased homes (and in some cases, wives and children) for a good chunk of the year.

After everyone mumbled greetings to each other and began noshing on take-away hotel coffee and pastries, the drive began, as did the entertainment—movies on the back-bus TV, skate videos on the one up front. Watching one of the latter, Vallely lit up with a rare smile when a security guard attempted to block a skater and both ended up on the ground. "I never understand what those guys are thinking," he said. "Get the fuck out of the *way*." In the rear lounge, someone pulled out a copy of *American Movie*. "What's that?" Shaun White asked. Dubbed the Flying Tomato, he was both mascot and punching bag, admired for his youthful bravado and big-air skills on both skateboard and his usual piece of gear, a snowboard.

He was told the film was a documentary about an independent filmmaker from Wisconsin.

"Any death or killing?" he replied.

Told no, he lost interest. The mood was restrained and mellow, the tinny melodies of cell phones chirping around the bus as skaters took care of business, read, napped, and played cards.

Since the previous demos had been so cramped and nerve-racking, it had been decided that an impromptu session at a remote spot would be the cure for the skaters' frustration. The designated unannounced stop was a relatively new park in Grand Junction, Colorado, in the west-central part of the state. The bus exited the highway and wound its way down maple-tree-shaded streets, and there it was—right behind a high school, an Enter at Your Own Risk sign stuck to the chain-link fence that surrounded it. "Oh, wow," Hawk said, putting aside the book he was reading—Mötley Crüe's autobiography—and gazing out the window. Preparing for battle, the skaters went through another of their periodic rituals—replacing the grip tape on the decks or tightening the wheels and trucks of their boards, tasks they diligently attended to themselves. (They were rock stars, but without road crews.) Then they disembarked and rolled into the small, homey park with concrete bowls and a small street course.

On the way in, they casually walked past a half dozen local kids who could only stare with open, dental-checkup mouths at what was happening before them on this late Saturday afternoon. It had been enough of a stunner to see the imposing Hawk tour bus pull up; to then see one familiar face after another march into the park was too much for some of them to grasp. The kids stood, gaping, as Hawk strode by, then Margera, then Burnquist—giants they had read about or seen on television who were now walking among them. It was as if Dave Matthews had walked past a coffeehouse in a small town and decided, impulsively, to drop in and give a concert next to the cappuccino machine. "I'm used to looking at magazines and videos," said fourteen-year-old Cameron, who shook his head as if he were trying to awaken himself from a feverish dream. "This is the craziest thing I've ever seen." In decades past, fresh-faced, clear-skinned types like Cameron and his two buddies, Nick and Jeremiah, would have been found in the local sandlot, practicing their swings and catching fly balls. But today, the baseball and football fields next door were deserted, and instead the trio held skateboards and wore T-shirts that sported the logos of action-sport companies. They had been skating for several years and repeated what had become the mantra of their generation's interest in these activities: There were no coaches, no schedules, no forced practices. As one pro skater after another pushed off on his board and began practicing tricks in the otherwise empty skatepark, Cameron ran off to buy a disposable camera.

By now, the athletes were skating for no one but themselves; the park, unlike others, also allowed BMX bikes, so Rick Thorne was able to haul out his stunt bike and pedal around as well. Hawk himself sat out most of the session; in a cruel irony the day before, he had turned one of his knees into a grapefruit not by skating but while white-water rafting, part of the wacky-shenanigans footage ESPN required for the TV series of the tour. But the fans, who were increasing by the minute as word spread by way of cell phones, didn't seem to mind. Burnquist began attempting a backside board-slide, ollie-ing onto a black iron rail and sliding down it backward, the board perfectly balanced. He was nailing the slide but not the landing, so he kept trying, displaying his masterfully elegant way of falling: Every time he came off his board after leaving the rail, his rubbery figure practically folded into himself, or he popped right into a handstand. Markovich climbed onto an RV and, as the crowd pointed and watched, gave thought to jumping off it into the park, but after a while, even he realized he might be tempting the gods too much and climbed back down. On another side of the park, Vallely began tackling a stall—skating up a ramp and smacking the wheels of his board onto the chain-link fence, then dropping back in. "It's a life lesson," he said later. "I never stop until I make it. This might be silly, but sometimes I think me pulling a trick is empowering people. I *have* to follow through. If I quit, what am I telling them?" He finally nailed it after a few dozen attempts. Several hours and many autographs later, the skaters returned to the bus, leaving behind a crowd still gawking at what it had just witnessed.

While the others skated, Hawk, still nursing his rafting injury, spent the time working on his computer and his phone. He was already thinking ahead to his Boom Boom HuckJam tour, which was scheduled to begin in just a few months. Lining up sponsors had been difficult, since the concept of action-sports stars playing arenas as if they really *were* rock stars was an untested idea. But thanks to his sister and comanager Pat, Activision and a few other corporations had finally been convinced to cough up enough money to offset the $6 million production cost; Hawk himself had had to shell out over a million of his own dollars to hire the production company that built stages for 'N Sync to construct a magnificent European birch vert ramp exclusively for the HuckJam. The idea for the tour, he said, derived from the overcrowded conditions of the Gigantic Skatepark Tour. "The lesson we learned from this tour is that the audience for skaters isn't just skaters," he said. "Now it's parents and people who play video games. It's now a spectator sport. Which isn't *bad,* but it's strange. You're used to everyone being in the know and knowing our reputations. Now it's people showing up and blurting out '900!' at a *street* demo."

Just then, Hawk glanced out the window and spied a very young and nubile blonde talking to a few of the skaters. He had witnessed many such scenes before on this tour, and he just chuckled and pointed at the sight. Later, after the bus had departed and was back en route to the next stop, Salt Lake City, he looked up and saw a flash of blond hair entering the bathroom. *"Hello?"* Hawk said in genuine disbelief. The last thing he needed, for his life or his family-entertainer image, was a potentially underage fan aboard bringing unwanted controversy. As he would later recall of that moment, "I was like, 'I don't even wanna *know.*'" Instead, he merely cocked an eyebrow and decided to take a wait-and-see attitude.

Hawk was the leader of a leaderless community, and by disposition he was not a very commanding ruler; he made his presence and wishes known in subtle ways. When he was dissatisfied—for instance, with the way a trick had been filmed for a video—he would either fall silent or say "Whatever." Even his wife, as he wrote in his autobiography, would talk to him about his hard-to-read expressions. "At times Tony bores the hell out of me, because he's not the most dynamic personality," Vallely, who had known Hawk over a decade, said. "But he always tries to put the sport and all the other athletes first. He never goes, 'Yeah, I'm the best.' It's not who he is." Confrontation did not suit him; he let others, including his new comanager, who also worked with musicians like No Doubt and the Offspring, handle the particulars. Even after all those years in the spotlight, he exuded shyness and a degree of social awkwardness. His agreeable smile could quickly recede. Around strangers or fans who approached him, small talk did not come easily, as if he were trying to figure out if they were tuned into his world or attempting to exploit it as so many had done over the years. With autograph seekers, he never failed to say hello and scrawl his signature on whatever they wanted to have signed. Then, if he couldn't beat a fast retreat, he and they would stand around hesitantly, until the fan eventually left. One of his tour nicknames was the Hummingbird, since he tended to spend evenings in his hotel room rather than carousing with his peers.

Thanks to the protracted drive ahead of them—an estimated eight or nine straight hours to Salt Lake City—there would be no barhopping that night, so the party came to them. Things started calmly, with a game of blackjack, but by nine P.M., the beer bongs had emerged and the loud music became even louder, the bass lines of Eminem and AC/DC songs rattling the bus walls. Entire cans of beer were poured into a plastic bong and disappeared into the skaters' mouths, followed by increasingly boisterous cheers. Eventually, several skaters switched to coffee bongs. At first, Hawk stayed in the back, working on his laptop and answering e-mail—he was a renowned gadget and electronics freak—but eventually he, too, joined in, lurching into break-dance moves as songs by Nelly, Pink, and the Red Hot Chili Peppers blasted on. The Chili Peppers' "By the Way" had become the tour's unofficial theme song, cranked up before each and every demo. It played again this evening, many times, along with "Cabron," a flamenco-rock number from the band's latest album that made for an even easier half-sober sing-along. Eventually, everyone was raging—standing, singing, jumping, yelling, and imbibing in the narrow aisle of the bus, the air thick with brawny, sweat-drenched machismo. The young blond stowaway, who was close to legal age, sat and watched quietly, smiling amusedly as the athletes let out steam that had been repressed the previous few days.

The emcee, Sal Masekela, who had witnessed his share of revelries while working for action-sports clothing companies and *Transworld Skateboarding* magazine, opted to take a breather in the back. "We just arrived at the reality tollbooth and passed right through it," he murmured sleepily as he pushed aside backpacks and settled onto the floor. Moments later, Vallely and Sumner came crashing through the door that separated the front of the bus from the back, and Masekela jumped up, startled and angry: An inch or two more, and his head would have been cracked open.

"That's gonna be a problem," Hawk said, straight-faced, staring at the unhinged door.

*   *   *

As the party commenced, Bob Burnquist sat quietly in the rear of the bus. His face was long, narrow, and unshaven; with his black glasses, baggy jeans, and lack of shoes, he looked like a scholarly slacker. Balancing a laptop on his knees, he was more than happy to show off the latest digital photos stored on his hard drive—aerial shots of his house in Vista, California, complete with a massive $110,000 vert ramp that was, in the words of one visitor, "like Noah's ark." His neighbors, Burnquist said, had moved in after the ramp had been built, so "they knew what they were getting into." Every time he heard a particularly loud crash or barrage of shouts from the front of the bus, he smiled ever so slightly. He had been there before, many times, and often in much worse condition.

Growing up in São Paulo, the son of a Brazilian mother and an American father who had moved to the country to work in the agricultural industry, Burnquist's troubles weren't bad at first. He had started skating at eleven when a friend borrowed and never returned his soccer ball; in exchange, young Bob took his friend's fiberglass board. He had dabbled in soccer in school, but an asthmatic condition—caused by growing up in a drafty old house and the local pollution, he said—curtailed his participation in any rigorous team activities. When a concrete skatepark opened up three blocks from his house, he found a second home.

For his twelfth birthday, he asked for a better board, one of the heavier Brazilian models. His father bought one for him, and together they assembled it in the family garage one weekend. His hobby, though, almost came to a halt when he was skating downhill one day; his board flew out from under him and was crushed beneath a passing truck. "It was the most devastating thing to me," he recalled. Eventually he received another, but it only proved a temporary distraction from the repressive environment around him, one of devastating poverty, drug trafficking and its accompanying violence, and water shortages. By his teenage years, he was sniffing glue and buying cheap cocaine on the streets, sometimes from the older skaters he met in the park. "I was trying to run away from things," he said. "I found an exit. Sniffing glue took me to another place. I got addicted to escape. Now, I can't believe I did that—putting that gnarly chemical into my body. And I'm *asthmatic*." He realized his drug use was getting the best of him when he stayed out so late one night that he missed an important skateboard photo shoot the next morning. In 1994, he met editors of *Thrasher* while they were visiting Brazil; Burnquist's bilingual education—he spoke Portuguese and English— proved helpful to the Americans, and in return, they invited him back to San Francisco, where he more or less moved in 1995. That year, he won first place in Vancouver's international pro skate competition, the Slam City Jam, and Burnquist's life and career were never the same. He was brilliant at both vert and street skating, his tall, loosey-goosey body easily adapting to both styles, but he was perhaps best known for perfecting the art of switch—riding not with one's normal foot forward but with the other, a tactic that would hobble most other riders. "You get to the point where new tricks are harder to find," he recalled. "I just fell into it." Hawk, who was nearly ten years his senior, was in awe of him: "What Bob has been doing is stuff I could never conceive of when I was younger. In my wildest dreams, I'd say, 'What if we did this and this?' He's out there making it happen."

His Brazilian background was far from the only thing that set Burnquist apart from his fellow skateboarders. He had a calm, Zen-like demeanor and had become a spiritist Christian who did not believe in pain medication (he wanted to *feel* the injuries, he said). He did, however, subscribe to theories of reincarnation and always seemed to be reading one book or another on the subject. Whereas other skaters projected a wizened ruggedness and cynicism, Burnquist emanated the mellow, affable vibe of the marijuana advocate and practicing vegan he was. He had passed on a Mountain Dew endorsement deal because, he said, "The product and what it does to you and attaching it to sports figures—kids shouldn't be drinking that and eating pizza. I know I'm going against the grain, but that's how I feel." ("We've had Pepsi interested and candy bar companies," his manager, Steve Astephen, said. "He won't do it, no matter how much money it is. He's a *hippie*.") He was a twenty-five-year-old with a wife, a one-year-old daughter, and the respect of tour skaters, who knew he was chilling in the back and would join in when the time was right.

Eventually Burnquist did precisely that; even he realized that cutting loose was not an entirely bad idea. Before long he was dancing atop the marble table to yet another playback of "Cabron" until everyone was too drunk or too caught up in the moment to do anything but shout along with it. It kept going, for hours and hours— driver Rogan would later say that the bus was rocking back and forth so powerfully that he had to work to keep the vehicle on the road— until finally, around three in the morning, the bus pulled up to the front of the Salt Lake City hotel. The Red Hot Chili Peppers were no longer heard; everyone had grown so sick of their CD that someone had thrown it out the window of the moving bus. The riders staggered off, checked in, and finally crashed. By that point, most of them had been up almost eighteen hours straight.

"It's been mellower than past years," Masekela said the next morning, words that could not have been more surprising. "We were *super*rowdy two years ago. When we first got the bus and we thought we were the Backstreet Boys? You have *no* idea."

Here was the thing about skateparks that truly set them and their sport apart from softball, football, and the rest: The more flawless the venue, the less satisfactory. Private skateparks were now popping up around the country in shopping malls, complete with admission prices and guidelines; pads and helmets had to be worn, liability forms had to be signed. In those settings, skateboarding and capitalism truly merged, since the concept called for parents to drop off their children and then shop until the kids were ready to drop from too many drop-ins. Some of these venues were satisfactory, but to many skaters, they felt like sterile prisons. "Too clean, too well-lit, it's in a mall—it doesn't make sense," Vallely said. "This wave of concrete parks being built around the country—it's cool, but I'm used to fighting for my space, like at a warehouse."

They, or Vallely at least, got what they wished for when the bus arrived the next afternoon at the Proving Grounds skatepark in Pleasant Grove, Utah, just outside of Salt Lake City. The park was located on the grainy fringes of the town, jammed next to an auto body shop, the smell of gasoline and the whiff of dust in the air. It had neither the beautiful vistas nor fresh mountain air of the park in Aspen; it was not even outdoors but inside a large, hangar-style structure that had once been a whirlpool factory. When the owners had taken it over two years before, they discovered hundreds of empty hot tubs inside. The interior, with its white cinder-block walls, overhead fluorescent lighting, and buttressing posts swathed in worn duct tape, was even grodier. Ventilation was a foreign concept, the only relief stemming from several huge fans that attempted, with limited success, to cool the place down—a futile gesture given both the close-to-hundred-degree temperature outside and the hundreds of spectators already packed into the place. Several local police stood guard outside. ESPN's contract required that any beverages sold on the premises not have labels (so as not to antagonize the tour's sponsors), so park employees had had to buy cases of Pepsi and Coke and spray-paint the cans. Overall, the event did not promise much in the way of glory.

Such quick judgments, however, were the domain of untrained eyes. Maybe it was the leftover energy from the previous night's bus bacchanal. Maybe it was the inspirational, one-for-the-Gipper speech Vallely gave before the bus arrived at the park, detailing how he had visited a sixteen-year-old skater in a local hospital who had been paralyzed after a diving accident. ("It's so important to seize the moment," he told the skaters, looking down, as if not used to such public pronouncements. "We have the power to do it, we owe it to these people and we owe it to ourselves." Everyone applauded, and even Masekela put aside his outrage over the door-crashing incident and hugged Vallely.) Maybe it was the sight of thirty-two thousand square feet with an eight-foot wall ride, a handful of rails, six-foot quarter-pipes, and other enticements. Maybe it was the simple fact that the event was actually organized, with the eventual thirty-five hundred fans in attendance kept behind barricades and the skaters having room to roam as a result. Maybe it was, as Vallely also mentioned in his speech, that the tour was winding down and that these skaters might never congregate again under one roof. Maybe this was their moment, just as it was skateboarding's moment, one that might not come around again with such intensity until they were old and worn and could only fantasize about executing some of the tricks they were doing at this point in their lives.

Whatever the reasons, it was instantly clear that this stop would be different from the last few. Once again, the bus ground to a halt near the park's entrance; once more, the skaters and Thorne grabbed their gear and walked, briskly and single file, into the structure, past crowds and a few chunky security men in rent-a-guard T-shirts. For the thousandth time in their lives, they dropped their boards to the ground, took in the array of ramps, wedges, walls, and rails before them, and pushed off in search of possibilities, options, and the gnarliest move possible. As usual, they all went their own ways: Some instantly ollied onto the rails in the middle of the park, others rode up to the ramps and dropped in. Hawk was among them; his knee was feeling much better, and even though street riding was not his specialty, he was ready to make up for lost riding time. The sound of polyurethane wheels grinding on the floor and boards *clack-*

clacking as they hit walls began building into a cacophony. Amidst it, Masekela took the microphone and began shouting each skater's name, and the demo more or less began.

And then something clicked. It was hard to say when, since everyone was going at once, crisscrossing each other, lost in their own world or following a particular line and seeing what part of the course he wanted to try. It was an ant colony filled with skateboarding ants, and the crowd didn't know where to look. Before long, Margera was doing backside boardslides; Thorne was pumping his bike up a wall and attempting a backflip, missing once, twice, before nailing it the third time. The crowd screamed wildly at each completed trick. The riding was superb and smooth, from Burnquist to Alex Chalmers, who went up the eight-foot wall. Then shouts of "Bam! Bam!" began filling the air, and there was Margera, who had climbed atop one of the electrical boxes up the wall; it was clear he was about to drop in on the ramp below. The idea seemed lunatic, and the crowd went momentarily silent. With that diabolical look, he let go of his board and, as it fell, jumped down onto it in midair. When he hit the ground, though, he fell off it. *Ohhhh,* went the crowd. He climbed up again, the applause increasing. ("We're daredevils in a way," Hawk said earlier, "but we're pretty calculated with what we're trying. We know if we really think we can do it. We're not just throwing caution to the wind. That's one misconception. And whether we like it or not, people *do* like to see the falls.") Margera tried again, and again fell. Then, suddenly, Vallely was up there, too, on a nearby beam of his own, and he also launched off—holding the board with one hand, dropping in and planting his feet back on it halfway down, only to miss himself. The crowd couldn't get enough; it was all they wanted to see. By then, Vallely and Margera began taking turns attempting the move, the crowd shifting its attention from one man to the other. Finally, after five attempts, Vallely pulled it, staying on his board after he hit the ground and skidding into the barricades and the crowd, and the place felt as if it had been hardwired with several thousand volts.

They were feeding off each other's creativity now, and no one could or would dare stop them. Given the roster of talent, the crowd must have felt it was watching the equivalent of a basketball game with the sport's biggest names letting loose on the same court at once. Anything and everything in the park that wasn't nailed down—and some that was—made for a potential trick. Before long, Thorne was moving an aluminum ladder over to a rolled-up canopy above a garage door, then climbing up onto it with his bike, and he, too, was dropping in off the same height—seven feet—onto a five-foot quarter-pipe. Then Ellis was up there beside him, repeating the trick on his board. Markovich, who always seemed to gravitate toward the riskiest, most potentially limb-damaging move, was zooming down a ramp, flying into the air, and attempting a vaulting frontside grab over a twelve-foot gap. He couldn't stay on the board, but kept going back again and again and again; with each attempt, his long hair grew sweatier and stringier, his torso grimier with the dirt from the floor he kept hitting, his expression more frustrated. At one point he crashed and didn't get up, the crowd quieted, and Zaritsky ran over and talked to him until, finally, Markovich stood up and returned to try once more.

Each time a skater pulled a trick, his compadres on the tour offered a victory salute, smacking their boards against the coping in a succession of *clack clack clack clacks*. After an hour, their T-shirts were like wet paper towels stuck to their skin. What had initially looked unpromising had turned into an astonishing display of athleticism, determination, and imagination. Here, in their element, they truly were rock stars. Real rock stars had become increasingly packaged and programmed; after Kurt Cobain died, it was rare to find someone who sliced himself up, literally or figuratively, onstage with such determination. By then, rock rebellion meant the likes of

Marilyn Manson, whose S&M-ghoul persona covered the face of
little more than an old-fashioned entertainer. When it came to
witnessing a truly rebellious act, the sight of a self-lacerating skateboarder destroying a park, staircase, handrail, and possibly himself
must have hit harder than concerts by the biggest bands of the
moment.

After over an hour, the spectators, who ranged from preteen boys
to curious parents, had drifted outside, where Hawk's Boom Boom
HuckJam vert ramp, specially imported for the occasion, was temporarily set up; it looked like the world's largest subway tunnel sliced
in half. Vert skating was far more technical and, in many ways, hard-
core athletic than street riding. When the skaters dropped into ramps
that could be as intimidatingly deep as thirteen feet, shooting up the
transitions and into the air and pulling off a complex series of bends,
twists, and grabs, it was not hard to imagine the day when the
Olympic committee would come calling, just as they had done with
snowboarding and its comparable moves. To its detractors, vert
skating had become the province of a new breed of career-minded
action-sports jock, yet even vert skeptics like Vallely could do little
but stand atop the ramp and watch, in amazement, as Hawk,
Burnquist, White, and others effortlessly jettisoned into the air,
contorted their body in unimaginable ways, and dropped back in.
As Anthrax's version of Public Enemy's "Bring the Noise" erupted
from large speakers, Hawk went for a frontside five, or a rodeo flip,
which he'd invented back in 1983 and hadn't attempted in years.
Burnquist pulled off something no one had seen before: a kickflip to
fingerflip to fakie, which, in essence, involved flipping the board
beneath him while in midair. White proved the advantages of starting
in snowboarding with a backside rodeo, a backflip in which he did a
backside half-twist. "This is the way it normally is," said Hawk
partner Morgan Stone by the side of the ramp.

Months later, reflecting back on the third and last tour, Hawk would have mixed feelings: "Honestly, it wasn't as fun for me as the other two were. Too many . . . *people*. You know? It just felt like too much pressure." He would come to prefer the HuckJam expedition, a show as intricately choreographed as an Ice Capades gig, albeit with punk bands performing live alongside the vert ramp during its first run, in 2002. When that tour finally got under way, it would do reasonably well, often grossing between $300,000 and $500,000 a night and pulling in an average of ten thousand per arena. Due to its production costs, it would barely break even, but it made enough to guarantee a second run the following year.

For now, however, moments like the Pleasant Grove demo were the ones the skates cherished. Whether they were trying to pull a new trick or reconquer one they hadn't attempted in years, their chosen sport was not simply about self-reliance but self-esteem, not just bravado and anything-goes creativity but constant hurdles. As any skate aficionado would affirm, the sport could never truly be conquered; there were simply too many tricks and variations, to the point where mastering just one move could take hours, days, months, even a lifetime. To the professionals, skateboarding was not kids' stuff; as long as their bodies would allow, it would be adult education as well. "To this day," Burnquist said, "what keeps me doing it is freedom. The accomplishments are all mine, no one else's. We have to know we can do things ourselves and not rely on others. There's a whole process of learning a trick that's about growing and character, and you try to transfer that to your life."

The demo finished, the skaters collapsed in the bus, red-faced and exhausted, while others wandered out into the crowd milling around outside. The teenage stowaway from Grand Junction was met by friends and family members who volunteered to drive her back home. Girls approached White for an autograph or a kiss; even Hawk stepped out to meet fans who might have thought he was a video-game creation rather than an actual, living-breathing human. Ellis, meanwhile, had skated both street and vert and looked it. He was crouching on the bus's front bumper, head sagging, helmet off, his face covered in perspiration beads. A group of fans gathered around him, and even though his body was aching and he felt like dropping, he dutifully signed their helmets and posters. As much as anyone on the tour, Ellis played the part of intimidating rock-star skater, but for a moment, he dropped his laddie-lout image and tried to deflect the reverence directed his way.

"I'm just the same as you—only lucky," he huffed out.

"Are you saying I'm not lucky?" one kid shot back with an I-dare-you smile.

"Not *today* you aren't," Ellis snapped. Then he smiled slightly. "I'm just falling, eating, and sleeping. That's my job."

Out of earshot of the fans, he looked over at a busmate and said quietly, "I left out a few things. On purpose."

4. CORE-MART
scenes from the world of shoes, videos, gear, and the industry within

The process commenced on crisp, cloudless mornings like this, in hulking, utilitarian buildings like this tucked away throughout Southern California. In this case, the structure was off-white and bulky, and the area was a leafy block in the industrial-park section of Santa Fe Springs, just south of Los Angeles. Only the logo, immediately recognizable to anyone with the remotest awareness of the new sports, distinguished the building from the similarly nondescript warehouse complexes flanking it. Above the receptionist, a silver skateboard was attached to a plaque that read FOOTWEAR COMPANY OF THE YEAR 2000. Once visitors were permitted to enter, they were handed laminated passes and escorted into a muted, businesslike compound of white walls and latte-colored carpeting. Other than the award in the lobby—and that, by strange coincidence, the building's address was Shoemaker Avenue—the only hint of the company's livelihood were the photographs of snowboarders and skateboarders that lined the otherwise undistinguished hallways, and the second-floor conference room called, tongue fairly deep in cheek, Skate "Board" Room.

Like all such rooms, this one held an elongated conference table that stretched down its middle. Unlike such rooms, however, the slatted walls resembled those of a shoe store, complete with small plastic shelves that held samples of the roughly seven hundred sneaker styles and color schemes sold by the company. The shoe-emporium motif was not accidental, since the firm, Vans, was serious about its foot products and had been since the earliest days of the Vietnam War. To outsiders, sneakers were sneakers, but not in *this* room, where the company's trademark shoe—a black-and-white checker-board-tile model—was displayed alongside those as beefy and rugged as mountain boots, as casual as loafers, or as simple and uncluttered as moccasins. And those were just the skateboarding models: The BMX shoes, with pegs on the soles for better pedal gripping, were also on display, and prototypes of new snowboard boots were being examined in cluttered cubicles across the hall. The shoe colors ranged from mustard yellow to charcoal gray to late-night dark, and most models sported the company's trademark wide-pattern sole, which resembled a waffle iron that had been nailed onto its bottom.

As Colin McKay had said during the Hawk skatepark tour, the action-sport army did indeed number in the millions, and the army needed gear. They craved sneakers and skate decks and wheels and bicycle frames and logoed T-shirts and compact wallets and watches and helmets and wrist guards and elbow pads and skullcaps and waterproof pants and belts and puffy shorts and hooded sweatshirts and jeans (preferably slim, at least for the moment), as well as backpacks in which to carry it all. They lived to pore through the hundreds of photos that appeared in the dozens of magazines that diligently covered the sports, and they eagerly kept up with the ceaseless blitz of long-form videos they could watch, study, and rewind to learn how to master the tricks themselves. If they wanted to practice in the solitude of their own backyard, they could even buy portable slant ramps for $200.

To serve this market, a vast industry had emerged that, like the Vans building, was both sizable and covert, above and below the radar. These were not the Madison Avenue corporations the athletes eyed suspiciously but rather their own, endemic companies founded or run by current and former skaters, bikers, and surfers. Most were based between Los Angeles and San Diego County, in towns like Vista and Garden Grove, yet the industry also extended from coast to coast and over to Europe and Asia, employing hundreds of thousands of people who conceived, designed, manufactured, marketed, and hyped anything and everything designed for professionals, amateurs, weekend riders, and those who simply yearned to live vicariously through the sports. Ironically, it had become more costly to participate in the new do-it-yourself sports than in the ones they aimed to replace: A top-quality skateboard, complete with wheels and trucks, could run $150 (far more than a basketball or a baseball mitt), and all the necessary gear for snowboarding—board, boots, bindings, and so forth—could easily add up to $500. In 2002, the research firm Corporate Marketing Information estimated the combined annual clothing, shoe, and accessories market at $9.9 billion, although that figure was hard to gauge since few of the companies were public and most were not especially eager to talk up their fortunes. Whatever the figure, no one denied there were many products to be sold and much money to be made from what had become an inordinately bustling sector.

Vans was neither the most au courant nor cutting-edge of these businesses—smaller, feistier ones with more attitude and street credibility continued to rise up to challenge it—but it was the most inveterate and established; its fortieth anniversary was on the horizon. By now, Vans not only made sneakers and boots but visors, caps, pants, snowboarding vests, and socks ("action sport socks," to be more specific), which were sold in both its own outlets as well as JC Penny and Kohl department stores. The previous year, Vans had scored an all-time-high net income of $15 million based on sales of $341.2 million. That number was minor league compared to the

billions Adidas and Nike grossed—basketball shoes still commandeered the footwear market, of which the action-sport-shoe sector
amounted to less than 10 percent—but it was an impressive figure
nonetheless. Just as important, Vans had survived good times and
bad, sales surges and recessions, popularity swings and backlashes. Its
tenacity made it something of a metaphor for the sports: as skateboarding or BMX or snowboarding went, so did, in many ways, Vans
itself.

In this competitive climate, where exacting customers could turn on
a company at any moment and declare it unworthy of their support,
stasis was death. Therefore, three times a year, the company rolled
out roughly a dozen new skateboard and BMX sneakers and snowboard boots. On this morning, the time had come for the design
department to look over ideas for the following year, since shoe
planning started a year to eighteen months ahead of time. A half
dozen young men, all in T-shirts, sneakers without socks, and loose
shorts with massive pockets, began congregating in the conference
room. Before the meeting began, Chris Strain, a marketing executive
with tousled hair, a polo shirt, and a congenial manner, popped in
and previewed for them a new television spot featuring British
skateboarder Geoff Rowley, whose signature shoe was one of the
company's strongest sellers. "The more anguish I have in my life, the
more despair, the more I love to skate," said Rowley on the TV
screen. With his accent and long, stringy hair, he could easily have
passed for an original member of Oasis.

"That's dope," said one of the designers.

Standing nearby was Dana Guidice, the vice president of product
development, who sported a small goatee, dark, spiky hair, a chain
tattoo that circled his ankles, and sunken, late-night-out eyes. Spread
out before him were a dozen shoe prototypes. For the following
season, the department was preparing a line that would include many
different models: twenty-three "men's classics," fifteen "signature

models" (named after specific athletes and designed with their input), twelve for "skate performance," two for "skate casual," and six for BMX. The line would also incorporate thirty five sneakers specifically for young boys, seven for girls, and three for toddlers. Each shoe would be test-marketed before it arrived in stores; signature models would bounce back and forth between company and rider several times, the rider making alterations until the final version was firmed up. Although the athletes were not designers, they could tell when, say, a stitch line could potentially result in an irritation or rub or the mesh was not airy enough. "Skaters come in and work with the designers," Guidice said as he pointed out models displayed on the walls. "Some want a heavier or beefier shoe, others want a lighter one. They want you to take away this or that. Skaters are very exacting in their preference. I worked with Shaq on his sneaker, and he wasn't nearly as discriminating as the least discriminating skater." He shook his head a little and flashed a wry smile. "All of them have shoe fetishes."

In a room beneath them that was the size of an airport hangar—complete with a high, chain-link fence that only seemed to be lacking drooling guard dogs—were the fruits of his department's labor. Extending from floor to extremely high ceiling were metal shelves stacked with box upon box of shoes. Forklifts beeped and whirred, preparing for the next shipment that would be arriving directly from manufacturing plants in Asia and then be transported to skate shops or malls around the country. Back upstairs, the Chinese food delivery arrived, the door to the Skate "Board" Room closed, and the time came to determine, as best possible, what style of shoes would be in demand in another year and a half and what would and would not be considered fashionable by the company's young, demanding customers.

"Today, there's twenty-five companies we're competing with," said Steve Van Doren, the company's gregarious vice president of promotion and events as he sat in his office wearing a Hawaiian shirt. Van Doren, who was forty-five, always seemed to be wearing a Hawaiian top no matter the locale. "Every time I open up a magazine there's a new company. A lot of competition. That wasn't the case twenty years ago. Now, the technology and faxes and e-mails and transportation have made it available for anyone to start up their own company. Everybody wants a little piece of what's out there."

At one point, even calling it an industry was a bit ridiculous. Van Doren could recall a time when the entire action-sport business amounted to a handful of California-based skateboard companies like Makaha and Gordon & Smith; since wakeboarding, BMX, freestyle motocross, snowboarding, and the rest did not exist in the early sixties, neither did their gear. In March 1966, another addition to the nascent industry arrived with the opening of an Anaheim sneaker store owned by Paul Van Doren. Van Doren, Steve's father, had spent twenty years working for the Randolph Rubber Company, a prominent Boston shoe manufacturer; he was then transferred to Orange County to help straighten out the company's West Coast manufacturing plant. After a falling-out with the owner, Van Doren gathered his children together and told them not to worry, but he was going to start his own company and fulfill a dream: to manufacture shoes and sell them in his own stores, bypassing wholesalers. Thus, with three other partners including Paul's son Jim, began the Van Doren Rubber Company. The name befitted a condom business more than the makings of a board-sport empire, but the shoes—particularly the first one, a blue slip-on—attracted surfers and skaters alike for two equally important reasons: their trademark sole, which gripped boards inordinately well, and their affordability (the sneakers were initially priced between $2.49 and $4.99). When the Zephyr team skaters, particularly Tony Alva and Stacy Peralta, began wearing them in the midseventies, Vans' status as the leading skate-shoe company was sealed. Mainstream prestige arrived a few years later, in 1982, when Sean Penn, as rascally surfer dude Jeff Spicoli, prominently flashed his Vans in *Fast Times at Ridgemont High*.

Action-sport companies were allowed to expand, but, as Vans would learn, such growth had to be done carefully and delicately, without upsetting or alienating the core constituency. For the Van Doren Rubber Company, the eighties were the beginning of a bumpy ride that would last well over a decade and come to symbolize the treacherous hills and valleys of the action-sports industry. First, the company overextended itself by attempting to venture into baseball and basketball sneakers, resulting in a Chapter 11 bankruptcy filing in 1984. "It wasn't our niche," Steve Van Doren said, "and it was costing too much." The company changed hands in 1988 when the family sold it to the investment firm McCown De Leeuw & Co., Inc. and officially shortened the name to Vans, but its troubles weren't over. Within the industry, Vans was seen as taking from the community but not giving back, resulting in a low net income of $1.4 million by 1994. The year before, Walter Schoenfeld, who had founded Brittania Jeans before selling it to Levi's, had taken over, but Vans' roller-coaster ride didn't end there: Business was up when Schoenfeld shifted some manufacturing from the United States to Asia; down when he retired, after which the company again slumped; and back up when he (and his M.B.A. son Gary, who later succeeded him) returned in 1995, eventually closing Vans' last American factory and shifting all manufacturing to Asia. "It's a public company and you have to grow your business," said Steve Van Doren, defending the company's business plans. "You can't just do it by staying in the core shops."

By the late nineties, Vans had learned innumerable lessons from its stumbles. The New York firm Weber Shandwick Worldwide was hired to buff Vans' image, and the firm's statement of purpose on the Vans account encapsulated the shoe company's refined strategy: The goal was to "leverage Vans' hip, cool, fun brand image across a wider range of media outlets . . . without the appearance of 'selling out' in the eyes of their core audience." Even after Vans parted with the agency, the message lived on: Vans could go mass market, but only to a point. The company began working overtime to return to the good graces of its customers and market. To demonstrate support for the sports, Vans started up competitions, bought into the annual Warped Tour to solidify the bond between skating and mall punks, and began building skateparks in malls from Colorado to New Jersey. At nearly every event, Steve Van Doren, the last link between Vans old and new, could be seen setting up his outdoor grill and making hot dogs and hamburgers for the athletes. By 2000, Vans was back on track, with revenue up to $12.1 million based on $273 million in sales.

Despite the company's best efforts, controversy continued to linger, especially when it came to lost American jobs. "With every company, you go through growing pains," said Strain. "The plants were California-based, and the cost of doing business here had increased to such a degree, and the opportunity for being competitive in the footwear market was offshore sourcing." One problem, though, was that Asian factories reportedly allowed for the use of a particularly toxic glue not allowed in the United States that endangered the lives of their employees. "There was some toxicity to [the glue], but that evolved and changed," said company designer Steve Mills. "That was out there a while back, but the industry as a whole realized it and changed the way they build product." Vans narrowly avoided a public-relations nightmare, even though many in the community remained wary of the way it dropped U.S. manufacturing (which, in fairness to Vans, was commonplace with its competitors).

In the main, Vans had sufficiently rebounded, which couldn't be said of other companies launched during the same period. Most had collapsed, including the skateboard manufacturer Makaha, which nearly went under after skating's midsixties crash and didn't recuperate until the following decade; by then, founder Larry Stevenson had been diagnosed with Parkinson's and his boards were mass-produced plastic models. Those companies that had survived continued to face rough patches. Airwalk, named after a skateboarding trick, had made a fortune with skate shoes in the eighties, but the following decade the company took its products into chains like Foot Locker. Skaters and skate shops alike felt Airwalk had sold out its product and image; sales deflated and the company became the industry's reference point for dramatic missteps. Malls, it was determined, were to be avoided as much as possible. "I don't want to see our stuff in JC Penney or Target," said the head of one company. "Our brand is too important." But the balancing act remained tricky. "You can't be *too* core, because nobody understands you," said manager Steve Astephen. "It's a battle every day."

To its dismay, Vans now faced a myriad of new rivals. The action-sport world was no longer simply about gear, but fashion; not just activity, but lifestyle. Up until the mid-nineties, the industry was small, but those frontier days ended with the mainstreaming of the sports and televised spectacles like the X Games. An entire, separate industry sprang up to clothe and accessorize skaters, bikers, boarders, and their fans. Depending on the year and the fashionability of each company, those buyers flocked to Billabong, Quiksilver, Nixon, Oakley, Volcom, Pacific Sunwear, and an array of other manufacturers of shorts, T-shirts, sunglasses, hats, and whatever else would be deemed part of the life.

The backbone of the industry, though, remained the shoes. They were no longer called sneakers, nor should they have been; the footwear had become so technically advanced that the old term seemed quaint. Over several decades, skate and BMX sneakers had transformed from relatively slim, everyday-use models (like Vans' thin-soled originals) to chunky, puffed-up foot protectors with almost as many features and selling points as the most exorbitant basketball sneakers. Even though a prototypical basketball sneaker had ten times the number of components as a skateboard shoe, action-sport footwear became akin to a government lab experiment. Vans shoes included "hidden ghillie lacing" (to protect laces from wear and tear) and "compression-molded ethyl vinyl acetate" for shock absorption. Launched in 1994 by skaters Damon Way and Ken Block and named after its parent company (Droors Clothing), DC Shoes catapulted the product another step further. Inspired by cross-training shoes, DC developed a nylon lace loop to prevent lace breakage during tricks. Other innovations, like padded tongues and collars, toe protectors, and air cushioning, were inspired by the enemy—high-tech soccer and basketball shoes—as well as hiking boots and walking shoes. "We just used that inspiration and said, 'Why can't we make skateboard shoes function for our sport like basketball shoes function for basketball?'" recalled Block. "No one had ever put a heel cushion in skateboard shoes. It's insane. These kids jump down stairs every day and land on their heels, and no one had thought, 'Wow, why don't we try to prevent heel bruises?'" The company's DGT (dynamic grip technology) system utilized, in its words, "three different durometers of rubber" for the ollie and heel areas; an "aerotech ventilation system" kept feet cool. The company also boasted of a mysterious, sci-fi-sounding element called PAL AB2000, described in its authorized biography, *Agents of Change,* as "a revolutionary hybrid composite of polyurethane-coated cowhide leather that flexes like leather but is highly resistant to a skateboard shoe's worst enemy—abrasion." As much as the corporate-sponsor booths at the X Games, the transformation of the shoes demonstrated that action sports had graduated from a laissez-faire pastime to an exacting, high-pressure undertaking.

DC was just one of the scrappier, streetwise companies that sprang up to take on Vans. Sole Technology, owned by French skater Pierre Andre Senizergues, was home to the mainstream brand Etnies and its hard-core-market siblings éS, Emerica, and 32 (the latter snowboard boots). Even Nike and Adidas soon entered the action-sport shoe market, which, according to John Shanley, athletic and footwear analyst at Wells Fargo Securities, amounted to annual retail sales of close to $450 million. Mirroring the dot-com explosion with which it coincided, the industry overall generated profits that just a few years earlier would have been deemed ludicrous. Billabong expanded from an Australian surf-shorts company founded in 1973 to a $60-million-a-year-profit business by 2002, buying Von Zipper sunglasses and Element skateboards along the way. The result, by 2002, was a bewildering assortment of choices: One mail-order catalogue listed 119 different skate shoes sold by eleven different companies, which one observer referred to derisively as "the Cartel."

The reason for the infusion was obvious: For everyone involved, the footwear market represented a potential soft-soled gold rush. The shoes retailed for less than basketball wear, averaging between $40 and $90 per pair, but if a company hooked up with the right rider at the right moment, the rewards were plentiful. According to *Sports Edge,* amateur skateboarders were primarily influenced "by what their favorite team rider is wearing" as opposed to price and their friends' choices. If that rider had a signature shoe in stores, everyone could make out well. Royalties ranged from one to two dollars per pair, leading to success stories that continued to be talked about with a hushed reverence: the DC model that made between $60,000 and $80,000 a month for one skater; the teenage athlete who took home $30,000 a month with another company; Geoff Rowley selling over six hundred thousand pair of his Vans shoe, at $65 each. The shoe's life span depended on its sales as well as the popularity of the athlete after which it was named: They could be on the market for months or years, and it was often hard to tell if they were bought for their connection to a particular athlete or for their aesthetics. For the riders, a signature shoe meant potential fiscal rewards unlike anything else in their line of work.

By the dawn of the new century, a combination of potential revenue, competitiveness, and additional shoemakers made for a very different business from the one of a decade before. "Back in the day, everything was a lot smaller and easier and a bit more fun," admitted DC president Block, whose company used a lab in Korea to test materials. "It wasn't such a serious business with such a large risk of loss. If I'd gone out of business the first couple of years, I'd owe a couple of people a total of forty to fifty thousand dollars. Today, our line of credit is millions and millions of dollars." When DC began selling its products in Nordstrom stores in 1999, the company lost five members of its skate team, who objected not so much to the store as to the terms of the deal. Even the notoriously iconoclastic DC ads had to be curtailed. "My liability concerns with an ad are a lot different nowadays than they were ten years ago," said Block. "I put alcohol and different language in them ten years ago than I would today. I have a hundred-million-dollar business and I'm trying to grow it to one hundred ten or one hundred twenty or whatever. I don't do that by putting out a real risky ad that shows a guy with a gun in his mouth. That may be funny to me and you, but to a twelve-year-old and his dad picking up a skateboard magazine, it'll turn away more people than it's going to entertain. Unfortunately," he added with a sigh, "everybody's gotta grow up, you know."

Within conference rooms like those at Vans, however, the dilemmas were much more prosaic. With his crew of designers, Guidice began figuring out which styles would be appropriate for department stores; a separate line of skateshop-only shoes would be considered another day. Later, another problem emerged: The shoes had become so intricate and corpulent that a consumer revolt was in the making. In Vans' case, the company had learned that a particular type of molding for the shoes' uppers was not connecting with customers. "It's something our consumer wasn't really looking for," says Vans' Steve Mills. "Vans has a very simple, user-friendly technical product.

We don't put a lot of bells and whistles on our uppers. We tried that, and it didn't work for us." By 2003, in a scenario becoming more than familiar to all involved, it was time for Vans—and the industry overall—to return to basics to ensure its survival.

Although the industry was largely rooted in the West Coast, not every business was based there; in fact, one of them could be found by peering into a glass storefront in grubby midtown Manhattan, near the corner of Broadway and Thirty-eighth Street. Beyond the glass was an unassuming lobby the size of a pizza stand. Only when one entered and descended down a flight of wide, carpeted stairs was another, entirely different sight revealed: an airy, gleaming subterranean world—said to be a former bank vault—of windowless offices, labyrinthian corridors, a showroom with black leather chairs, and high, metal-beamed ceilings. Everywhere, strewn on floors and mounted on walls, were skateboard decks. "We call it the bunker," said a lanky man with an unruly goatee, black sneakers, and untucked dress shirt who stood at the base of the steps.

Eli Michael Gesner was a thirty-one-year-old graphics designer and one of the owners of Zoo York, the city's preeminent skateboard and skate-clothing company. It was fitting that Zoo York was underground, which corresponded with New York's longtime skate scene. The community dated back to the seventies—in fact, Zoo York was named in honor of the Soul Artists of Zoo York, a collective of graffiti artists and skaters that came together during that time—but, for understandable reasons, it had never attained the visibility or cachet of warmer-climate scenes in California or Florida. The reasons were as geographic (icy winters and high-humidity summers were not conducive to outdoor riding) as they were legal (Mayor Rudy Giuliani's quality-of-life campaign included a 1996 law, albeit one not rigidly enforced, that targeted the "reckless operation" of skateboards on city streets). "In California, everyone you know surfs, all their dads were surfers, and skateboarding is an integral part of the culture," said Gesner, who grew up in the city and estimated there were, at one time, only "thirty or forty" Manhattan skaters. "I have vivid memories of me and my two or three friends skating down the street and constantly turning heads, like, 'What the hell is *that*? What are you doing?' You were really ostracized and alienated."

Alienation no longer set the tone. Brooklyn now had its own skatepark, and Manhattan had two. Still, many riders opted for the steps, ledges, and railings of office-building plazas—but only after dark, and until guards inevitably evicted them. "Everyone goes home at night, and then the skaters go out," said Jeff Pang, Zoo York's rangy team manager. "There's a lot of stuff going on in the middle of the night." On the wall of Pang's office was Zoo York's official map of "NYC Skate Spots." The Upper East Side, the chart indicated, should be avoided since "most of the fancy apartment buildings don't have a lot to skate." Much preferred were the legendary Brooklyn Banks, a line of red-brick inclines located under the Manhattan side of the Brooklyn Bridge and adjacent to police headquarters. The Zoo Yorkers had only positive things to say about the cops and their tolerance of skaters; indeed, every day at the Banks on-duty police would watch, with mild amusement, as rider after rider bombed down one of the banks and either stayed on the board or crashed.

Zoo York's existence was a testament to the emergent culture of action sports, but it was also indicative of a larger business trend. The concept of athletes running companies dated back to the Dogtown era, when riders like Alva and Peralta began their own skateboard firms. But the practice solidified in the nineties, when Tony Hawk and BMX rider Mat Hoffman started businesses of their own and took their destinies, no matter how shaky or unpredictable, into their practice-scarred hands. Zoo York was the creation of two skate-boarders—Gesner and tall, laid-back New Jersey native Rodney Smith, also in his early thirties—along with former design-studio manager Adam Schatz. The three founded Zoo York in 1993 with $30,000 and a rented space in Greenwich Village. Like an aggressive subway rider pushing into a crowded train at rush hour, the company elbowed its way into an industry long dominated by businesses thousands of miles away. Zoo York's decks, made of the same seven-ply wood common to most boards (and manufactured by one of a handful of wood mills in the United States and Canada), were splattered with city imagery—the "we are happy to serve you" design found on Greek-coffeeshop cups, graffiti-style interpretations of the Zoo York logo, or homages to the kung-fu movie posters found in sleazoid Times Square theaters before the Giuliani administration drove them out.

The aim, said Schatz, was to depict a "raw, dirty New York City feel" to counteract the sport's sun-doused West Coast image. Similarly, the company's offices and videos pulsed to the beats of hip-hop, not the punk common to other skate companies. "If you look at other skateboard teams, it looks like the same type of person skating," said Schatz, who resembled a harried city owl. "They're all blond and beach-oriented. Here the skateboard community is comprised of every ethnicity, background, and musical influence."

"They're a lot more sophisticated mentally, more culturally aware," Gesner chimed in, sitting in Schatz's deck-crammed, graffiti-art-strewn office. "You go to the Met to skate the steps and then it's like, 'Wow, there's a new show at the *Met?*'"

Like their equally skilled West Coast counterparts, though, New York skaters were not especially known for their rigid attention to procedures. The following day, an informal meeting was scheduled for Zoo York's sixteen team members, who hailed from the Bronx, Brooklyn, Westchester, and New Jersey. As with every other skate, snowboard, or BMX company, Zoo York had a team of salaried athletes (both skaters and, most recently, BMX and motocross riders), although calling it a team was something of a stretch. The objective of the meeting was to discuss an upcoming promotional tour of European skate venues and to bring everyone up to speed on the trip, set to kick off in a few days. But by two P.M., only one skater was in attendance—Danny Supa, a twenty-three-year-old African-American in baggy jeans and gleaming white sneakers; a mildly mischievous smile lurked beneath his black baseball cap. "Those other guys, they're never in," he said with a chuckle. "They're all off skating."

To pass the time, Supa—one of the few African-Americans in a world that was largely white—sat in a small room as an editor at a computer terminal assembled a rough cut of Supa's footage in an upcoming Zoo York video. His board on the floor next to him like a faithful pet, Supa recalled how he had first learned to skate as a child in the Bronx—"People would laugh at you. They thought it was a white-boy sport or something." Like many of his peers, he preferred midtown, especially the revered Time-Life Building plaza ("It's *super*-smooth," he said admiringly). "Our boards would shoot into windows and there'd be security guards and dogs and cops," he recalled of trips to that and other sites. "The normal everyday thing. But it's not as bad as Philadelphia. Those guys would chase you and ambush you." Supa dropped out of high school during eleventh grade to become a pro and was now earning, by his estimate, $7,800 a month from his combined sponsors: Nike for shoes, Zoo York for skateboards, Independent for trucks (the metal devices to which the wheels were attached), and Von Zipper for sunglasses. As with athletes in all of these sports, he also stood the chance of making a few extra dollars from so-called photo incentives: If a core skate, bike, snow, or motocross magazine did an article on him, and if the photos prominently displayed the logo of one of his sponsors, the sponsor could pay him anywhere between a few hundred and a thousand dollars.

The rise of photo incentives revealed the clout of the action-sport press, which had itself become a formidable enterprise. The magazines had been around almost as long as the sports, dating back to

The Quarterly Skateboarder of the sixties (later renamed *SkateBoarder,* then *Action Now*). But in the eighties, a new generation of publication invaded newsstands. *Thrasher,* founded in 1981 and embracing a defiant, annihilate-all-posers ethos, was joined two years later by *Transworld Skateboarding,* started by a group of adults who felt *Thrasher*'s punky "skate and destroy" credo was not sufficiently upbeat. Twenty years later, both magazines had become phonebook-thick glossies featuring more advertisements than articles; it was not uncommon to leaf through four-hundred-page monthly issues only to discover that half of those pages consisted of full-page ads for shoes, decks, clothing, and other gear. The Transworld empire, encompassing eight magazines, was eventually bought up by AOL Time Warner in 2001 as part of its purchase of Times Mirror publications. (In a revealing clash of cultures, two years later the editor of *Transworld Skateboarding* and two other top staffers would quit in protest after Time Warner placed inappropriate ads, like one for L'Oréal shampoo, in their magazine.) By then, dozens of magazines covering the skate, snow, moto, water-sport, and bike world jockeyed for readers, each offering a distinct perspective. Skaters in search of uncompromising punk-rock attitude went to *Thrasher, Big Brother,* or *Slap;* freestyle-motocross fans who wanted to keep it gritty had *MX Machine,* launched by *Hustler* publisher Larry Flynt (also publisher of *Big Brother* and, briefly, the edgy snowboard magazine *Blunt*). The circulation numbers for each of the magazines hovered only between 50,000 and 250,000, but advertisers knew their discerning readers viewed the magazines as much as catalogs as editorial products and were plugged into the caffeinated-energy, perpetual-adolescent point of view, as well as the inside references to athletes and companies that ran through them all. ("I'd like to think readers want articles, but we're a photo book," admitted one editor.) As one rider was quoted as saying in *Big Brother,* "Skating with a boner is the fucking best."

Supa was no stranger to the magazines, having appeared in Zoo

York ads and feature articles in skate magazines. But for him and his peers, videos were equally important. Turning his attention to the computer monitor, Supa watched himself ollie onto a concrete ledge, set to a Notorious B.I.G. song he'd chosen. When the director hit the pause button, freezing Supa's image on the screen, the skater smiled approvingly. Then his Palm Pilot–style phone went off; other plans were in the making. Since one of Supa's fellow riders was still recovering from elbow surgery, a Zoo York team photo shoot had also been postponed. A rainstorm was in the forecast, meaning riding was out, so Supa opted for heading to a friend's uptown restaurant. "Some guy is going to eat a fifteen- or nineteen-pound lobster," he said, "and we're going to go watch him." The meeting would have to wait for another time, if at all.

Once the videos had been edited and the skateboards constructed and the shoe designs finalized, all the products wound up in the same places. These were the core shops—the small, cramped independent stores, usually situated in outlying parts of town, that were aimed exclusively at the hard-core action-sports crowd and any groms and outsiders who dared to enter. About two thousand skate shops were sprinkled across the country (general board-sport stores constituted another eight to ten thousand), and in one way or another, most of them resembled Tekgnar, Austin's long-standing contribution to this sector of the industry.

Tekgnar—a combination of *technical* and *gnarly,* two skating terms—was located a few short blocks from the Capitol Building, where once-governor George W. Bush had presided. Sandwiched in between a pizza parlor and a yogurt shop, it also faced fast-food stands and gas stations. The windows and inside walls were splattered with stickers and posters for companies like Vans and Alien Work-shop. Displayed in the storefront window was a reminder of the days when the sports weren't seen in soda commercials—a vintage street sign that read No Bicycles or Skateboards on Sidewalk. Inside, the floors were cement gray and paint-splattered. On one wall were rows of skateboard decks, the artwork of which had become the modern equivalent of psychedelic posters of the sixties or clever product-parody rave art of the nineties. Fists, skulls, demon imagery, and multicolored beavers dominated; on one, a well-dressed white couple out on the town smiled at each other over dinner, the man saying, "Tastes like shit," the woman responding cheerfully, "It *is* shit." Beneath the decks, housed in steel cages that added to the store's skate-apocalypse atmosphere, were displays of thirty-four varying types of wheels and ten different sizes of trucks. In the middle of the store sat clothing racks with baggy shorts and shirts, followed by a wall of shoes. CDs of local punk bands like Simian Dreams and Yuckmouth were for sale behind the front counter. In its every crammed square foot, Tekgnar was both store and shrine.

At one time, Tekgnar had been situated inside a mall, said its owner, Laurie Pevey, a woman with long, sandy-brown hair and an unwavering stare. But she had never felt at home there—"too corporate; it wasn't our image"—and had moved to their present location three years before. Pevey stood behind the counter giving advice to a mother who wanted to purchase a skate shirt for her son ("The kids like them baggy, and I like to wear them that way, too," Pevey explained) and asking customers to contribute to a jar soliciting donations for a new skatepark. A private park already existed in Austin—albeit one that charged $12 for four hours—but Pevey and others felt a free, open-to-the-public skate area was also needed. "We've been fighting for a park for ten years," she said. "The city has to recognize it's a legitimate sport. The city bureaucrats think it's more important to build a golf-Frisbee park," she snorted, "which we have, believe it or not."

Displayed on the wall behind Pevey and extending to the glass case beneath her was another ubiquitous part of core shops—the video boxes. One by one a stream of kids—white, Mexican, black, some-times alone, sometimes accompanied by patient parents—walked over and peered at them as if they were sacred objects. Every month, an array of these videotapes and DVDs bombarded the market, sporting titles like *Misled Youth* and *Fulfill the Dream* and not much else. Adding to their mystique, packaging and credits were minimal. To outsiders, they must have seemed like straight-to-tape movies, complete with unrecognizable "stars." In reality, they were thirty-to-sixty-minute movies, many shot on super 8 or digital video, in which a select group of riders performed trick after trick after trick to unrelenting metal, thrash, or hip-hop. They were, as many pointed out, like porn—one action shot after another, with few distractions like plots or dialogue—and the metaphor extended to the way in which customers drooled in anticipation before watching them. Whether they focused on skate, snow, moto, or bike moves, the videos tracked the progression of the sports in the months since the *last* batch came out; things were moving that fast.

The roots of the extreme-video circuit lay in the surf movies of the sixties, but the contemporary world of action-sports theater had begun in earnest in 1984. Stacy Peralta, the ambitious, flaxen-haired member of the rebel-minded Zephyr skate team of the seventies, had realized, especially after breaking his arm twice in a row at competitions, that he needed to plan a different future for himself. Though only in his early twenties, Peralta decided he wanted to be a player rather than full-time rider, and in 1978, he became co-owner of the Powell Peralta skateboard company, serving as its team manager, among other tasks. To promote the boards, he and a friend came up with the idea of filming the Powell Peralta team—otherwise known as the Bones Brigade—and giving the tapes to skate shops to play during business hours; they would be, in effect, infomercials. "I had been in a lot of bad skateboarding movies," Peralta said of his stunt work in the seventies. "I always thought it would be so cool to be in a great skateboarding movie, but they never were. They were *stupid*. So this was my revenge." Taking six months and an unexpectedly exorbitant $18,000 to make, the first full-length tape, *The Bones Brigade Video Show*, opened with Peralta watching a faux, coiffed television newscaster report on the state of his sport. "This is a skateboard," the talking head said, holding up a low-rent model. In response, Peralta smashed an ax into the TV set, pulled out a deck, and, smiling at the camera, said, "Now, *this* is a skateboard." What followed was a half hour of nonstop footage, the likes of which few had seen on a television screen. Young Lance Mountain, cruising around Hollywood and Venice Beach, did handplants off a concrete plaza; a young, blond stick figure named Tony Hawk pulled half-pipe moves that left older spectators watching with open jaws; Mountain and Steve Caballero rode on their backs, street-luge-style, down a street. The "premiere" was held at the home of Hawk's parents, Frank and Nancy, complete with pizza and cake; it was, Peralta recalled, "like a sweet birthday party."

Two decades after it was made, *The Bones Brigade Video Show* seemed impossibly old-fashioned, both in its tricks and its soundtrack of wet-noodle blues-rock. But at the time, it was revolutionary—the *Birth of a Nation* of action-sport movies. Since he was a rider himself, Peralta filmed the team while skating alongside them or in a wheelchair for mobility, which lent the footage a knowingness and intimacy rarely seen in skate footage and captured the energy of the sport better than any magazine layout could hope. Once word of mouth about the *Video Show* began spreading, the company decided to sell it, and thanks to a coincidental bit of timing—the newly flourishing VCR market—thirty thousand copies, at about $30 each, flew out skate-shop doors. "Little did we know we were making history," Peralta recalled. "Didn't have a clue whatsoever." A sequel was in order, and soon enough the Bones Brigade videos became a series, a sort of Bowery Boys on wheels. The next tape, *Future Primitive*, arrived in

1985, followed a year later by the ambitious *The Search for Animal Chin,* which featured a rare-for-video plot—the Brigade attempting to track down the title character, a mysterious, inspirational skate-boarder missing in action. Animal Chin was Peralta's metaphor for the increasing corporate hold over skating. "We wanted to show kids, 'Look, it's okay to make money, but don't forget the first thing about this is *fun,*'" he recalled. "At the time we didn't want com-panies like Gatorade to come in and sponsor contests. We wanted to keep it pure if we could." *The Search for Animal Chin* included digs at the media and a sleazy skateboard-company owner who bragged of "thirty million bucks" in revenue. In their journey to find Chin, the team traveled from San Francisco to Hawaii. They never tracked him down, but their adventures along the way, complete with stiff, ad-libbed dialogue—vert-ramp exhibitions, Hawk ollie-ing over a chain-link fence—were the point. "That's the pure fun of skating," intoned the narrator. "And as long as skaters keep searching for Chin, they've already found him." The fourth video, *Public Domain,* codirected by iconic skate-culture writer and photographer Craig (C.R.) Stecyk and released in 1988, included a larger cast of skaters, sweeping shots of cement parks that gave them the look of urban sand dunes, newcomer Mike Vallely cruising around the D.C. mall and in front of the White House, and for the first time, casting and styling credits.

Like the magazines, the Bones Brigade videos were proudly silly and juvenile and encompassed cornball skits, toilet humor, crash footage, parodies of commercials, and non sequitur humor. They made the world outside skating seem like a depraved, corrupt place, especially compared to the purity of the skaters' ambience and existence. The message was simplistic, but it touched a hefty nerve from California to the streets of Brooklyn, where young skaters like future Zoo York member Jeff Pang watched the tapes until they wore out. "Seeing Tommy Guerrero's part in the beginning of *Future Primitive,*" recalled Pang, "I took to that because he was in the hills of San Francisco and I was like, 'This is New York City and we can do that city stuff here, too.' " Before he himself briefly became a member of the Bones Brigade, Vallely watched *Future Primitive* with skating friends at one of their houses in Edison, New Jersey, Vallely's home. "When the video was done, we tore out of the house and went out into the streets and had one of the most insane sessions ever," Vallely recalled. "Totally annihilated our hometown."

Peralta himself bowed out after 1990's *Propaganda*, citing burnout. "At first it was an exploration, and then it was, 'I have to do this to feed the machine,'" he said. "It didn't inspire me anymore." (He went on to work on everything from one of the many, numbing *Police Academy* sequels and a Bravo cable series before directing the rousing 2002 documentary *Dogtown and Z-Boys* on himself and his old teammates.) But the industry he had helped pioneer along with frequent collaborator Stecyk and company co-owner George Powell did not fade with him. Skate, snow, and bike videos quickly became an industry and underground art form unto themselves. Most adhered to the Bones Brigade formula of tricks broken up with skits or footage of the riders horsing around. Among the early practitioners was a young, Maryland-based BMX-shop employee and magazine photographer named Spike Jonze (née Adam Spiegel), who, in 1991, made *Blind: Video Days* with codirector Karol Winthrop. Only twenty-four minutes long, *Video Days* was steeped in the developing style of street skating. To the Jackson 5's "I Want You Back," pipsqueak genius Guy Mariano skated in an underground garage and over garbage cans in balletlike moves; artist and skater Mark Gonzales skated between cars on a bustling street. Future actor Jason Lee, then a close-cropped bleach-blond rider in baggy green shorts, also appeared. *Video Days* wrapped up with footage of the skaters in a car, drinking beer while driving and, ultimately, "crashing" violently; the sardonic last shot listed each of their birth and death dates. *Video Days* unleashed a new, more aggressive wave of videos, which came to include those by the skate company Plan B, the *Road Fools* series of BMX tapes, and the macho antics of the *Crusty Demons of Dirt* moto compilations.

The videos, some produced by skate and shoe companies and others by independent firms, kept coming—between five hundred and eight hundred new releases a year by 2003, with titles like *Unbreakable* and *Expendable Youth*. At every demo, contest, or road trip, it was easy to spot the "creeper"—or video maker— darting around the half-pipe, ramp, mountains, or streets shooting footage. Given that the tapes were relatively inexpensive to film and sold for between $20 and $30, the industry within the industry quickly grew into a $50-million-annual business by 2003. Break- even points varied depending on production and promotional costs, but could be as few as five thousand copies sold; selling twenty thousand units was the equivalent of a hit. The tapes turned respectable profits for their producers and transformed skaters, snowboarders, and BMXers who couldn't be bothered attending ESPN events into cult icons.

Few of the videos were works of art—fish-eye shots and slow motion were prevalent clichés—but few claimed to be. They were, at heart, instructional tapes much like those made for home exercise or dance. What the action-sport versions added was a sense of danger, vicarious thrills, and exuberant nihilism. The point was not simply to see a bike, snow, or moto trick done and to learn from watching, but to see it pulled in as forbidden a locale as possible. Such was the case with the most anticipated tape of 2002, the Flip skateboard compa- ny's *Sorry*. Its nonstop barrage of surreptitious grinds, kickflips, and ollies, all filmed in deserted nighttime parking lots and similar no- skateboarding-allowed premises, took viewers to places many wouldn't dare venture, complete with genuinely startling crashes and bloodied skaters. Particularly creative were John Lydon's sneer- ing introductions to each segment and Finland-born street-skating icon Arto Saari's part, which began with fake footage of paramedics taking him to a hospital after a "crash" and then flashed back to the insane moves that had supposedly led to it. Tapes like that—and the darkly energetic and renegade *Dying to Live,* from Zero, released the same year—were the ones most coveted and talked about, the ones that took the Bones Brigade classics to their next, intense level. At the same time, others were attempting to move beyond the skate-porn parameters and make cinematic minimovies, most notably the ambitious black-and-white *Hallowed Ground,* a combination skate compilation, art film, and travel documentary featuring the Hurley skate team. Shot on film, a rarity in a digital-video world, the video depicted skaters revisiting their starting points—Bob Burnquist in a particularly dreary Brazilian ghetto, for instance—and, in doing so, took two years to make and cost a higher-than-usual $120,000, epochal by extreme-video standards. "Hopefully people are sick of seeing the same old run-of-the-mill skateboard videos," said its director, Scott Soens. "I love those things for going out and getting amped on skateboarding. But I wanted something for *after* you're done skating, something anyone could sit down and watch." The only problem was Hurley itself: Shortly after *Hallowed Ground* was released, the two-year-old surf-apparel company was sold to Nike. In a review of the film in *Big Brother,* Pat Canale wrote, "It's ridiculously hypocritical for a Nike company to pretend it's got roots."

The success of the videos also led to the inevitable problems. As riders became busier, their schedules crowded with contests, appearances, and other duties, the tapes took longer to make and cost more. To push more units, distributors began selling them in chains like Target and Wal-Mart, which in turn infuriated core-shop owners, who weren't able to offer the discounted prices the chains could. There was also growing concern that, as one video producer put it, "They make skating look easy." At demos and contests, fans and spectators expected their heroes to pull particularly difficult tricks immediately, not realizing it often took weeks of filming one move in order to nail it perfectly.

But the tapes, like the sports, were too far gone to be corralled. At Tekgnar, Pevey said, tapes like *Dying to Live* and *Sorry*—and not those featuring X Games–associated athletes like Burnquist—were the ones flying out the door the fastest. *Dying to Live* was on its way to selling over one hundred thousand copies nationally, and both tapes had made indie-rock stars out of underground skaters like Saari and Rowley. Rowley's signature Vans shoe was one of Tekgnar's best sellers, and thanks to Saari, the store sold about fifty Flip skateboards a week, more than from any other company. Boards were only part of the equation, though. If the deck didn't break in a few months, there were bearings, wheels, and trucks to replace, in that order, which was what lanky store manager Brent Cowley was doing across from Pevey. As a mother watched, Cowley replaced the mangled trucks on her son's board.

"Is it normal to replace one since Christmas?" she asked as Cowley went about attaching new trucks and wheels to her son's deck. It had only been three months since the holidays.

"Yeah, that's about right," Cowley drawled. Using a razor blade, he carefully cut a swath of grip tape to fit atop the board. Finally, the board was ready to roll again. The bill came to $65 for ten minutes' work.

5. SKATETOWN AND CABIN B-BOYS
going extreme at summer camp

The caravan of station wagons and sport utility vehicles, each containing at least one skateboard or stunt bicycle, slowly wound its way into the middle of Pennsylvania. It had been this way every Sunday between the months of June and September for every one of the preceding thirty years, and certain parts of the routine never changed. The parents, children, and bags of clothing crammed inside each car came from hundreds or thousands of miles away, yet they all wound up on the same road, 45 East, that sliced through the eleven hundred square miles of Centre County. Through their windows, the families glimpsed the hundreds of small—in some cases exceedingly small—businesses in the area: the weathered churches, the gas stations that appeared deserted despite their Open signs, the roadside café with a stereo that quietly played "You Are My Sunshine," "Big Rock Candy Mountain," and other mountain folk songs. They drove past lumpy green hills and expansive pastures, cow farms, HAY FOR SALE signs, and buggies steered by hunched, elderly Amish women. For nearly an hour, they navigated their way along the serpentine twists of 45 East, to the point where many of them must have thought they had misread the directions. Finally, with a marked sigh of relief, they saw the sign they had been hoping to see, right across the street from an antiques shop: the name of the camp, accompanied by symbols of each of the specialty sports played there. For the mothers and fathers who had driven their children this far, the locale must have appeared as odd as the activities their kids would be practicing, and as incomprehensible as the lingo they would use while doing them.

Upon seeing the sign, they all pulled onto an asphalt road and checked in at the front office, where they wrote down the name of their health-care providers and, in conjunction, their credit-card numbers; they also signed waivers that guaranteed they would not hold the owners of the camp responsible in case anything happened to their offspring. Once their children were assigned to a cabin, they returned to their cars and, as the teenagers stared eagerly out the windows, soaking up the surroundings, they drove down Big Air Drive and officially entered the grounds of Woodward Camp, the country's dominant and most established summer enterprise devoted to the world of action sports.

After locating the appropriate cabin, the families would park and unload, the father usually dragging along one or two skateboards or a bicycle as his child darted ahead. (The cabins for the BMX crowd were easy enough to distinguish, since dozens of bikes were strewn chaotically in front of them.) Wearing inquisitive, What-do-we-have-*here?* smiles, the parents would follow their kids into the cabins and glance over the dozen bunk beds, weathered but functioning air conditioners, and wood interiors that made the rooms appear murky even on sunny days. It all *looked* fairly normal, from the slope of green mountains in the distance and the horse farm next door to the arts-and-crafts shop and the large outdoor grill encrusted with charred meat. The massive green field next door, which the camp also owned, was kept purposefully empty to maintain a sense of isolation.

But as the parents quickly realized, little was traditional about the camp, where hundreds journeyed each week to master skateboarding,

BMX, and in-line skating (and, for an equal group, gymnastics). Their teenage children were outfitted in baggy minicargoes (the phrase *gym shorts* was never uttered, nor were they ever worn) and loose-fitting T-shirts that displayed the name and logo of one skate or action-sport sneaker or clothing company or another. After checking in, the kids would always lead the way; the grown-ups, in their tucked-in sport shirts and pressed slacks, would trail behind. Together they would begin making their way down paved, serpentine roads that led them past dark brown buildings the size of airport hangars, each with a baffling name—Egypt, Lot/8, the Cage. Inside was a sight even more vexing, a series of wood ramps, jump boxes, grind rails, ledges, and quarter-pipes that resembled an overgrown, out-of-control version of the skateparks in their hometowns. Eventually they arrived at Titanic, a twelve-foot-tall vert ramp that induced vertigo in any novice who stood on its deck and looked down, and then the Rock, a massive concrete pool. At each stop, the same thing happened. The child would expertly explain that this ramp was for *these* moves, and those artificial stairs and benches were for *those* tricks. All the elders could do was listen intently to every word their children spouted and respond with an amazed "Wow!" or "How *about* that!"

Finally, after a leisurely tour of the nearly dozen structures and bowls, the families wound up back at the cabins. As their bunkmates watched, the kids awkwardly accepted a kiss or hug, and then, at last, the folks were in their cars and gone for a week, if not more. At last, the children would have the chance to envision a world in which there would be little to do but skate, bike, and eat. They would be far from the cops who always seemed to be harassing them or handing them tickets, and far from the SKATEBOARDING PRO-HIBITED signs that now stretched from Los Angeles to the eastern tip of Long Island. For eight hundred of their parents' dollars a week, they were free.

*   *   *

The official brochure for Woodward Camp described its heap of cabins as "rustic," and so it was with Cabin 18; its plank deck and white roof lent it the look of a barracks. What distinguished it from the other cabins was its trailer-home length—it contained four separate rooms—and its incoming residents. The cabins were organized by age and sport; 18's campers would all be skateboarders between the ages of eight and fifteen. Each room also had an OSI, or open skate instructor, who was equal parts teacher, counselor, and babysitter. "We call it the skateboard ghetto," said Mike, leaning against the front porch, checklist in hand and rumpled jeans on body. A husky twenty-one-year-old with a doughy face, wavy brown hair, and an expression always somewhere between bemusement and sarcasm, Mike was the OSI for cabin 18A. Joining him on the porch was the 18B instructor, Tim, who was five years older and wore Docksides, had an earnest face, and parted his brown hair in the middle. Mike was studying art at a college in Alabama; Tim was a high-school teacher in Athens, Georgia. Both had been skateboarding since they were little, and both had taken these $180-a-week summer jobs because they promised to be a very different, and potentially entertaining, type of seasonal employment.

"It's so bizarre to come to a place like this," Tim said as he swept the porch and watched cars pull up and deposit fledgling skaters around him. "Moms dropping off their kids in minivans to go to a *skateboard* camp." He shook his head in disbelief.

"Yeah," Mike said, shading his eyes from the late-morning sun. "Kids get arrested for doing it elsewhere." Killing time as a patch of hazy heat began to settle over the camp, they talked about their love of skating, their favorite videos, and their ambivalence toward high-voltage events like ESPN's splashy X Games.

"It's cool to see it on TV," said Tim.

"Yeah," Mike acknowledged, "but it's kids all one-upping each other. It's turning into baseball!"

Then came another voice. "Hey, Mike—I made this!" Mike turned around, and there was Greg, the kid from Grand Rapids with the spooked-out face, spiky hair, and eyes set wide apart. In one of Greg's hands was the head of a green teddy bear; in the other hand were the mangled remains of the doll's body. Greg had turned the bear's torso inside out, transforming it into a grotesque hand puppet. His grin revealed how proud he was of his accomplishment, and the few campers who had already checked in gathered around to take a look and laugh along. "That's what I have to deal with all day," Mike said, rolling his eyes, even as he well knew how it felt to be that age and that much in love with skateboarding, and what it meant to be at a place like this.

By midafternoon, the thirteen-, fourteen-, and fifteen-year-olds who had been assigned to Mike's room had all arrived. There was Greg the bear mangler; his Grand Rapids sidekick Brandon, who wore green-tinted braces and had a dark complexion that reflected his Asian background; Nick, who had the shag haircut, sideburns, and denim jeans of a seventies stoner despite having been born the following decade; and Danny, a shy, awkward-looking New York City kid with frizzy hair who had once played basketball but gave it up because, he said with a monotonal snort, it was "*boring*." They neither looked nor acted as if they were members of their schools' honor societies, and they carried themselves as if they weren't ashamed or embarrassed about it. After dropping their bags and boards into the cabin, they began congregating on the porch with Mike. They flipped through the latest issues of *Transworld Skateboarding* and *Thrasher*, dwelling on photos of in-vogue riders. They talked, dismissively, about how overly padded and high-tech skate sneakers had become, almost like those absurdly expensive basketball shoes. ("I like to be able to feel the board," Mike concurred.) They chattered about upcoming skate videos as if they were summer-movie blockbusters, listening raptly as Danny told them his mom would be mailing a copy of the much anticipated *Sorry* tape directly to him at the camp: they had heard it was the greatest skate video of all time. Danny had asked his mother to send it via UPS, but given how remote Woodward was, the package would take an extra day or two to arrive. They all looked a little disappointed.

"UPS *sucks,*" Danny said into the dirt.

In theory, a place like Woodward should not have existed. Training facilities prevailed in the worlds of traditional sports, where drills, workouts, and team practice were the established regimen. In action sports, though, it was generally accepted that the best way to learn was by watching and rewatching videos in slow motion, studying photos in the core magazines, and then, either alone or with friends, attempting to pull a trick in a nearby street, skatepark, parking lot, or backyard. (Snowboarding may have been the exception; formal lessons were particularly useful.) Ability did not matter as much as perseverance. "When we started skating, no one ever said you had to be good at it," said skater and past Woodward visiting pro Mike Vallely. "You just *did* it. There was no 'You're not good so you should quit.' If you sucked at baseball, you eventually stopped playing baseball. But if you sucked at skating," he chuckled, "you just kept skating anyway."

Yet it was a sign of how established and commonplace alternative sports had become that proper instruction was welcomed, and that businesses eager to fill that burgeoning need had sprung up. According to the American Camping Association, 12,000 day and resident camps existed in the United States as of 2003; of those, 2,300 were privately owned, for-profit enterprises. Of those 2,300, only a dozen were dedicated to one or more action sport, but the number appeared to rise every season. Snowboard camps now dotted the West Coast just as signs for Extreme Camps in the middle of Long Island began to be stapled to telephone poles. In 2002, Point X, devoted to everything from skate to motocross, had opened in Temecula, just north of San Diego. Then there was Woodward, the oldest and most respected of them, the place where, each summer for decades, campers had come to learn how to ollie, grind, jump dirt, and do tabletops. Another sign of how integrated the sports had become was that each of Woodward's fourteen weeks this summer was sold-out, and the waiting lists numbered in the hundreds. If they were lucky, the kids fortunate enough to get in would receive pointers and tips from one of the many pros who stopped by at one time or another every summer, from Ryan Nyquist and Koji Kraft to nearly all of the name skaters who had been on Tony Hawk's skatepark tour. Ground had already been broken on Woodward West, a new facility in California; that the locale was once home to a golf course was an irony lost on no one.

To the surprise of some, including the boys of Cabin 18, Woodward Camp shared at least one attribute with other, more traditional summer getaways around the country: rules and schedules. By six P.M., the last member of Cabin 18, Room A, had shown up—a small, blond-haired kid named Bo whose claim to fame was his mother's supposed acting role in the sex-romp movie *Porky's*. ("He says there are naked pictures of her all over the house," Mike relayed enviously.) With all the campers accounted for, Mike gathered everyone together and announced he would take them on a camp tour before orientation was to begin. Smiles both enthusiastic and mocking rippled through the boys, and Mike and his motley pack of skate rats were on their way.

Mike had never been a fan of rules, especially when he was a young skater worshiping Plan B videos and vert skaters like Colin McKay and Danny Way; even now, he was only going to follow orders begrudgingly. The group, a ragtag bunch in T-shirts and sneakers and faded jeans, made a left onto Woodward Avenue, past the Morton Building with its kidney-shaped bowl. Mike pointed to structures in the distance. "Those are the girls' cabins—stay away from them!" he said with mock seriousness. Here was another Woodward rule: no fraternizing between the action-sports kids and the female gymnastic students with whom they shared the campgrounds. *"Why?"* the boys implored back.

Then they arrived at the building where those same gymnasts cushioned themselves during practice by jumping onto foam balls, and several of the Cabin 18 boys asked if they could steal a ball or two for a souvenir. "No!" Mike snapped.

"That's the infirmary," he then announced, arriving at one structure. "If you got any medicine, even Tylenol, put 'em in there. I'm supposed to tell you that." The kids followed behind, talking, smirking, or barely listening; Nick had by now put on his SKATE-BOARDING IS NOT A CRIME visor. Arriving at the volleyball court, Mike lackadaisically said, "Here's volleyball. You can play whenever."

Behind him and out of earshot, one of the cabin boys said, "Or *watch* someone play volleyball."

Eventually, they made their way up the hill and over to one of the largest of the structures, Lot/8, which had wood-beam ceilings and an assortment of ramps and half- and quarter-pipes. Kids began streaming in from each of the open doors—a swarm of the skinny, the chunky, the long-haired, the close-cropped, the wholesome-looking, and the punk-style. If Woodward made one thing abundantly clear, it was that these sports no longer attracted merely one type of adolescent.

Soon, orientation began and the kids quieted down. Three counselors welcomed everyone and, as the campers listened attentively and the overhead fluorescent lights buzzed, laid out the rules. Campers had to be in their cabins by ten fifteen P.M. each night; lights were out at eleven. Skating was not permitted inside the cabins. Helmets and pads were required. "Razor scooters are not allowed," another said, "and it's not just because it's not cool." The kids laughed at the mocking reference to that *kids'* toy. Finally, another counselor warned, "No PDAs"—public displays of affection—"with girls. And no foul language. We don't want that here. Drugs are illegal. You can't have them here. This is a training facility. If you have it, get rid of it."

After a half hour, the session was over, and it was time for testing, in which each camper was given thirty seconds to prove what he could do on a board or bike in order to be placed in a class with those at an equal level. In the Cage, one runty kid flew down a ramp on his BMX bike and fell. He picked up his bike and was about to resume his run when a counselor, sitting on a ramp above him and taking notes, interrupted, "Wait a minute—you're bleeding."

Sure enough, blood was streaming down the kid's nose. At the instructor's request, the camper walked over to where the teachers sat and looked up at them silently, an Oliver in oversize clothing. The kid appeared startled, but not because of his injury: Neither he nor his peers were accustomed to anyone, especially adults, watching over them and asking them if they were hurt. Generally, their parents stayed *away* from their parks, which was fine with the riders.

"Let us see you," one trainer said. "Does it hurt?"

"No."

"You want to keep riding?"

"Yeah." He completed his run and was then sent to the medical room for a checkup.

At a skate-testing area nearby, Graham Kelly, a brown-shagged assistant skate director, addressed the lumpy line of kids: "If you've never dropped in before, come and talk to me." Like the others, he would watch as each camper stepped onto his board and glided down the six-foot-high miniramp. Some, like Danny from Cabin 18, were tentative, others a little more assured. Kelly and the other teachers made notes on each camper and in particular kept their eyes on those with long pants or long-sleeve shirts; most likely, those were the kids attempting to sneak by without wearing pads. "As more campers come in, it has to be stricter," Kelly said, sitting alongside the ramp as a stray skateboard shot past his foot. "More rules have to be reinforced."

One kid approached Kelly after his testing was done. "Can I skate back to my cabin?" he asked. Generally, this was not allowed during the first day; campers tended to be so excited when they arrived at Woodward that they wanted to skate immediately, leading to a higher rate of first-day accidents than anyone cared to see.

But Kelly had a change of heart. "Sure," he said. "Just don't stop at the parks." The kid was gone before Kelly could finish his sentence.

Although the concept of a school or camp devoted to nonball sports was relatively new, Woodward itself was not, and a peek into its history was nailed to a wall at the Canteen, the camp store that sold everything from pizza to Woodward caps and sweatshirts. Housed in an old wood frame was a collage of black-and-white photos, dated 1979, that depicted teens practicing gymnastic moves on mats and parallel bars as heedful instructors looked on. In other shots, kids leapt into pools and were serenaded by a bearded man with an acoustic guitar emulating one of the sensitive troubadours of the time. The images were unabashedly wholesome and innocent, and they seemed to take place in an entirely different time and universe than the one in which Woodward now operated.

In another photograph, a strapping, square-jawed man with short, dark hair and sideburns was standing next to two students and beaming with evident pride. His name was Ed Isabelle, and over two decades later he could still be found striding around the grounds he had cofounded. Isabelle was now a fifty-eight-year-old with a head of silver hair, but the set jaw and drill-sergeant air of his vintage photo were still part of his demeanor, and his white shorts and Woodward polo shirt revealed a build that remained trim and muscular. He'd loved team sports once, especially as a teenager in Springfield, Massachusetts, in the late fifties, when he had played baseball in an interregion league, pitching and playing third base and right field. Then one ninth-grade afternoon, something in him snapped during a game. He pitched well—hence his nickname Dizzy Izzy—and threw a runner out at first, fielded a catch at third, and knocked in two home runs. But for all his effort, his team still lost, 4–2. "I personally played a great game," he recalled, the old disgust still lingering in his voice as he sat in his plaque-lined Woodward office. "I was walking home and threw my baseball glove across the street. Never played again. I got bored silly. I think these kids are going through the same thing.

"In our society, everything has gotten more and more controlled. There was no baseball diamond in my town, so we'd go in the street and play. All of a sudden they built baseball diamonds. So you'd go there and play, and pretty soon there's only certain times you could play at the city park with the baseball diamonds because there's a fence all around it and they closed the gates. It starts to get *controlled,* and they form *leagues* where the only way you can play is to be on one of the *teams* in the leagues, and you can only play on the team at a certain time when the whole team gets together. So pretty soon you've been restricted so much that you play baseball in the *summer,* you practice Wednesday afternoon from *four* to *six,* and on Saturday mornings you have a baseball game. That's it. Our society with traditional sports has restricted and controlled the environment so much. Kids need freedom."

Isabelle's disillusionment with baseball also made him realize he didn't want to rely on anyone else to succeed. Gymnastics, a sport he had loved as a child, was the answer; for him, being one-on-one with a high beam symbolized the ultimate in self-reliance. He acquitted himself well at that sport, later attending Penn State and, after graduation, taking a job as assistant coach in the school's gymnastics department. Then, in 1969, a friend of one of his buddies asked if a gymnastics camp would work near the school, which was in State College in central Pennsylvania; the friend had seen a farm for sale in the area. The two drove thirty miles out to the rural burg of Woodward, where they inspected the ninety-acre spread with farmhouse and barn, the latter of which had a floor that just happened to have the same measurements as a gymnastics mat. "I said, 'Yep, we can do gymnastics here,'" Isabelle recalled. "No market study, no nothing." With another partner chipping in, it was theirs for $35,000, and Woodward Camp, America's newest school for gymnasts, was born.

The facility opened the following year, immediately drawing six-hundred young and aspiring gymnasts—then and each successive summer—who trained in the converted barn. The camp did fine, helping to churn out stars like future Olympic gold medalists Lilia Podkopayeva and Vitaly Scherbo, but Isabelle was, by his account, "coach, counselor, and business manager," and by 1977, extra hands and funds were needed. A local jack-of-all-trades, Paul Ream, who had built a Laundromat and ice-cream stand on the property of his house in nearby Aaronsburg, put in $50,000, and he and his son Gary, who had received a business degree in management and had been given a crash course in the food-service industry while training at the Roy Rogers fast-food chain, came aboard as partners. The parallel-bar vaulting, pool jumping, and campfire serenading continued apace, and Woodward seemed set for life.

No one could have anticipated the crisis that soon befell them. Woodward relied heavily on the Olympics to stoke the nation's interest in gymnastics; after the 1972 and 1976 games, camp attendance had shot up. Then came the summer of 1980, and as Isabelle growled, "The *peanut farmer* boycotted the Olympics." To protest the Soviet Union's 1979 invasion of Afghanistan, Jimmy Carter took the United States out of all competitions in Moscow that summer; West Germany, China, Japan, and Canada—sixty-five countries in all—also went along with the ban. As a result, the Soviets snagged four gold gymnastics medals—eighty gold altogether—and smaller nations like Bulgaria and Mongolia saw their athletes decorated on television. It was a bad global joke to everyone except those at Woodward, who rightly sensed as soon as the boycott was announced that there would be no spike in the years to come. "It's at this low point and it just kept getting lower," said Isabelle of attendance during those dire times. "And we thought, 'Man, we gotta do something else with this camp.'"

They had heard about BMX, this new type of bike racing and riding, and decided to roll the dice on kids in small-wheeled bikes who raced downhill and performed seemingly insane tricks on ramps and dirt courses. The influx was small at first—fourteen BMX racers showed up for the debut of the program in the summer of 1982—but the impact was, from the start, considerable. The girl gymnasts looked out the window of class one day and saw scruffy, helmeted young men on miniature wheels. "These *wild boys* showed up," recalled gymnastics coach Nancy Claar. "The little girls were attracted to them because they were the bad boys." Despite the attraction, though, the girls were not necessarily understanding; to them, BMX was simply not a sport. "Of course, we didn't like it," Claar added. "Gymnasts are purists. They are so disciplined, and here was a sport that seemed so free and had *no* discipline."

What Ream called "a huge cultural change for the camp" also affected the bicyclists: Everyone expected that they, like other athletes, would want to train with, say, a ten-mile ride to warm up. "By Thursday they all wanted to go home," recalled a staff member. Gradually, the two camps within the camp reached a détente. It hadn't taken long for the gymnasts to see that bike stunt riding involved more athleticism than they had first thought. The BMX program was so successful that, in 1987, the camp began a skateboarding program, although that, too, was an adjustment for everyone. "Skateboarding came down the driveway with an attitude," Ream said. "Basically, you had kids who weren't listening to rules." From the start, rule number one made it mandatory to wear helmets, of which skateboarders have never been particularly fond. But they, too, learned to adjust, and when skateboarding went through one of its downturns, in 1992, the camp embraced in-line skating, otherwise known as Rollerblading. Gymnasts continued to dominate attendance at Woodward, but within a few years, the camp was as well-known within extreme-sport circles as it was within tumbling ones. Each year brought a new skating or biking ramp, culminating in the Rock, the concrete bowl that had cost the camp a half million dollars to install.

By the time the boys of Cabin 18 arrived, Woodward was as bustling as the sports it championed. The camp employed between 250 and 300 staffers each summer, which included 40 gymnastic staffers, 35 dining-hall employees (who doled out three thousand meals daily), and hundreds of counselors, instructors, and supervisors. The combined payroll was $1.4 million. The day-to-day running of the camp had passed from Isabelle to Ream, who was forty-eight and tall, had dark pepperish hair and a mustache, and spoke in the deep, garrulous voice of a radio announcer. Ream declined to divulge Woodward's profit margin, but it was not hard to see that the camp made for good business; the nearly ten thousand campers each summer added up to $8 million in admission fees alone.

The roads that connected the cabins, gyms, and skate and bike buildings each had names as if they were suburban streets, and the idea made sense: Woodward felt like a town within a small town (in this case, a very small one—Woodward township's population was only two thousand). And like any town, Woodward Camp had certain guidelines. Ream almost dropped BMX in the early nineties, not because the sport was slumping but because the new breed of riders who checked in had become "just not proper for camp," he recalled. "Language, timeliness—it was just getting a little too rebellious." There was the time a bunch of skaters showed up to film video parts; when Ream later saw the tape, he realized they weren't wearing helmets, and all the skaters were turned away the next time they showed up. "We said, do your thing—just don't do it here," said Ream. He respected the sports enormously, but he also wanted civility: "When you come here, you have to come in and ride and you have to conduct yourself. We've had buses come up and we've said, 'Sorry—we can't have rough words here.' You have to be good with kids." With the exception of the occasional troublemaker, who would be asked to leave, everyone adjusted to the rules. The staff members who cruised around in golf-cart-like vehicles, keeping an eye out for trouble or foul language, made sure of that.

To the staff, these incidents were beside the point; the bigger picture was that Woodward fostered a balance between discipline and unbridled freedom. "The worst thing we can do in society is create a sterile environment, and there are people out there who would like to do that," said Isabelle. "They'd like to create an environment where nobody is ever at risk. Instead of joining the real world, you do it vicariously through a video game. Then you develop high cholesterol and become overweight and diabetic. The next great epidemic, they tell me, is obesity. Me personally, would I put up with my son breaking his wrist but being healthy when he's forty or fifty? Any day. Sounds cruel, but . . ." He let out a hearty "Heh!" After thirty years, the system hadn't changed him, and it wasn't about to now—not him or his campers, not this season or any other.

Monday, the first full, nonorientation weekday at Woodward, had the makings of a beautiful day to ride. The air was sweetly scented with morning dew, the horses brayed in the distance, and the sun began inching out early in the morning. First, however, there would be class. Woodward required all campers to take two hours of instruction each day before they went off on their own, and morning sessions began promptly at nine thirty A.M. As the time approached, groggy teenagers straggled out of their cabins, stopped by the dining hall for a bowl of sugary cereal, then made their way to whichever building they had been assigned. The streets became increasingly clogged with small bands of kids trudging along, clutching skateboards, or posses of bike riders or in-line skaters. The STOP, LOOK AND LISTEN signs dotting the grounds were clearly meant as much for pedestrians, who were in the minority, as for the campers.

They were at once a tribe and a group of individuals, both in society and at Woodward. The baby boomers had been the first to test-drive these sports, back during the first skateboard craze of the sixties, and their successors, dubbed Gen X, had driven skate, bike, and snow to new levels of popularity in the eighties and early nineties. But now the torch had been passed to Generation Y, or the Millennial Generation, as writers and researchers Neil Howe and William Strauss had dubbed them. These were the children born after 1982, seventy-six or so million of them, and they constituted the majority of the Woodward campers, who had to be at least seven years old to attend.

There were already indications they would not be taking their cues from Gen X. As Howe and Strauss wrote in *Millennials Rising: The Next Great Generation,* this generation was more confident and goaloriented, and less pessimistic, than their predecessors. From his trolling around the grounds, Ed Isabelle had witnessed this shift firsthand. "They may want people to *think* they're not smart, because it's part of the culture," he said of the current crop, "but they're very smart kids. They're getting self-discipline and they're motivated to learn; they want to succeed. Learning a trick is a microcosm of being successful. Every time they succeed, they're building confidence that's gonna help them for the rest of their lives."

These were the children of the Internet, a generation that had grown up with technology and was accustomed to taking matters into its own mouse-holding hands. "Individuals in our nation now feel they have total control over what they can do, *when* they do it, how they do it, and through what means," said Rich Luker, a social psychologist whose Chicago-based research company, the Leisure Intelligence Group, focused on adolescence. "We no longer feel this need to be connected with other people." For Luker and others, the jump to action sports made for a very short leap. "The culture of action sports is the culture of technology, which is there are no rules," he continued. "In team sports, there are rules. You can do it *this* way; you can't do it *that* way. In action sports, your reward is doing things differently from the way anybody else has done them. It's less about direct competition and more about the ascension of excellence in expression. That's the essence of the technological age. It's not about beating someone else anymore. It's about perfecting what you do on your own."

As Luker and other analysts were quick to note, this generation still followed baseball, football, and basketball; the appeal of those sports would never cease. But Gen Y were born of a faster-paced culture; they were the offspring of not only the Internet but video games. For them, team sports were simply too snail-paced, too sluggish, and not nearly kinetic enough. The idea of waiting two hours for a rush paled next to skillfully and quickly completing a skate, snowboard, or bike trick. When the producers of Nickelodeon's *Rocket Power* cartoon show were casting about for other activities for their young skateboarding characters, ball sports "felt so sedate and static," said coproducer Eryk Casemiro; ultimately, none was included. This was a generation that had never known a world without competitive skateboarding or events like the X Games, and who viewed professional athletes with skepticism. Everyone had been told how many millions of dollars baseball players made each season and how they still seemed to complain, threaten strikes, or leap from team to team.

In a *Sports Illustrated* baseball poll conducted in 2002, 75 percent of the respondents—*fans* of the sport—said they had not forgiven baseball for a strike eight years before, and on the subject of a pending labor dispute between owners and players, the overwhelming majority were "fed up with both." It was telling that in action-sports video games, players could dramatically alter the appearance of each skater, snowboarder, or biker; with a few clicks, their favorite rider could wear the most asinine of shorts, the loopiest of haircuts, the corniest of sandals. Nothing—not sports stars, certainly not musicians—was sacred anymore, another result of the Internet's impact on Gen Y: Since they were able to imitate the moves of their icons by way of their computer, how special *were* those icons?

In the School building, class began, as always, with stretching. In the dining hall beforehand, several of the students had frowned or blanked when the topic was brought up; warming up was a strange and foreign concept. In class, the instructor made them extend and twirl their arms, sit with legs extended, and connect hand to ankle. Those who participated kept glancing around at the others to see if they were doing the stretches correctly. Others, the wool-hatted kids in the back of the room, ignored the teacher altogether and talked throughout the whole session.

It was then time for instruction, and the sounds of polyurethane wheels and bike tires rolling across cement and atop ramps made of Skatelite (a popular wood-and-plastic composite that made for a grippy surface) quickly began resounding around the camp like pockets of gunfire. Lot/8 became an ant farm of bikers and skaters following each other down ramps and pipes to the accompaniment of thrashy punk. As a young, bearded instructor looked on, young BMXers streaked down a ramp and jumped into a pit of blue foam balls that cushioned their falls. "Don't get scared and ditch your bike," the teacher said after one rider had done just that. "That's when you get hurt. Hold on to that bike, don't let it go." Another rider took his foot off his bike in midflight, leading the instructor to bark, "Put that foot back on!" The kid emerged, sheepishly, from the foam pit. Expletives were not allowed in the school, but somebody had circumvented that rule by carving words and phrases like *Billy H Sucks Ass* and *Pussy* into some of the foam balls.

In another building, Danny, the reserved, Brillo-haired thirteen-year-old from Cabin 18, had to learn to drop in. He had never done it before, since his skating had been confined to the streets, curbs, and building plazas of Manhattan, but he knew it was time and was clearly nervous. "Dropping in takes courage," he had murmured beforehand. "Waiting and courage." He walked up onto the ramp, carefully planted his feet on the deck, appeared ready to move, then hesitated. He turned to his instructor and asked again how it should be done. After a few more pointers, he extended the nose of his board over the coping, jammed his foot down on the nose, and sailed down into the pipe, his tall frame looking tense, his arms extended out for balance. He made it down, but at the bottom his scuffed-up board shot away from him. The instructor told him to try again, and with a frown he climbed back up the ramp once more. The same mistake happened again. Finally, on his third attempt, he pulled it: He dropped in, stayed on the board, and rode halfway up the opposite wall. He walked away with the most fleeting of smiles on his face.

Each day at Woodward would take on this rhythm—practicing the same move several times until it was mastered well enough, then moving on to another as teachers, who looked like older versions of the campers, offered tips. Some campers found the classes irksome, but just as many looked forward to them, and in this appreciation, those who ran the camp noticed a shift. In the eighties, when instruction was first introduced, it had been greeted warily, but this new generation of riders was different—more serious and more driven about their sports and more aware of its potential economic rewards. "When you get kids thinking of fashion and music and culture and risk-taking and computers and sponsorship and how it flows, it teaches you a lot," said Ream proudly. "And overall what is that? That's just about anything associated with capitalism and business." And as everyone noted, they were *young:* It was not unusual to see kids who could barely reach the top drawer of their dresser pulling an ollie or bunnyhop. "Back before the X Games, it was a recreation," said Isabelle. "All of a sudden you have kids for whom the sport becomes competitive. I don't know if it's good or bad, but they're becoming much better athletes." The sight was both heartening and disconcerting—and most likely, inevitable. These sports were real sports now, and there was no going back.

Later that afternoon, a thunderstorm that had been threatening to strike all day finally did, with a fury that mocked Woodward's bucolic surroundings. As a Foo Fighters song played in one of the bowls, the sky ripped apart and the torrent began. Everyone ran for cover, some into buildings and others, like Jeff and Craig, onto the covered porch of the Canteen. They were both twelve, both from nearby towns in Pennsylvania, and both BMXers who had already been riding for several years.

Sitting on a bench, they anxiously watched bullets of rain pelt the campgrounds and soak the outdoor bowls. They talked about sponsors and most admiringly Dave Mirra, the sport's biggest, most financially successful star. With their short hair and chipper, revved-up demeanors, they could have been Little Leaguers. But that activity held little interest for them. Jeff had been to a basketball camp before but left unimpressed: "You have a coach, and you can't pick what you can do." Craig, too, preferred these sports: "You don't have a coach yelling at you. And you don't have a certain way of doing things."

Craig looked over at the Outdoor Street course, yearning to get back on it once the weather improved.

"It's not really street," said Jeff.

"Yeah, it is," Craig said.

"You don't even know what street *is*!" Jeff snapped back. "This isn't street. It's park. It's street ramps on sidewalks." Whatever it was, he wanted to ride it again soon; to his delight, he had finally landed a no-footed can-can today.

"I wanna do a fufanu," said Craig.

"Those are *hard*," replied Jeff.

They were asked about the gymnasts, and both giggled mockingly as only twelve-year-olds could. "We're in the cabin next to them," said Jeff, "and we yell out the window at them."

As the storm intensified, Jeff grew more serious. "I'm paranoid of storms," he said quietly as lightning cracked near one of the buildings. "I saw a tornado touch down once. You see that tree?" He pointed to one about fifty feet away. "It was that close." Weather was one thing, but he was asked if he was afraid to drop into a steep ramp.

"Not at all," he replied.

He tried not to think about the taunts, put-downs, and derisive comments he had been hearing for years, always aimed at the sport in which he participated and took great pride. Part of him had become accustomed to the scorn, if only through its relentlessness. But the cracks and lack of regard still gnawed at him, and he could still not fully comprehend why they persisted.

"People have to recognize what we're doing and move beyond their prejudice," said the bearded young man with the wire-rimmed glasses and brown Caesar haircut. "We're devoted, totally, three hundred percent. We're out there doing crazy things and people don't even acknowledge it. They just write it off." He shook his head. "It's not good. People don't really know what Rollerblading's all about. They just have this image of a dad rolling down the street. We're like, 'That's not what we do. We're jumping off twenty-five stories over there.' We have our own things to offer."

Each summer, Woodward welcomed not only campers and instructors but visiting pros, who were given free room and board and allowed to use as many of the facilities as they desired in exchange for interacting with the kids. This week, one of those pros was Nick Riggle, an in-line skater—or, to use the parlance of outsiders, a Rollerblader, a reference to the name of the long-standing company that dominated the in-line market. Sitting on a bench near the outdoor grill, where campers had queued up a few hours earlier to devour as many burgers and hot dogs as they could, Riggle looked far more studious than most in his sport, which reflected his upbringing as the son of a Methodist minister. "It's like a meditative exercise, man," he was saying as dusk began to fall and the clacking of boards in the distance continued. "If you're too scared, it's hard to concentrate on what you're doing. But if you're very solid and focused, and you can concentrate, it's like meditating. There's nothing else."

This particular summer, the sport-by-sport breakdown at Woodward amounted to 3,500 gymnasts, 3,100 skateboarders, 2,400 BMXers, and 2,100 in-line skaters. Each group arrived with an image and a reputation. The BMXers, said one counselor, were "more independent" than the others. The girl gymnasts were seen as the most competitive within their own ranks. ("I'm in a cabin with them," one of their overseers said, "and they look like they're ready to cut each other's braids off. You can *feel* the tension.") Yet when it came to overall disapproval verging on wrath, in-liners were in an antileague of their own. All one had to do was bring up the subject to skateboarders, BMXers, even counselors, and merciless ridicule ensued: "What do you do without ramps? You're a *roller skater!*" Or, "They stole our moves." Or, "Their parents are like soccer moms." Tension between different action-sports factions had existed for years, especially between skaters and BMXers. Under the category "jihad," an issue of *Thrasher* had listed "Fuck BMX." But those were minor, lingering irritations compared to the impression many, both inside and outside Woodward, had of in-liners. In *The Answer Is Never,* writer Jocko Weyland summed it up when he referred to Riggle's profession as an "unspeakably contemptible eight-wheeled scourge."

It hadn't always been that way. The sport was the brainchild of Minneapolis hockey player Scott Olson, who, around 1979, began retooling ice skates to work on regular surfaces by replacing the blade with ball bearings. He and his brother's fledgling company, Rollerblade, quickly led the market, which grew steadily for most of the eighties. Early the following decade, though, in-line skating went from cult pastime to craze. The exact numbers were hard to verify, but estimates of ten to twelve million participants by 1994 did not seem out of line; nearly four million pairs of skates (some of which cost as much as $400) were sold in 1992 alone, driving the industry to $319-million heights that year. Success on that scale never fails to breed contempt, but in this case it led to outright hostility. For some, the reason was timing. By coincidence, the rise of in-line skating coincided with slumps in skateboarding and BMX, and those athletes looked at the Rollerbladers with their four- or five-wheeled shoes zipping past them and saw nothing but people stealing their tricks and garnering all the attention, publicity, and sponsorship money while they, the skaters and bikers, had been driven back underground yet again. It was humiliating, and they would never completely forget it.

In the action-sports world, mainstream success was a tricky business; everyone wanted a taste, but *just* a taste, since the risk of alienating the devout was too great. Eventually, in-line skating fell victim to this trap, as overambitious companies cranked out more pairs of the things than people wanted to buy. Even worse, in the eyes of the skaters and bikers like Tim in Cabin 18, "Everyone's *dad* was doing it." In-lining became a family affair, which clinched its fall. The blader-haters saw the article in *USA Today* in 1993 in which a group of women—"including grandmothers and homemakers," the article noted positively—were interviewed about their interest in blading ("It's very social but it's also good exercise," they said), and they cringed and laughed. It didn't seem to matter that in-line contests at the X Games and other competitions revealed that the athletes could pull off difficult tricks—like double backflips on vert ramps—every bit as challenging as skating or bike moves, albeit with a certain balletic style that didn't mesh with the hard-grinding approach of skateboarding. It didn't matter that one could wander the paths of Woodward and see in-liners standing on a long stretch of rail and grinding down it, maneuvering each kink and twist with flailing arms and displaying impressive balancing and coordination skills. It didn't matter that there were an estimated one to two million competitive, aggressive in-liners and, if one factored in the part-timers and parents, some twenty million overall. It was still supremely uncool, and those twenty million could have it.

Nick Riggle had been hearing those condemnations since the time he tried on a friend's pair of in-line skates in 1992. The sixth-grader was instantly smitten with the feel and sensation of gliding along. The following year, still game on team sports, he had tried his hand at football, and the memory was still bittersweet: "I didn't like football, man." He talked in a gentle, prematurely wise manner and carried a copy of *The Tao of Physics*. "When you get in there with pads, man, I don't know. I like crashing on my own, not someone else crashing into *me*." He decided to become a nonrec—a nonrecreational skater—and practiced in the skatepark near his home in Santa Rosa, California, where he first encountered the askance looks of the skate crowd. "The vibe wasn't good," he recalled soberly. "Wasn't good. Skateboarders didn't like Rollerbladers. Like it was a threat or something. I'd like to think it's that simple. But in a way, the attitude toward Rollerbladers is almost out of contempt, like a deep prejudice."

With the help of the California Proficiency Exam, he left high school halfway through his junior year, and, thanks to a growing number of sponsors, soon became a pro in-liner. His immersion came in particularly helpful when his parents—his mother the minister, his father an employee of a surgical supply company—split up when he was eighteen. After that, he grew even more entranced by skating, his escape from the pain of his family life. "You really gain a sense of individual qualities, of 'I'm doing this, I'm doing something for myself,'" he said. "It's pretty powerful when you're young." Things happened fast after that: He filmed a video part, placed respectably at one X Games in San Francisco, and developed a growing reputation that lingered to this day. A number of campers at Woodward recognized him immediately.

"When I want to do something that's big, or something someone else might not do, part of it is because it's something no one's ever done before," Riggle said. "It's like breaking new ground. That's really exciting. But another part of it is that you question yourself: 'Can I do that?' It's a matter of seeing how far you can go. I've gone too far before and screwed up," he said with a laugh, a reference to those times when he had broken his arm, wrists, and hand. "There's a limit." He paused. "It's fun, man. It's just fun." He laughed. "That's the easiest way to put it. We're not *trying* to destroy that person's plant box. We see it as an opportunity to be artistic."

And now it was over. A few months before, for largely financial reasons, Riggle had retired just before turning twenty-one. At most, he had made $40,000 one year, but just before he quit, his annual take-home had dropped to $23,000. He had heard the stories of athletes, especially skateboarders, making six-figure salaries and could not even imagine such a payday for himself. "The hard thing is that we're not making money," he said, referring to his fellow in-liners. "And when you get to be twenty-one and you're not making enough money to live on your own, you gotta quit, man. There's nothing you can do about it. You gotta make money, you know?"

Besides, signs that his sport was in decline were all around him. The
Rollerblade company had overextended itself and had dragged down
the profit margin of its parent company, the Italian clothing chain
Benetton. Sales of in-line videos had plunged from their heyday in the
early nineties. He had heard that ESPN had put on some sort of
awards show earlier that year and that in-line was conspicuously
omitted. "That's the way it is, man," he said with a shrug. He'd felt
such a bond with the other athletes; to him, in-lining was halfway
between skate and BMX. Like a skater, he'd even been banned from
his local skatepark for riding without pads, which felt too restrictive
to him ("you can't bend your knees as much"). He tried to argue that
the cop had written down the wrong time on the ticket, but they
hadn't bought it. Given a fine, he was told he would be jailed if he was
caught again without pads. He was a societal outlaw like the others,
but it still did not seem to matter. He would always be an outsider in
an outsider's world.

"There's tolerance now," he admitted. "I wouldn't say mutual
respect. There is a tolerance like, 'We don't like what you're doing,
but we'll tolerate you.' It has gotten better." He was told that the
merest mention of in-line skating, both at Woodward and in the
world beyond, still provoked stinging put-downs. "Oh, totally,
yeah," he said, nodding, and offered a slightly sad smile. "Unfortunately there are still Ku Klux Klan members, you know."

He would soon be back in college, studying philosophy with the
hope of eventually becoming a teacher. In that regard, he felt the
lessons learned during his five years as a professional in-liner would
come in handy. "It was good for me," he said, "because I got to see
how other people can act when they don't like what you do. Which is
a good lesson in life because it's wrong. It's fundamentally *wrong*.
And to experience that, that strongly, was good. It sucked, but . . . it
definitely made me stronger. I got a lot of crap when I was little for
being a Rollerblader. And I learned a lot from it, man. I can see how

stupid people can be. How ignorance can distort their whole world-view, their whole view of life."

The evening had grown still and dusky and the curfew had passed, meaning the campers were now ensconced in their cabins. Other than the fireflies gently buzzing overhead, the only sound was that of the teachers' wheels connecting with Skatelite; it was now their time to ride. One by one, the saucer-shaped lights at each of the outdoor facilities blinked on, casting an otherworldly, bluish glow to the camp.

"What can you compare this to?" Riggle finally said. "I can't think of anything. It's heaven."

It was time for the staff to meet and discuss how the week had been progressing, so two dozen skateboard instructors congregated at a long table in the Lodge. A miniature hotel with fireplaces and arm-chairs, the Lodge was the place where ESPN executives and other visiting dignitaries would stay. Tim and Mike from Cabin 18 were there, as were skate instructors hailing from Florida, Kentucky, Alabama, and Illinois; making a rare guest appearance at one of these get-togethers was camp boss Gary Ream. The two skate directors chairing the meeting started with the usual run-through of the rules: Instructors were not allowed to wear headphones or use cell phones while on duty, and they always had to keep an eye out for kids who used unacceptable substitutes for elbow pads. "Always look out for socks," one warned, and everyone nodded or chuckled in agreement.

There was nothing amusing, though, about the spate of injuries that had dogged the camp. No one denied that bumps, bruises, and far worse were part of the Woodward experience; as Isabelle stated earlier, "I've never told anybody that a child coming here is safe. 'Cause they're *not*." In case anyone (especially parents) missed the point, the alarm was sounded in the application. "Warning," a small box read. "By the very nature of the activities, skateboarding, in-line

skating, and freestyle bicycling all carry the risk of physical injury . . .
The risk of injury includes minor injuries such as bruises and more
serious injuries such as broken bones, dislocations, and muscle pulls.
The risk also includes catastrophic injuries such as permanent pa-
ralysis or even death from landings or falls on the back, neck or
head."

In spite of safeguards, it had been a rough few days. The trouble
had started the week before, when one of the BMX instructors had
been jumping dirt during his off time. As campers and fellow
instructors watched that evening, he pedaled up into the air, came
back down on the ramp on his front tire, and was thrown off the bike,
landing on his face. A helicopter rushed him to a local hospital, where
he now sat, paralyzed from the waist down. There were reasons to be
optimistic—his most recent visitors reported he had regained some
feeling in his legs—yet the incident had sent a chill through the staff,
who talked about it in hushed, somber tones. T-shirts with the
instructor's name had quickly been printed up and were being sold
to help raise funds for his medical expenses.

Then there were the kids who had injured themselves during testing
and had to sit out the entire week. They still attended classes but sat
by the side of the ramps with their crutches, crestfallen and murmur-
ing "It's not fair" to anyone who would listen. The training room,
home to the camp's medical personnel, was accustomed to a slew of
sprained ankles and wrists, but in the last few days, two wrist
fractures, an ankle dislocation, and a broken finger had already been
reported. Cabin 18 had been hit as well: Nick, he of the seventies
sideburns, had been hobbling around since his arrival. Just before
coming to Woodward, he had been skating and had landed with his
foot on the side edge of the board. He had felt the mysterious bump
but had ignored it: "I gotta skate," he had said when asked about the
injury. Eventually, though, it hurt so much that he was driven off to
the same hospital where the BMX teacher was undergoing tests.

"We're not pushing kids to get hurt," said one of the skate directors at the meeting. "We want them to know they can do it. But we don't want them in the hospital. The kids have been dropping like flies today." Everyone nodded gravely, although there was little they could do to prevent any of these incidents.

The meeting moved on. A dark-haired skate teacher with a British accent said he had been spoken to while riding off-duty without a shirt. "I never knew there was a big issue with this," he said. "Why can't I?" At this, Ream, who had been silent much of the time, spoke up, his resonant voice commandeering the room. "There's a difference," he said, "between being professional and being trashy." Shirts were mandatory, and that was the end of that; the teacher who had brought it up shrugged and accepted it. After half an hour, the meeting broke up, and Mike, looking as if the Lodge had been the last place in Pennsylvania he had wanted to be, ambled back toward Cabin 18. On the way, he ran into Brandon, the green-braced kid, and together they grabbed seats at one of the picnic benches near the Canteen as another Woodward day wrapped up.

Brandon was happy with his headway; thanks to Woodward, he had learned how to carve a bowl. In between quips and put-downs, he talked about what it was like to be a skateboarder in Grand Rapids, especially when it came to girls. "They say, 'You're a stoner who smokes weed,'" he griped. "Then they go out with rich *preppies* who smoke weed." He had more serious plans in his mind: The kids in Cabin 17 had doused him with water, and he was plotting his revenge. "If you poop on someone," he said to Mike, "*no one* will mess with you." It was only a question of how to get a pile of feces into his enemies' rooms.

A fellow camper came by to hang out and said, a little too loudly, "Fuck."

"Did I hear what I think I heard?" a nearby counselor in a golf cart barked, turning in their direction. Brandon apologized, but the counselor still came over. "Okay, let's go," he told them all; it was now ten P.M., time for everyone to make their way back to their cabins and prepare for bed. With that, Brandon and Mike drifted past the street course and the infrequently utilized basketball court and returned to Cabin 18.

Rules notwithstanding, sleep still seemed to be hours away. Some of the campers, like Brandon, had cut classes that day and had spent the afternoon inside the cabin, beating the ninety-degree temperatures that had engulfed the camp and made it difficult to skate or practice BMX. Greg, Brandon, Danny, and Nick, who was now on crutches, beckoned a visitor inside and pointed to something they had scribbled near the door: "ACP Represents." What did it stand for? "Anal cherry poppers!" they roared in unison, reducing themselves to hysterics. This was, again, a violation of camp regulations, which did not allow writing on cabin walls.

"Look at our wall of acne pads!" said Greg. Sure enough, one portion of the cabin was peppered with a handful of white circular pads, as if a food fight with pimple products had taken place.

Talk turned to the facility. "There are way too many rules," said Nick. "We're just kids." He said he wanted to stick his crutches up the butt of a particularly aggressive camp official and demonstrated with a cabinmate.

The topic of in-line skating came up. "They're all five years behind our style," said Greg, who would hurl a large chunk of plastic at one startled in-liner the following day.

"They think they're better than us," said another bunkmate, "they think they're like . . ."

"Jocks," said Nick.

"Yeah, jocks!" another said.

"I don't like team sports," Greg said. "You have to depend on everyone else. And if someone screws up, everyone does."

"We don't give a fuck about anything," Nick added with a shrug. "We're just a bunch of dumb-asses."

To demonstrate their craziness, Greg lit up an incense stick and, as the others egged him on, stuck it in his mouth. The sticky-sweet scent was bad enough; it was hard to imagine how it must have tasted in his throat. The Cabin 18 boys all laughed, screamed, and flicked the lights on and off as Greg pulled the stick out, grabbed a plastic jug of water, and chugged it down. For all the changes that had been wrought in the action-sports world—all the money, corporate involvement, and interest of the Olympics—certain aspects refused to die. There would always be teens who wanted to ride, whenever and wherever they wanted and with no restrictions, and there would always be adults who wanted to encourage them while making sure they were adhering to certain guidelines.

In his bunk, Mike put on a Bob Marley album and watched the proceedings with numerous shakes of the head and a bemused smile. In another half hour, he would flick off the lights for the last time and pray for the boys to finally crash for the night. There was only so much a skate counselor could do before the station wagons and sport utility vehicles returned once again, taking Greg, Brandon, Danny, and the others away, and another group arrived to taste as much freedom to ride as the adult world would allow.

6. EAT DIRT TO THE BEAT
the music-sports connection

"Music and skating have always gone together," Steve Caballero was saying. "It's about creativity and adventure and the rush you get from writing a song or learning a trick—the spontaneity of it. They're both raw, not polished."

Caballero, an elfin thirty-six-year-old with bleached hair, was squatting by the side of a metallic vert ramp. He was wearing shorts and a sleeveless, oversize T-shirt that exposed bony arms; his head was cocked to the side. Cab, as he was called, had been skateboarding professionally longer than just about anyone else. He had started in the late seventies while growing up in San Jose, California, and had joined the Bones Brigade the following decade. At the time, Caballero was so revered that when teenage Tony Hawk joined the team, he had to prove his mettle by chewing a piece of gum stuck between Cab's toes. Caballero had invented a number of innovative skate tricks—especially the Cab 720, or two 360-degree turns on the half-pipe, a move many snowboarders would later adopt—and had come to represent not only longevity and diligence but credibility; unlike other skaters, he had never formed his own company and still appeared relatively independent. When it came to music, Caballero also knew of what he spoke. He had been listening to punk for over two decades and had even played in several hard-core bands; one of them, the Faction, had recently reunited. "It's a lot safer to be a punk now than back in the eighties," he said as he prepared to climb up an aluminum ladder to the top of the ramp. "It's more accepted. You won't get your ass kicked if you have different-color hair."

To hear Caballero, though, one had to listen close. All around him was music: the jackhammer drumming and boisterous shouts of punk, the jumping-bean rhythms of ska-rock, the staccato rhyming of hip-hop. It was all happening at once, a jumbled cacophony that not even the sound of polyurethane wheels scraping against metal could muffle. The occasion was the annual Warped Tour, a traveling festival of vent rock, action-sports sideshow, and clothing, jewelry, and food vendors. Inaugurated in 1995, Warped had become a mainstay of the summer concert season; on this particular afternoon, it had taken over a large dirt field on Randalls Island, one of two interconnected isles off Manhattan right in the middle of the East River. Circling the vendors were stages presenting the music long associated with Caballero's sport, as well as with BMX, in-line skating, and motocross, which were also part of the day's attractions. Early in the day came Flogging Molly, a California band that mainlined pogo-punk rhythms into traditional folk melodies and instruments, even more so than the late, lamented Pogues had done. "Bless me, Father, for I have sinned / But then again, so have you" went the line to a song condemning the Catholic Church. "This is a new song," announced a skinny punk-band member on another stage. "It's called . . . 'Your Face or Your Knees'!" One band dedicated a song to the police who had harassed them; on another stage, a singer announced, "We'd like to dedicate this song to all the assholes and motherfuckers in the audience!" The Icelandic trio Quarashi offered up a tight, snot-nosed homage to the beer-spouting, nonpolitically correct side of the Beastie Boys. The eight stages were within such close proximity that musicians were easily able to assess their competition across the way and make disparaging comments about them. The previous day, at a tour stop in Camden, New Jersey, one punk band, encased in leather and studs as if 1976 had never ended, summed up the prevailing attitude when its singer addressed the mosh pit: "Whenever you go to work or to the mall, do people fuck with you? This is for everyone who tells you you can't be who you are."

By midafternoon, it was 3rd Strike's turn to add to the sonic mêlée. The sun was raging full on, but theirs would not be music for basking in the warmth. The four musicians dutifully assumed their positions onstage to the accompaniment of doomy symphonic music and began whipping up a merciless maelstrom of cement-mixer guitars and tub-thumping drums. Eventually, the band's singer, Jim Korthe, a thick-bodied man in a sleeveless silver basketball shirt and shorts, emerged from the wings; with his shaved head, weight-lifter arms, and swarm of tattoos, he could have passed for a contestant at a prison talent show. Propping one leg on the stage monitor, he began singing, grimly and without any display of pleasure—hard labor set to a beat. When the shout-out chorus arrived, everything cut loose: Korthe began rapping while hoisting his frame up and down, and the guitarists flagrantly lurched about.

"Put your fucking fingers in the air!" Korthe ordered the crowd afterward. "Let's see if we can kick up more dust out there. I want a big-ass dust cloud." Eager to comply, the small but multiplying audience in front began leaping up, down, and into one another. Within minutes, Korthe got his wish: The once-empty dirt patch before him had become a circular whirlpool, dirt particles whooshing into the air. The smarter ones in the crowd had already wrapped do-rags over their heads to protect their faces from the soil being whipped up. In doing so, they resembled gang members, but at least they could breathe. One of them wore a T-shirt that announced I HAVE TROUBLE REMEMBERING NAMES—CAN I JUST CALL YOU ASSHOLE?

3rd Strike continued its sonic tirade for the next half hour, Korthe singing and bellowing songs about the overpowering influence of the media, suicide, drug addiction, and friends killed by drive-bys; they also performed a hip-hop-influenced cover of Black Sabbath's "Paranoid." "This is for everyone who grew up without a father," Korthe said as the band started "Walked Away": "Abandonment how I can taste it / My resentment time to face it" went the chorus. The topics shifted, but the musical template established by the first song remained: metallic guitars and melodic twists in the verses gave way to full-on gangsta intensity in the choruses. The music of two different groups of societal underdogs, suburban and urban, merged on the stage. This was the sound of 3rd Strike, its generation, and the new type of sports that generation had claimed as its own. Remarkable in its incessant rage, the new rock was unlike anything the music had produced in its fifty-year history. Overhead, jets headed for LaGuardia Airport could be seen but not heard.

It was hard to ascertain the first song written about any of the so-called extreme sports, but it was easy enough to determine the first successful one. In 1964, skateboard enthusiasts Jan and Dean—Jan Berry and Dean Torrence, two California high-school buddies whose biggest hit, the previous year's "Surf City," immortalized another recreational pastime—decided it was time to write a tune about the four-wheel craze sweeping their state and country. Given that skateboarding had emanated from surf culture, it made sense that the duo, at the suggestion of Brian Wilson, lifted the song's melody from Wilson's Beach Boys hit "Catch a Wave" and gave it new lyrics and a revamped chorus: "Why don't you grab your board and go sidewalk surfin' with me?" The refurbished single, "Sidewalk Surfin'," was typical of the Wilson and Beach Boy knockoffs of the day: the virginal falsetto harmonies, the rinky-dink guitar riff, the chipper background voices (chiming in "bust your buns / bust your buns now!"). A mention of "the coffin" referred to a move in which skaters would lie flat on their backs on their boards and cross their hands like corpses—the forerunner of street luge. Issued during the peak of the first skateboard craze, "Sidewalk Surfin'" climbed to number twenty-five on the pop charts in the fall of 1964—and was quickly relegated to insignificance when the sport burnt itself out soon after.

Nearly forty years after its release, "Sidewalk Surfin'" sounded even more timid compared to the music that now served as accompaniment for skateboarding and its brethren in sports. Throughout the seventies, skaters in search of empty pools to carve opted for the dominant FM rock of the era—Alice Cooper, Jimi Hendrix, Led Zeppelin, and the like, the music of white, post-sixties, dazed-and-confused teenagers. When skating went subterranean at the close of that decade, new, more defiant music was needed to convey the sport's relegation to the fringes. Skaters found it in punk, whose appeal was obvious. Punk rock was antiauthoritarian, uncompromising, and born of a do-it-yourself culture, and it never wanted to stray far from its underground bloodline. Punk's unyielding thrash also made for a perfect complement for the new sports; its short, punching-bag songs matched the energy of riding, and it adrenalized the athletes as much as the spectators. "It was hard to find places to skate and hard to find places for an all-ages punk show," recalled Steve Martin, a hard-core musician and part-time skater who went on to head up Nasty Little Man, a music publicity firm. "It was the same mentality—you were an outsider. They were both cultures of exclusion."

Mike Vallely was a green teenage skateboarder when he witnessed his first punk show, featuring Black Flag, at the City Gardens in Trenton, New Jersey, in September 1984. "Henry Rollins came out and started pacing the stage, back and forth, like a caged animal," he recalled. "I was like, 'God, look at this guy—he's so intense!' He's dripping with sweat before the show even starts. Then he hits the first vocal and the place erupts. I get crushed against the stage; the energy is insane. It was one of those times where you never want to leave that moment. I realized that somehow, some way, I wanted to be in that same position; I want to make people feel like that. That's where a lot of the intensity I have in my skating comes from. It's from that moment, that experience."

Thousands of kids around the country had the same encounter, at different concerts and with different bands. Almost immediately, the unruly, coercive music and its like-minded sports met and embraced. *Thrasher* was more than happy to include reviews of hard-core bands and interviews with the likes of Rollins. From the pile-driving frustration and ennui of Black Flag to the thrashed-up reggae/ hard-core of D.C.'s Bad Brains to, later, the marching-orders fury of Bad Religion—just a few of the bands pouring out of clubs and garages—little of the music made it onto radio or MTV. Yet that, too, was fitting, since skateboarding never made it onto network sports specials either. The corny blues-pop of *The Bones Brigade Video Show* gave way to more aggressive soundtracks as well; released just a few years later, the video *Red Hot Skate Rock* featured the Red Hot Chili Peppers, a new L.A. punk-funk band, alongside footage of Hawk, Caballero, Christian Hosoi, and others. Spike Jonze's *Blind: Video Days* had Jason Lee and Mark Gonzales, among others, riding to Hüsker Dü and Black Flag. Some skaters, like Vallely and Caballero, formed bands of their own (original Bones Brigade skater Tommy Guerrero went on to make steamy handmade-techno albums), and many of the musicians were riders as well; Beastie Boy Adam Yauch was known for skateboarding from his home in Brooklyn to his publicist's office in downtown Manhattan by way of the Brooklyn Bridge.

Soon, the music and the sports would be dragged together into the mainstream. Punk's breakthrough arrived when Green Day, a northern-California band who had made several indie albums, began drawing in a widespread audience. Their ascent began just a few months after Kurt Cobain's death, and the timing was not coincidental.

The new punk rarely if ever preached the Sex Pistols' old message of "no future." Their songs had the brawny energy and concision of punk, but their personae were lighter, friendlier, and more accessible, especially for MTV; even when they mocked themselves, the self-inflicted wounds were cartoonish slaps. An audience looking for alternatives to Cobain's self-destruction found it in bands like Green Day and Offspring, where nihilism was relegated to the bench. It was telling that when the Clash-invoking Rancid entitled a 1995 song "Disorder and Disarray," the topic wasn't a white riot but whether the band should sign with a major label. Compared to grunge and the alternative scene, which were consumed with diffidence and inner turmoil, the new punk was downright uplifting and empowering—a surprising, and very punk, gesture in and of itself.

Again, the music and sports were in sync. In 1995, the year Green Day's *Dookie* went platinum, ESPN inaugurated its biannual X Games, broadcasting skateboarding, BMX, and in-line skating to the masses. As with the new punk, the X Games lent the sports a more buffed, professional presentation, all the better for mass consumption and business interests. (It wasn't long before Green Day and the likes of X Games star Hawk were deemed corporate cogs, and the debates about what constituted real versus fake punk, and real versus tele-vised skateboarding, began.) The ways in which indie rockers grappled with corporate-label offers mirrored the inner struggles of action-sport athletes and their big-ticket sponsorships. Through it all, the music served the same purpose: maintaining the beat and thereby the momentum. Moving beyond punk, board-sport rock also encompassed alternative hip-hop, ska, hard-core rap, and cut-and-paste DJ scratching, all with a veneer of cheery insouciance and a caustic attitude. If team sports were the equivalent of classic rock, then action sports were the sound of a successive generation that had little if any need for the sounds of boomers past.

The gnarlier the sports became, the uglier and more visceral the music. The rise of high-intensity offshoots like freestyle motocross, with its shadowy, motorcycle-gang atmosphere, coincided with the ascent of nu-metal—heavy metal taken to its bludgeoning extremes and infused with hair-tugging angst—as well as the blend of metal and hip-hop known as rap rock. A survey conducted in 2002 by *Transworld BMX* ascertained that the preferred genres of the magazine's readers were hard rock/heavy metal, at 67.6 percent; punk, 50.8 percent; and rap/hip-hop, 45.2 percent; with country at 6.4 percent; the top five favored bands were blink-182, Linkin Park, System of a Down, Korn, and Limp Bizkit. Rock had once been all about tension and release; with these genres, it became all tension. It was hard to imagine such music—low on melody, high on bludgeoning rage—topping the charts. At one time, it had also been inconceivable that fast-food chains and car manufacturers would incorporate skateboarding or snowboarding imagery into their commercials. But by the dawn of the twenty-first century, both scenarios had occurred.

Then again, by that point everything felt extreme: The anarchic aspects of the music and the sports were of a piece with youth culture. It was no coincidence that one of MTV's most popular series of the late nineties, the nonstop slew of self-hazing rituals known as *Jackass*, sprang out of skateboard culture. P. J. Clapp, the future Johnny Knoxville, had begun making videos for *Big Brother,* the proudly insolent skate magazine, in which he and his friends crashed into whatever was available. Eventually, MTV noticed and signed up Knoxville, and he and his posse of hyena-cackling insubordinates became stars of television (and later, feature film), where they subjected themselves to smashups, falls, trips, and concussions that were precisely like those in action-sport videos. One of Knoxville's gang was Bam Margera, which cemented the bond between this video punk rock and the sports. The hilariously deranged *Jackass* was simply part of a cultural trend in which nuance and subtlety fell out of favor.

Hollywood blockbusters grew more bombastic and radio and television talk-show hosts more emphatic, and television commercials aimed at that demographic delighted in screaming—quite literally—in viewers' faces. Whether they liked it or not, skateboarding, BMX, motocross, and snowboarding became caught up in something much larger and much more uncontrollable.

In the meantime, the music, the harder and heavier the better, was everywhere: blared at contests and demos, featured in skate and snow videos, included in video games like Hawk's Pro Skater series. On the annual Sno-Core tour, college-radio bands played as footage of snowboarding tricks and crashes was shown on a nearby screen. (Imagine the Grateful Dead playing the Fillmore in 1968, but with sports videos behind them instead of swirling lights.) Every action-sports gathering, from competitions to charity events benefiting organizations like breast-cancer research, featured stages with power-punk bands or rappers. For her second run at the 2002 Winter Olympics, snowboarder Kelly Clark dropped into the half-pipe while blink-182's "Dammit" blasted in her Walkman; she went on to win the gold medal. In a concoction that was both natural and straight out of a science-fiction film, Burton teamed with Apple for the Burton Amp, a snowboarding jacket with an iPod stitched into it.

The next step in the bond between the sports and skatepunk rock was full-fledged tours featuring bands and athletes. By 2002, earlier attempts, like the Swatch Vision tour of the eighties, gave way to a T-Mobile–sponsored sports/music tour and, most prominently, Hawk's Boom Boom HuckJam extravaganza, at which the skateboarder and an assemblage of top-dollar skaters and BMX and motocross riders—Bucky Lasek, Mat Hoffman, Dave Mirra, and Carey Hart among them—were accompanied by live performances from punk veterans Social Distortion and Offspring. When it became apparent after the tour's first few performances that the audience was younger than expected—not sixteen-year-olds, but ten- and twelve-year-olds with parents in tow—the musicians had to adjust: The amps were turned down so as not to damage juvenile ears. "I also asked the guys who had questionable lyrics in their songs if they wouldn't mind being *kind*," said Hawk's sister and manager, Pat Hawk. "And a lot of these guys, they're dads anyway, so that wasn't really a problem. The bands who had lyrics like that were really cool about it."

Long before the Boom Boom HuckJam—seven years earlier, to be precise—the first major, long-term attempt to cement the bond between the two worlds began with the Warped Tour. By the middle of the afternoon of the tour's Randalls Island stop, the circus was in full effect. The skate demo featuring Steve Caballero attracted a small but fervent crowd by the side of the vert ramp. Shortly thereafter, concertgoers at another end of the grounds looked up and saw motorcycles flying into the air and over a trailer truck. A demonstration of BMX tricks was taking place in the middle of the concourse, and curious ticket buyers watched, for a few minutes at a time, as bikers, fenced in as if they were zoo animals, jumped off small boxes and wedges. The thousands of teenagers wandering through the maze of tents, booths, and food vendors wore T-shirts that either advertised punk bands or skateboard companies; a Woodward Camp shirt was also spotted. "Moshing and crowd surfing strongly discouraged—if you do so, you assume your own risk and liability," announced a sign at the entrance that read almost exactly like ones found at skateparks.

"It's simple," Warped founder and organizer Kevin Lyman said, talking about the connection between the tour and the sports it presented on the sidelines. "It doesn't take a whole lot to learn how to skateboard. This music is just as simple as the sport. Kids aren't intimidated by it."

With his spiky coif, wrinkled T-shirts, and cargo shorts, Lyman, who was forty-one, was the embodiment of the punk-rock entrepreneur. In the late eighties, he had witnessed the connection between action sports and music when he hired the Chili Peppers to play atop a vert ramp at a skate/music show, paying them only a few hundred dollars. Warped had sprung out of such loose, freewheeling combinations of gigs and demos in Southern California. Lyman was ambitious ("I knew how to talk on the phone. And I was one of the only ones *with* a phone"), so, in 1995, he and a skateboarder friend decided to take the idea nationwide before anyone else stole it from them. With only about a dozen bands, a climbing wall, and a few skaters, BMXers, and in-line riders, the Warped Tour launched. Looking for increased funding the following year, Lyman turned to Vans, which was looking for ways to grow the sport and sensed a music tie-in could boost its credibility.

At first, the tour felt like a novelty that would go the way of others, like Lollapalooza, which eventually died from complications of cultural insignificance. Warped, however, continued to grow with each year. The first summer, 1995, it sold 78,850 tickets; by 2001, that number had jumped to 467,415, and the tour grossed $6 million based on average per-show grosses of $251,000. Among the many musicians and bands who had joined up for one leg or another over the years had been Eminem, Green Day, Limp Bizkit, blink-182, Sum41—an eardrum-rattling smorgasbord of the new music. The crew for the first tour numbered about fifty, Lyman said; 2002's expedition, which hit a record forty-seven cities, included nearly six hundred along with twelve trucks and forty-one buses. The profit margin was helped by the notoriously low wages the bands were paid and by Lyman's open embrace of corporate sponsors anxious to connect with an audience of cash-wielding teenagers. On Randalls Island, Domino's Pizza, Mrs. Fields cookies, and Snapple all sold their products at booths. Warped had become the embodiment of the new antiestablishment establishment.

Just as the sports appealed to a generation that had many options and wanted to sample them all, Warped was the ultimate in festivals for those with ADD. Overnight, the Randalls Island field had been transformed into a punk-city outdoor mall, complete with body-piercing booths and eight stages that presented, one after another, a total of seventy-eight bands. Over ten hours, the crowd was in constant motion—stopping by a booth that offered "vibrating tongue rings" for $40, then wandering over to catch a band on a nearby platform. They would rarely stay for long, since there was always another group, another food vendor, another hemp-clothing stand to check out, another tent under which one of the hard-rock bands would be signing autographs or selling their CDs: Death by Stereo next to the Deviants, next to Five Iron Frenzy. The people who wandered those grounds ranged from kids with studded-leather belts and Mohawks to those who looked straight out of their advanced-placement classes, and all stepped carefully over the cans and bottles beginning to litter the grounds. "It's the greatest discount shopping day in a kid's life," Lyman boasted. "Everything's below retail."

Despite the tour's growth, two constants remained. One was the cries of cooptation ("Its alignment with punk's ideals offers a false sense that concertgoers are getting involved in something more meaningful than free samples of chocolate soda and rides on surf simulators," wrote Daniel Sinker in a scathing investigative piece in *Punk Planet* magazine in 1999). The other standby was music genres. The festival adhered doggedly to its idea of presenting only blood-vessel-bursting punk, hard-core, and metal bands, with an occasional dash of hip-hop or ska. Wandering through Warped, one would think punk never died, and that grunge, teen pop, techno, and other styles that blossomed in the nineties never existed. (At least one company paid the price for signing up: Right Guard had been a sponsor but ended the association when concertgoers began taking the small samples of Xtreme Sport deodorant being handed out and hurling them at the bands.) In the distance, skaters could be seen dropping in and grabbing big air on the ramp; across the field, motorcycle riders bulleted into the sky, hands and arms shooting out in midair. No one in the crowd gave the sights a second thought.

The sign on the back door of 3rd Strike's bus read DANGER/ENTER AT YOUR OWN RISK. Their set over, the band was chilling in its traveling home, where it would live for the next month or two, taking showers at venues or at truck stops. On a couch inside, Jim Korthe, thirty-one, slouched sullenly in the same clothes he wore onstage, while guitarist Erik Carlsson, twenty-seven, looked, with his shaved head, narrow face, and all-black clothing, like an introspective hunger-striker. Half-empty bottles of water and juice were strewn around.

The presence of nonalcoholic beverages was meaningful, since like many of its peers, the band had lived extreme lives that served to complement its music. "I was a troubled kid," Korthe said. His head down, he spoke so quietly that at times it was difficult to hear him. "Had mental problems. Bipolar. Take medicine. Real violent when I was young. Kinda was looking for that father figure I didn't have. My father was in the war in Vietnam, and when he came back, he wasn't the same. I was raised by my mom and two sisters. So I was looking for that brotherhood I didn't have." The search led him to gang life, which he entered around 1988 and stayed in, he said, for the next seven years, as part of Wilmington's Wilmas, a notorious gang near his hometown of San Pedro, California. "I got locked up a lot of times. A lot of bad things happened. Shot at. Lost a lot of friends. Kinda fucked-up. I'm still affiliated." He pointed to the tattoos on his arms and legs. "But I'm not active. My homeboys like what I'm doing. I lived a violent life, man. Anyone who glamorizes that really hasn't lived that way, or they wouldn't do that."

Korthe had played drums in a California speed-metal band, but then discovered hip-hop and R&B oldies. Eventually, he and a guitarist friend, Todd Deguchi, formed a band called Dimestore Hoods that made a few albums and appeared on the first Warped Tour. For his part, Carlsson had grown up not far away, in Irvine, listening to the likes of Tool and Rage Against the Machine and eventually moving to San Francisco to attend music school. "Unfortunately," he said, "I got heavily involved with drugs. That kind of took over by the end of my tenure there. I made it through school but I was heavily strung out. Pretty much hanging on by the end of my rope." He returned to Southern California and, he said, "made attempts to get clean and it didn't really work. I was still up to the same old stuff for years down there. One day I woke up and I was like, 'I need to do something different.'" He finally checked himself into a recovery house in San Pedro; even there, he relapsed and was kicked out. But this time, fortune glanced his way: The next person who took him in was a friend of Korthe's. Despite having pawned all his equipment for drug money, Carlsson auditioned for the new band Korthe and Deguchi were putting together, and the fledgling 3rd Strike—named after California's "three strikes and you're out" conviction rule—was about to be hatched.

Hollywood Records, the music division of the Walt Disney Company, eventually signed the band and invested a considerable amount of money—millions, it was rumored—to break them. Not only had the label placed the band's songs in ESPN's *Ultimate X* IMAX film, but it had also hired the film's director to make a video featuring motocross riders, further establishing a tie-in with the new sports. Korthe was never terribly specific about his background, but at least one Hollywood Records executive didn't doubt his history during a band dinner following their signing. The service was terribly slow, and by the time everyone's food had arrived, Korthe had already wolfed down his meal. "That's how you gotta do it in county jail," he said straightforwardly. "You gotta eat fast."

The label's interest in the band made sense, since 3rd Strike's brand of hard rock—part rap, part metal—was in vogue, and Hollywood didn't have any other such acts on its roster. "We use the flow of rap, but it's presented really hard—it keeps the energy going," Korthe said, adding, "We're kinda hard to pigeonhole." By now he was standing and swigging a big bottle of iced tea. "Some people say we're hard-core. Some people say we're rap-core. Whatever the fuck that means. The energy of the show, we move around like a punk band."

"We've just all been into heavy metal, man," said Carlsson. "It's just metal minus a couple of guitar solos and lyrics about witches and weird shit like that." Korthe laughed in the background. "It's heavy metal but with a different edge to it through life experience. A lot of people who are fronting bands have actually been through a lot of crazy shit, so what they're talking about translates and is real. And it translates into something a little more intense."

In 3rd Strike's case, though, the onstage intensity was brief; due to the crammed schedules at Warped, they and most of the other musicians were restricted to roughly thirty-minute sets. Most bands wouldn't have been happy with such an arrangement, since it didn't allow time for building and peaking, yet 3rd Strike were not troubled by it.

"A half hour's perfect, man," said Carlsson.

"Nobody wants to hear a band for more than an hour," said Korthe. "I don't care who the fuck they are. I get bored."

"Unless you're watching some reunion tour or something," Carlsson added.

"Pink Floyd *The Wall* or some shit," muttered Korthe.

"I wouldn't want to listen to more than seven or eight songs from *any* band," Carlsson added. "We can play for forty-five minutes if we're headlining a show. *I* wouldn't want to listen to us for forty-five minutes."

"Yeah," Korthe added, "attention spans are real small now."

Korthe sat down once more and grew quiet. "My fiancée is coming out tomorrow," he said. "I was kinda losing my fucking mind. A friend of mine was killed and I said, 'Fuck this shit, I'm going home.' I told my manager, 'I'm leaving.' He goes, 'Well, we have to do this.' I called my girl and she goes, 'I'll come out.' She's on her way. She always calms me down. She's a good girl." He talked of his friend. "He was a homeboy, man. It hurts when a homeboy gets killed. It's fucked-up. I haven't really figured it all out because I've heard different stories from different people. Some say he was murdered, some say he killed himself. I gotta go home and figure it out. He's dead, no matter what." He stared out the bus window. "It always hurts, losing friends. In that lifestyle, that's what you have to expect. Sometimes you expect you're gonna be next."

Carlsson had his own concerns. "I just know that if I kept doing what I'm doing, being on tour and being around all those types of things, inevitably I'll go down really quick. So I've been doing my best to stay on the straight and narrow. We have a lot of people in the band with checkered pasts when it comes to drugs and alcohol, so we try to keep it sober on the bus. We were fortunate enough to get through a lot of those hard times in our lives before we signed up for this. It's kind of a blessing, man. If I started getting involved with that stuff when we got the deal, I would've blown our little lump sum of money all on drugs. Where would I be?"

"You'd be dead," Korthe muttered.

"I'd either be in jail because I'd get busted trying to score some dope on the road, or I'd OD," Carlsson said. "Nothing good would come of it. It's hard, you know. I like to party a little bit. When I'm home, I drink and party a little bit. But other than that, when I'm on the road, we made a little pact to keep it sober."

"It's good that we found each other, man," interjected Korthe. "'Cause we're helping each other out. We did so many fucked-up things in our lives that we're glad we're working together. We're stayin' alive together."

Carlsson asked about the book he was being interviewed for and when it would be published. He was told in a few years. "I'll probably read it in rehab," he said without the slightest hint of sarcasm.

7. LIGHTS, CAMERA, GRIND
madison avenue's
extreme makeover

B ill Carter did not know any of these people by name, but it did not matter; he knew who they were and what they wanted from him. He had been asked to speak at countless conferences like this, this one being the 8th Annual Sports Business Marketing and Sponsorship Forum at the Helmsley Hotel in Manhattan, sponsored by an organization known as the Strategic Research Institute. Over two days, representatives from Burger King, Keebler, Frito-Lay, Eastman Kodak, Dow Chemical, Pfizer, Quaker Oats, Texaco, Tropicana, Xerox, Sara Lee, Ralston Purina, Colgate-Palmolive, and the American Stock Exchange, among others, would drop by to attend panels with names like "Driving Retail Sales Through Sports Marketing," "How College Sports Are Evolving to Offer More Opportunities to Corporate Sponsors," and "Sponsoring Sports: Making Your Investment Pay Off." On this particular morning, they had assembled in the hotel's third-floor conference room for "Action Sports and Sponsorship," the panel on which Carter was sitting.

Carter arrived promptly and settled into one of the chairs on the dais. There, he glanced up and saw the chandelier dangling above and the reddish carpet and five rows of red-clothed tables before him. But most of all, he saw *them*—another group of solemn, very professional men and women in oxford shirts, ties, and solid-colored business suits; water pitchers, yellow-lined legal pads, and pens had been placed in front of them. Carter himself was wearing a waist-length denim jacket, sneakers, and jeans—his standard work attire—and his hair was a little longer and wavier than theirs. No one in the room, though, seemed to doubt his authority or cast a dubious eye on his wardrobe. They looked at him attentively, ready to learn how to break into a world about which they knew little but which promised untold financial rewards for the companies they represented.

Introduced as the founder of Fuse, Carter began his presentation by explaining how his firm, based in Burlington, Vermont, performed "corporate consulting, PR, event sponsorship, and event execution" in the field of action sports. In that capacity, he and his staff of thirty-five had worked with companies such as Pepsi and Gillette—advising them on advertising campaigns and marketing strategies, recommending alliances with specific athletes and skate and snow events, and in general, helping businesses that were largely clueless about this new universe look as if they had at least one or two inklings in their suit pockets. Carter could flash the furtive smile of the class clown keeping a prank to himself, but today, he was here to teach the hundreds assembled before him a few lessons in how their corporations could successfully infiltrate and penetrate a world of skateboarders, bikers, and snowboarders. A decade before, none of these firms had the slightest interest in doing such a thing, but those biases were as extinct as the roller-skate wheels once used on skateboards; everyone seemed to be pitching products at the segment of the population that either followed or participated in these sports. In so doing, companies could potentially reach some of the estimated forty million Americans between the ages of ten and nineteen, who, according to one estimate, had $250 billion in their collective backpacks to spend each year on cereal, fast food, snacks, and toiletries.

"What we found is that brands that got involved *early* and stuck with it are brands that are very successful with youth culture today,"

Carter said firmly. "It's a matter of being there and sending a clear message about your involvement with these sports. The trick is approaching it in a very different way than traditional sports efforts."

That trick, he continued as the attendees began scribbling on their pads, was to treat this culture and its followers with a sensitivity normally reserved for religious groups. "Teens are looking for *your* cultural permission to use their sports," he emphasized. "These sports are *not yours*. Teens are expecting you as a corporate brand to understand their culture and not paint it as new. It's new to *you*, but not to them. They want to see you support the sports not just on a mainstream level. They don't want fanfare. They just want to *see* it. What they don't want to see is a brand coming in with no grassroots support and just slapping a logo onto a high-profile event. Nine times out of ten, it's going to be a poor job."

To many in the room, such a strategy was genuinely startling. Their corporations never had to jump through such fragile hoops when working with football or basketball games; they were not required to prove the honesty of their intentions. They spent money to have their banners and placards at the Super Bowl or the World Series and rarely gave a thought to whether it was fine with the spectators in the bleachers. Yet here they were, being told they had to rewire their thinking or else all was lost.

At that point, an audience member raised a hand. "Can you talk about authenticity—the way to tap into that?"

Carter had heard this question many times before, and he responded with a quick nod and barely a flinch. Teens today, he said, were different from those of his generation in the eighties. "We grew up playing sports and watching them on TV," he said, his words echoing around the room on small speakers. "Today, they connect to these sports in a lot of ways we didn't ten years ago—through video games, the Internet, participation, TV, and videos." Appearing authentic, he said, involved utilizing all those forums. It could be as simple as making sure a brand logo was displayed in one of the computerized skateparks in a video game, or handing out the proper giveaway items at events like the X Games and its competitor, the Gravity Games. "When I see a sponsor handing out *key chains*," he sneered, "the message is clear: 'I didn't do my research and I'm handing out the same old junk.' I walk through another tent and they're handing out a specially made music tape with a DJ, and they're handing it to *teens*, not adults. If you're sixteen, what's cooler than something your parents don't know?"

Another open palm jutted into the air. "If you're a major corporation," came the question, "how do you get the word out to people without it seeming like a branding campaign?"

"You just have to build it from the grass roots," Carter said. "You have to demonstrate support for the sports. It's more of a cultural phenomenon than traditional sports has to deal with." His panel-mate, Wade Martin, the senior vice president of the company that ran the Gravity Games, chimed in, "I would say one of the refreshing things about these sports is that they're *tremendously* loyal to brands. There's a more direct connection there." Several times, both men evoked the brand that embodied this relatively new approach—Mountain Dew. PepsiCo, Dew's corporate parent, had first included these sports in ads a decade before, and the corporation had learned, sometimes the hard way, that simply inserting a skateboarder into a TV spot would not suffice. Over the years, Pepsi had pumped major capital into competitions and events around the country; the ubiquitous, brassy green-and-red Dew logos adorning half-pipes were intended to demonstrate to athletes and enthusiasts alike that the company was serious about backing the sports. For its effort, Pepsi had earned the begrudging respect of the community and, more important, had reinvigorated the Dew name and made a good deal of money.

After forty-five minutes, the panel wrapped up to make way for another, "Auto Sports, Sponsorship and Television." Carter and Martin walked to the back of the room, near the croissant-and-coffee tables, as one representative after another approached them and handed over a business card. The two men had delivered their message as bluntly as possible; now it was up to the corporations to either heed their advice or proceed, blindly, at their own risk. If they went ahead, cautiously and carefully, the rewards were considerable. If they didn't, they could become one more punch line in a skateboard or snowboard magazine, and no one in the room wanted that.

By the time of the Sports Business Marketing and Sponsorship Forum, it was possible to lead an "extreme" lifestyle simply by visiting the nearest supermarket or mall. Before heading for work, one could shave with Xtreme 3 razors, scrub one's teeth with Aquafresh Extreme Clean toothpaste, freshen up with dabs of Xtreme Sport deodorant, and if so inclined, apply one of Clairol's Extreme FX line of hair colors. During lunchtime, one could stop by Taco Bell for an Extreme quesadilla and, afterward, wolf down a bag of Xtreme Doritos, a stick of Extreme beef jerky, a container of Extreme Jell-O, or a box of Extreme popcorn. If such high-intensity snacks made one's mouth taste stale, Xtreme breath spray was there to assist. After school, young boys or girls could rev up with the X-treme wheels scooter sold at toy-store chains. To wind down at night, one could rent movies with titles like *Extreme Days* or soft-core drool-fests like the *Girls Gone Wild Extreme* video. Around the time of Carter's panel, these were only a dozen of the 1,141 products incorporating the word *Extreme* or *Xtreme* that were trademarked (and still active) with the U.S. Patent and Trademark Office. Collectively, they constituted a thriving subindustry of product signifiers that sent a forceful message: Use any of these supposedly high-octane products and unleash the repressed risk-taker, the extreme id, that lay inside.

The world had not always been this way. At one time, global corporations had little if any use for skateboarders, snowboarders, or bike and motorcycle stunt riders. By the eighties, as skateboarding experienced its third of four revivals, a gradual shift began to occur as a handful of major companies put money behind skaters and bikers or hired them for stunts in commercials. Even then, the funds were low and the returns not clear. The sports' undeniably sporadic nature— hot for a few years, then ice-cold again, in what appeared to be cycles of eight to ten years—made the big-money businesses especially nervous; as soon as skate or BMX hit a slump, the sponsors were among the first to leave the building.

Then came Dew Day, the invasion of Pepsi. Older Southerners most likely had dim memories of Mountain Dew in its earliest incarnation, when it was a regional soft drink first trademarked in November 1948 by the Hartman Beverage Corporation of Knoxville, Tennessee. The tarty lemon-lime concoction was most popular in the South, where its customers knew better than anyone else that the product name was local slang for moonshine. In 1964, Pepsi, then called the Pepsi-Cola Company and dating back to the turn of the century, bought Mountain Dew and took it national, instituting a series of bawdy, low-rent cartoon ads depicting barefoot, whiskey-fried moonshiners guzzling the drink and spouting slogans (incorrect spellings and all) like "It'll tickle yore innards!" The campaign was garish but effective: Within two years, Pepsi had quadrupled Dew's sales. In the seventies, Pepsi pursued younger soft-drink guzzlers with its renowned "Pepsi Generation" campaign, and with it, Mountain Dew went suburban. The revamped Dew commercials ditched the cartoons in favor of bowl-haired, irrepressibly social teens rafting, hiking, rock climbing, camping, even painting a house together— group orgies but with water and soda. The accompanying jingle, "Hello Sunshine, Hello Mountain Dew," emulated the exuberant, feel-good hits of John Denver. The campaign continued into the eighties, by which time it had adapted to the times by way of break-dancers, a synthpop variation on the jingle, and footage of skate-boarders and flatland BMX riders on quarter-pipes. (One of the skateboarders was a young Tony Hawk; a water-skier in another ad was fledgling actor Brad Pitt.) The outdoorsy nature of the campaign, the equation of the drink with a type of Rocky Mountain high, never changed; only the activities did.

The ascension of Gen X in the early nineties rumbled like an earthquake through the culture, and Pepsi rolled with it. A new group of twelve-to-twenty-four-year-olds—men specifically—was waiting to be tapped. In the $50-billion-a-year soft-drink industry, hooking customers early was vitally important; the peak soda-drinking years were twenty-nine to thirty-nine, after which consumers tended to switch to coffee or juices. It was only natural for Pepsi to see Mountain Dew as an entry point to that new generation. "Dew has a point of view and it is more male—we don't try to be all things to all people," said Dave Burwick, Pepsi's forty-year-old vice president of marketing for its soft-drink brands. Burwick wore a blue dress shirt and tan pants and had short, gray-flecked hair. His office was on the second floor of Building Five of the company's college-campus-size headquarters in Purchase, New York. Outside his window were lawns, ivy, fountains, flagpoles, and patrolling Pepsi security cars.

Mountain Dew was distinctive in more than just its fan base, neon-green color, and lemon-lime taste with a hint of orange. Although Pepsi executives did not like to discuss the topic, Dew contained more caffeine than standard sodas. A typical twelve-ounce bottle crammed in fifty-five milligrams of the compound, slightly more than Coke or Pepsi. "There's this whole energizing feeling you get from the product, partly because you can drink it quicker and there's lower carbonation," said Burwick. "It does have a little more caffeine. It's overstated how much, but it does have a little more than your typical cola. *Exhilaration* is really the word I would use to describe the brand. It's exhilarating." Recalled Bill Bruce, the lanky, affable BBDO account executive who was handed the Diet Dew account in 1993, "We're not allowed to talk about the caffeine in it, and you can't really say caffeine gives it a jolt. So how do you reflect that?"

No one had to look far for an answer. As it happened, a markedly different kind of exhilaration was in the air, one that brought together a new style of raw-throated, flannel-shirted rock and roll and, in tandem, the increasing popularity of the skate and bike culture first featured in Dew ads in 1985. It was particularly evident to BBDO, the eminent New York advertising agency that had been working with Pepsi since 1973. "The interesting thing about the early nineties was everything that was exploding," said Bruce. "It was music, culture, and the sports that had come out of it." Everything in the culture felt more caffeinated, so to Bruce and his coworkers, it was only natural to link the amped-up soft drink with the frenzied, synergistic, and conveniently teen-oriented sport culture around it. "There's a sugar-caffeine rush you get from Mountain Dew that's very similar to adrenaline," said Chris Strain, a former Pepsi marketing executive, "and that was the metaphor they were driving."

By the time Bruce was handed his assignment, Pepsi had already entered these waters, albeit gingerly. In 1992, the company had launched a revised, high-octane campaign for Mountain Dew created by another executive at BBDO. Premiering during the Grammy Awards that February, "Get Vertical" brought together windsurfing, motocross stunts, and the throbbing, old-school rhythms of fifties rocker Bo Diddley. But even for a first step, it seemed a little off, particularly in its use of Diddley, whose appeal to the grunge crowd was limited. Still, Pepsi liked the idea of connecting its product and the new so-called extreme sports—Dew, said Burwick, "was always about youth outdoors doing active things"—and the following year, the corporation jacked up its advertising and marketing budget to

$40 million, up $20 million from the year before, to make sure the general public got the message.

As Bruce realized, more than the sound of pop music had changed. Reflecting the upbeat self-absorption of the boomers, Dew campaigns from the sixties and seventies were cheery and wholesomely hedonistic. Gen X, by contrast, was more jaded and cynical, less about expectations than their lack of them. With that shift in mind, Bruce's first pitch to Pepsi made a direct, unavoidable link between attitude, music, and brand. His "1993 TV Creative Brief" was intended to "increase awareness and trial of Diet Mt. Dew" among "male teens/ young adults"; under "Executional Guidelines," it read, "Leverage 'full-tilt taste' and 'rush' as point of reference." The five-page storyboard that followed opened with a skier leaping out of a helicopter to "loud and raucous" music, then "cut to group of guys looking unimpressed" who spouted, in succession, "Done that. Did that. Been there. Tried that." They reacted the same way while watching cliff parachuting. But—aha!—they were knocked for an unsardonic loop when cans of Diet Dew popped into view. Suddenly the ironic four were curious and would begin "slamming down Diet Dews," in the words of the storyboard. The voice-over at ad's end would then announce, "You've never done nothing [sic] until you've experienced the extreme full-tilt taste of Diet Dew." In one rough draft, the new face of Diet (and soon to be regular) Dew was revealed, at once astute, clever, and unabashedly calculated. Bruce, who was in his early thirties and a fan of alternative rock, used songs by the Red Hot Chili Peppers and Soundgarden in a rough cut of the first commercial; ultimately, the company went with a track by the Supersuckers, another band from the roster of Seattle's Sub Pop label.

"It was all about connecting with Gen X, which in the early nineties was the big rage," said Burwick. "It was the whole idea of 'nothing fazes me.' We brought in this irony. That's when we had the whole twentysomething slackers 'been there, done that.' They're not impressed by anything. But they'd never tried a Diet Mountain Dew. 'Whoa—never tried it, never done it.' The whole idea was 'Hey, try this thing.'"

The new, upgraded spots, launched in March 1993 and dubbed first "Do Diet Dew" and eventually "Do the Dew" by BBDO, kicked off with a version of Bruce's first proposal, "Done That," which opened with a cliff's-eye-view shot of a long-haired BASE (Buildings, Antennas, Spans, and Earth) jumper leaping off a mountain, followed by a waterfall surfer. (BASE jumping, in which participants jumped off cliffs, mountains, roofs, and other elevated areas, was more hobby than sport but was linked with action sports by default.) Those scenes were intercut with footage of the four scruffy, shirtless, headbanded "Dew Dudes," who at one point literally screamed in the face of viewers.

The ad would mark the beginning of a campaign that comprised several increasingly irreverent new spots every year, each one upping the ante in connecting the beverage with action sports and the punky blare of the new music. Overnight, the hardy, clean-cut young men and women of Dew ads of the seventies and eighties were replaced with Dew Dudes variously wearing sleeveless flannel shirts, cargo shorts, and other fashion accoutrements of the Lollapalooza generation. Waterskiing and logrolling were gone; in their place were shots of motorcycle stunts (one performed by star freestyler Travis Pastrana), an in-line skater jumping from one roof to another with the help of a helicopter, skateboarders on vert ramps, mountain bikers roaring downhill, and BMXers and snowboarders shooting into crisp blue skies. A "parking attendant" in an ad of the same name used one of the vehicles under his watch to rev around the lot and onto the roof of an adjacent building: "What snowboarders do in the off-season," read the tagline. In "Route 66," street lugers zipped past man-made monuments like the Taj Mahal and the Eiffel Tower as John Lydon, the former Johnny Rotten, screeched out a version of the title song.

("He asked for decaf cappuccino with low-fat milk," recalled Bruce of Lydon's voice-over session, "and I thought, 'Oh, man, it's *over!*'") Even when the spots didn't explicitly feature action sports, the association was implied: In 2001's "Spaceship," the Dew Dudes commandeered a UFO and did what amounted to vert-skate moves in canyons and on ice banks—natural geological formation as half-pipe. One of the savviest Dew spots used footage of crashing skaters, bikers, and snowboarders to evoke actual skate and snow videos. It was just one indication of how well BBDO and Pepsi had done their homework; another was the time Bruce was snowed in at a bar in Alaska while filming a spot with snowboarders. "One guy was saying, 'I was knocking down this hill and I started stale-fishing,'" Bruce recalled. "I had no idea what he was saying, but I totally got the visual, and at that point I was in the bar basically writing down what they were saying."

"I really do think the Mountain Dew brand more than any other took alternative sports and put it on the map," Burwick said. "Bagel Bites can go and do the X Games, but what do Bagel Bites have to do with alternative sports? Our product, and the benefits of our product, are really rooted in energy and excitement." As blunt as the campaign was in connecting a thirty-year-old soft drink to the Kurt Cobain generation, it was also inordinately effective. By 1995, the third year of the campaign, Dew was on the rise, running up $2.7 billion in sales, up from $2.2 billion a few years before, and becoming the sixth best-selling soda behind Coke, Pepsi, Diet Coke, Dr Pepper, and Diet Pepsi. Sales jumped to $3 billion the following year, on the basis of shipments of 458 million cases; by 1997, Dew had risen to fourth place. To Pepsi's satisfaction, more people than ever seemed to be doing the Dew.

The increase in sales did not come without its share of learning experiences. Networks initially balked at storyboards for the ads, especially those involving BASE jumping, and forced BBDO to make

the athletes and stuntmen wear helmets. At a shoot with skateboarder Colin McKay on a temporary half-pipe built atop a Manhattan building, a stylist attempted to dress McKay in flashy
clothing he would never have worn. "It's people like you who give
skateboarding a bad name," McKay snapped back in an oft-
repeated remark, ultimately wearing a T-shirt and sneakers sporting
his sponsors' logos. For every athlete who signed on the dotted line
for a modest annual Pepsi salary, an equal number stayed away,
afraid of being tainted by association or appalled at the idea of a
massive corporation treading on the sports' notoriously grassroots
turf. "We were helping to facilitate their sport," said Bruce. "They
all wanted their sports to be more popular. Later, some of the posers
were giving us crap: 'I don't wear my hair like that, I don't listen to
that music.' They liked it when the sport was more underground."
(Eventually, the Dew Dudes were made "more aspirational, not so
much caricatures," said Burwick.) Dew executive Chris Strain
witnessed this clash firsthand when he attended the Slam City
Jam, the revered annual skate event in Vancouver. "This guy was
going off," Strain recalled, "and saying, 'Back in 1970-something,
Madison Avenue grabbed skateboarding and what happened to it?
It died. If *we* let Madison Avenue grab skateboarding now, we're all
done. It's the first sign you're out the door.' The skaters from
Thrasher and *Transworld* magazines were like, 'We don't want
to be in some stupid *fucking* Mountain Dew ad.' And I'm going, 'Oh
my God, they don't like my product!' "

The increase in sales also did not come without at least one major
tragedy. Putting together storyboards of "extreme" stunts was one
thing; filming them without inflicting serious injury on anyone
involved was another. During an early spot in which a Dew Dude
hurdled down a fifty-foot waterfall on a boogie board, a stuntman
hurt his neck. Regarding his shoot atop that New York building,
skater McKay recalled, "It was not safe at all . . . If my board went off

the roof, somebody would have gotten killed." (Luckily, nothing of the sort happened.) Then there was that day over British Columbia on December 14, 1995. For a spot called "007," BBDO had hired the skysurfing team of Rob Harris and Joe Jennings to film a segment in which Harris, dressed in a Bond-like tux, leapt out of a plane; Jennings, the cameraman, would jump in tandem and film the stunt midair. The day had been foggy, but suddenly, Jennings recalled, "the sky broke up and we just had an opening." The men piled into their small Cessna, Harris sporting three parachutes and Jennings a camera attached to his helmet. The plan called for Harris to go into a free fall, open one chute, cut it loose, and switch to one of his remaining two, all while dropping at 120 miles an hour. Harris and Jennings had done jumps like these many times before, including at the inaugural Extreme Games.

They jumped at an altitude of about five thousand feet, and everything appeared to be on track until Harris's final move. No one would ever know with absolute certainty what happened, but with about thirty seconds remaining before Harris would have hit the ground, two of his chutes appeared to become entangled. "You're just sort of hanging there and the first five or six seconds, you're kinda going, 'All right, buddy,' but it's not too bad," Jennings recalled, still shaken. "Then it turns into a nightmare." As Jennings watched—helplessly, his camera now turned off—Harris, a widely respected and admired skysurfer, plummeted to earth; from his perspective in the air, Jennings saw his partner's parachute inflating just as Harris hit the ground. One theory had it that Harris may have grabbed the wrong release handle, and that by the time he realized it, it was about "a half second too late," according to Jennings. Harris, killed on impact, would have been twenty-nine in just three days. As a tribute to him, and with his family's permission, a sequence of the same jump, filmed a day or two earlier, was used in the eventual Dew ad, making for an eerie posthumous tribute. "His parents were proud of his achievements," a Pepsi spokesman said, "and wanted him to live on in this commercial."

Pepsi and BBDO executives were shaken by the accident, but the campaign soldiered on. To ward off competition from Coke's similarly marketed new soda, Surge, Pepsi hired Bill Carter's Fuse firm to help sharpen its approach and ingratiate itself further with the action-sports crowd. Carter suggested sponsoring events and contests, and soon enough the Dew logo could be seen at Vans Triple Crown and X Games competitions. At those same events, the company hired young, affable, T-shirted "samplers" to work the crowds and pass out free soda. "Other sponsors, you see guys with clipboards talking to consumers," said Burwick. "Not us." Pepsi had learned that the most effective way for an institution to secure credibility with its targeted audience was to *not* act like an institution. X Games attendees were not supposed to know that Dew was part of Pepsi, which also owned Frito Lay, Tropicana, and Quaker Oats and was therefore responsible for all the Gatorade, Cap'n Crunch, Aunt Jemima, Doritos, Ruffles, Cheetos, Fritos, Rold Gold pretzels, Aquafina bottled water, and Lipton tea on the shelves of their local supermarkets. It was a lesson the company had been pushing all along: "They were like, 'We're not Pepsi—we're just a small *division* of Pepsi!'" Tony Hawk recalled of the time he filmed a Dew spot in the eighties.

Over a dozen years later, the plan was still in effect. "Being next to Bagel Bites and Slim Jim and some of these other brands [at the X Games], we have to think, 'Do we really want to be part of something that's becoming overly commercialized?'" Burwick wondered as he sat in his office. "That's always our challenge—how do we keep an edge? Mountain Dew is a huge brand, but we don't want people to *believe* it's so big because it wouldn't be very cool anymore. So we try to do stuff where we act like a small brand all the time, try to take more risks and do things differently and be a bit more edgy." He had to end the conversation; a contingent of ad executives had arrived from Manhattan, and the time had come to discuss another campaign.

What Bill Carter would later describe as a "huge turning point" in the intertwining of action sports and corporate America began with every indication it would be neither huge nor make a good point. By the end of the nineties, Fuse had been hired by numerous clients, most of whom, like Burton snowboards, had started as homespun companies within the community and grown with the sports; other than Dew, major corporations kept at arm's length. Then, one day in October 1999, the phone rang in Carter's Burlington office. On the line, much to Carter's surprise, was a brand manager for Gillette. The company, the executive said, was about to launch a new product aimed at male teens and was giving serious consideration to using action sports as part of its marketing campaign.

For Carter, the call could not have been more groundbreaking. Pepsi's Dew strategy had been important, but Gillette, founded at the turn of the century by King Gillette, a salesman who had conceived the idea of a disposable razor, was an even bigger fish. Employing 39,800 people and on its way to netting $9.2 billion that year, Gillette was a massive, all-encompassing corporation that not only manufactured and sold razors but shaving cream, deodorant, pens, disposable lighters, Liquid Paper, Oral-B dental-care products, and Duracell batteries. These were products aimed at the whole family, not just a segment of it. The corporation had been involved in team sports for many years—it had bought radio broadcast rights to the World Series exactly sixty years before—but, unlike Pepsi, it had steered clear of the alternative-sports scene.

As Carter quickly learned during his conversation, that was no longer the case. Although the company was headed toward $332 million in deodorant sales, Gillette needed to freshen up its decades-old Right Guard brand. Since that product's "point of entry," as it was called, was in the twelve-to-thirteen-year-old range, Gillette felt it was time to go younger than normal, especially in light of the blossoming Gen Y demographic. "Get them at point of entry," explained Gillette marketing manager John Stephans, "give them a product that delivers what they're looking for, and you could potentially have a customer for life in a very big demographic group." Stephans admitted the move represented "a quantum shift" for the company, which had never targeted that age bracket before. Gillette wanted to do it right, and hearing that Fuse had worked with Dew, it hired Carter and his coworkers to lay the appropriate groundwork.

Carter couldn't believe his good fortune until he heard that the product, a deodorant, had already been given a name: Right Guard Xtreme Sport. "It couldn't have been worse," Carter recalled. "What went through my mind right away was, I wonder how far down the road they are with this product, because if it's not already been fully developed, maybe we can get them to change the name." By then, *extreme* was officially word non grata to those in Carter's community; the easiest way to separate those who lived the life from those who didn't was to listen for the term, with its zany-death-defier implication, to come up in conversation. Before they had a chance to do anything about it, board-sport athletes were now part of an "extreme" universe that included everything from rock climbing to canyoning (hopping from rock to rock along riverbanks). In the general public's mind, there was little difference between an athletic trick and a simple stunt. "The term *extreme sports* already had a huge negative connotation to it within the community," Carter said. "The participants didn't see what they were doing as extreme. It alienated them. The objection is that action sports represents a genre of sport like any other sport, whereas the connotation of *extreme sports* was danger, not skill level. It was about jumping off buildings, which took a lot of balls but no skills."

No one knew for certain when the term was first associated with the sports; one guess was the rise of the phrase *extreme skiing* in the late eighties to describe that sport's progressive freestyle offshoot. From there, the word spread, like a benign virus, through the media landscape. "It's like calling someone insane or crazy or psycho," said BMXer Rick Thorne in a common sentiment. "It seemed kinda hokey. It's like the dude who claims he's punk rock but is just trying to be cool. We didn't want to be like that." Many companies listened to the complaints and reacted immediately. The Extreme Games became the X Games after one year; BBDO and Pepsi realized early on that the word was, as Bill Bruce said, "a turnoff" and mostly refrained from using it in Dew ads. In 1998, Vans went so far as to trademark the phrase *Core Sports* as a potential substitute. Finally, everyone decided on a new, less offensive term embraced by both athletes and the endemic businesses: action sports. In terms of the mass audience, the move may have been too late: *Extreme sports,* like it or not, had stuck, and only a massive public-relations campaign could change the situation. But within the scene, *action sports* it would be.

In Gillette's mind, the point was moot when it came to Right Guard Xtreme Sport deodorant. At a conference-room meeting in the company's Boston offices that fall, Carter and a coworker were informed that the name was set, as were the logo, packaging (a hint of metallic sheen, much like a computer), and launch date of June 2000. To Gillette, professional snowboarders or BMX riders may not have loved the word *extreme,* no matter the spelling, but the millions of teenagers who would potentially be drawn to the product wouldn't care one way or another. Much more important was the smell: Teenagers, according to Gillette research, preferred a strong, sweet fragrance, hence Xtreme Sport's potent, lingering scent. Besides, the company had already received positive feedback on the name from chains like Wal-Mart and Kmart. "Right Guard Xtreme Sport builds upon the sports heritage of the Right Guard brand," went a press statement issued in September 2000, just after the launch, "and updates it by capitalizing on the trend toward extreme or alternative sports that are individualistic, free-spirited, and high-adrenaline." If the public wanted to connect the brand with the sports and hence feel a little adventurous when they rubbed it on their armpits, that was fine with the company.

Carter decided to stay quiet. He didn't want to lose a huge client, and he figured that teaching behemoth corporations how to penetrate this large but elusive market was what he had set out to accomplish when he started Fuse in 1995 after working for two previous sports and entertainment marketing firms. Besides, Gillette had decided to pump $61 million into launching Xtreme Sport, complete with television spots featuring goateed, new-generation-gonzo comedian (and part-time skateboarder) Tom Green. What the manufacturer wanted from Carter was advice on buying credibility. Months before the product arrived in stores, banners announcing Right Guard Xtreme Sport began popping up at events like the U.S. Open of Snowboarding and the Vans Triple Crown series of bike, snow, and skate competitions. The marketing equivalent of a preemptive strike, the message was simple: You haven't heard of this product, and you may be suspicious of the name, but Right Guard believes in these sports and wants to help ensure that events such as these take place.

At almost the same time Carter was meeting with Gillette, another revolution was in the offing. In 1999, the first boxes of Activision's Tony Hawk's Pro Skater, part of a line of new action-sport video games, were shipped to stores. There had been board-sport games before, dating back to Nintendo's Skate or Die of the late eighties, and the market (especially snowboarding games) had become more profitable each year since, from $4.7 million in sales in 1995 to five times that amount just two years later. But Activision's launch was more significant. The company, which had begun in 1979 and initially made software for Atari, recognized that sports games constituted the biggest sector of the gaming business and that the demographic was growing younger. "The PlayStation market was at a midcycle point in 1997," recalled Will Kossoy, the company's vice president for global brands development, "and we saw opportunities to do something that would align nicely with where the demographic was going." The demographic's destination, studies indicated, was skateboarding and its affiliated activities, which also made for a smart business plan given that Activision's leading competitor, Electronic Arts, focused on team-sport games. Activision researched the field, discovered that Hawk's name was the most recognized, and set about wooing him. The skater was considering offers from two other video-game makers at the time, but Activision had a high-tech card up its sleeve: newly developed software by Neversoft that allowed players to freely wander around a computerized skatepark or terrain and not simply race, as in other games. ("We saw with teens the idea of freedom and the ability to roam free and do what they wanted to do," Kossoy said.) Intrigued, Hawk signed on, and Activision went to work—sending out early copies of the game to create buzz, expanding its marketing budget when that buzz appeared positive, and visiting skateparks and hiring focus groups to test out names. (Skate Jam, an early thought, was rejected because, Kossoy said, "it just wasn't cool.")

No one, including Activision, had huge expectations for Tony Hawk's Pro Skater when it was unveiled to the public; the company itself would have been happy selling a half million units. To everyone's surprise, the game took off, selling several million copies at about $50 each. In retrospect, its success was easy to understand. From its Hawk-approved environment and free-skate feel to the clothing and sneakers on the computer-generated skaters, even to the revenue-generating corporate logos displayed on the clothes and ramps, Pro Skater capitalized on two burgeoning markets—the sports and computer games. Both the original Pro Skater and its subsequent upgrades aimed for a realism rarely seen in the games, allowing skaters and game enthusiasts alike to know what it was like to get on a board, push off, and try to stay on while doing anything from an ollie over a bush to an attempted 900. Just as the sports had brought a new intensity and aggression to the sporting world, so did the games, which were louder (music courtesy of punk bands like Pennywise and NOFX and new metallists Papa Roach and the Deftones) and bloodier (graphic red spillage every time a skater or BMXer crashed). Before long, Activision had signed up sixty-five action-sport athletes to become characters in the company's line of BMX, surf, skate, wakeboard, and snowboard games. Electronic Arts came on board as well, with Freekstyle (on which motocross-inclined gamers could transform into freestyle rider Mike Metzger and jump through fire and other obstacles) and the snowboard-driven SSX Tricky. Although none of the games approached Hawk's numbers (sales of one hundred thousand and under were more common), a new, billion-dollar industry was hatched.

With the combined successes of Gillette and Activision, corporate America entered the arena with a fanfare it had never demonstrated before. It became impossible to glance through the business pages of trade magazines and not see an announcement for another major company buying into action-sports culture: Schick introducing its Extreme III razor. Heinz announcing Hawk as pitchman for Hot Bites, a line of frozen minipizzas targeting boys between nine and fourteen. KFC hawking its new Blazin' Buffalo Twisted sandwich with scenes of actor Jason Alexander (or rather, his stunt double) skating on a half-pipe. McDonald's unveiling a Happy Meal that included a miniature vert ramp. Mazda incorporating skateboard footage into a TV ad for a new vehicle. Ad after ad—for Visa, AT&T, Nissan, Chef Boyardee, Head & Shoulders shampoo, Old Spice's Red Zone deodorant—presented scenes of skaters, bikers, or snowboarders. Some were clever, others clueless, but they kept coming. According to Carter, it became standard for a corporation like Ford to spend several million dollars a year trumpeting its Ford Ranger pickup truck—ideal, the marketing suggested, for hauling around snowboards, wakeboards, and BMX bikes. Such marketing would include about a million dollars pumped into competitions and $200,000 on the combined salaries to a half dozen sponsored athletes. "Instead of the dominant players being the endemic companies," said Carter, "the dominant players ended up being Fortune 500 companies."

The skaters, snowboarders, BMXers, in-liners, and motocrossers could only watch, alternately stunned and caustic, as the influx of outsiders with large wallets approached them. They saw the money thrown in their direction jump, like big air, from an average of $20,000 for an annual deal in the pre-Gillette days to as much as $100,000 (and occasionally more) after. All they had to do was slap company logos and stickers onto their gear, appear in ads, and make nice. For their trouble, they would also receive enough free gear and clothes to last several lifetimes. Those who had been around a decade or more found themselves envisioning a level of income they had only dreamed about; those just starting out began using the word *career* in ways the veterans never had.

Along with the new paychecks, though, came conflicting emotions the athletes had never experienced before. They knew all too well the history of corporate infiltration into their world. They had seen the inane Hollywood skate movies of the seventies and eighties—kitsch classics with titles like *Rad* and the utterly nonsensical *Gleaming the Cube*, in which Christian Slater played a Cali skater who defeated a gun-toting villain by skating *into* him and knocking the gun from his hand—and were wary of being labeled sellouts by the kids who looked up to them. They wanted to be seen as hard-core and true to their sport, and a backlash triggered by overexposure—or an alliance with the wrong company at the wrong time—was all too plausible.

"They want the money and the notoriety but want their underground secret culture and don't want to let anyone into it," said one agent, with an air of exasperation, who handled a leading snowboarder. "The athletes don't *want* a lot of media attention." Even when they signed on a dotted line, they worried how they would come off; if an ad in which they were featured was cheesy or too slick and didn't mesh with their image, irreparable damage could result.

Yet they realized these paychecks might be the biggest they could see in some time, if ever. Product endorsements and licenses of their likenesses for toys, T-shirts, and action figures were the only avenues by which many of them would make substantial money. They weren't paid for television appearances at competitions, there were no teams or leagues to stand up for them or demand extra cash and considerations, and the prize money at contests varied wildly. ("Contest winnings at skateboard events at the X Games pay a fifth as much as bowling tournaments," claimed Pat Hawk. *Less than bowling. It's unbelievable.*") For most of them, college was not under consideration, nor were part-time jobs. Ultimately, they reasoned, it was better to take the corporations' money; if they didn't, one athlete or another would. Besides, the money would give them the latitude to practice their sport full-time. In many ways, they were like old-time Southerners: wary of the Northerners who appeared so condescending toward them yet still yearning for mass acceptance and the sense of validation that came with it.

So they signed on with one or more beverage, car, or hygiene companies, sometimes wholeheartedly and sometimes with a pang of reluctance. They did most of what was asked of them—appeared at autograph sessions, met with corporate representatives—and deposited the checks and bought two-level homes or SUVs or electronic gizmos. They could follow the example of the snowboarder who had linked with Right Guard Xtreme Sport early on, then asked the company to design a special sticker that reduced the product name to an acronym, RGXS, to avoid embarrassment. But those were exceptions. If Dew or Right Guard asked them to put a sticker on their helmet or board, they did it (granted, many were able to choose *exactly* where the sticker went, especially on skateboards and snowboards, and some athletes were highly superstitious and felt the stickers had to be in very specific places, like underneath and just below the nose). Most of the athletes did not have managers or agents; in many cases, they had no one, except a parent or family friend, who looked over their contracts to make sure a fair shake was in the works. Shortly, there arose a need for someone who could not only examine those contracts and try to score the best possible deals, but also someone who would, in the absence of leagues or unions (which were perpetually being talked about but had yet to open shop), help them decide which offers were acceptable and which were not. And this was the point at which men like Steve Astephen plowed into the picture.

Everyone in the restaurant of the Manhattan hotel was dressed either for a business meeting or a Sunday service, but he was not, and the brisk looks the waiters exchanged among themselves indicated they weren't sure what to make of the man in the boots and 76ers jacket, either. As he eased into his seat at a table, he did not notice or care. His face was droopy, heavy-lidded, and unshaven, his hair a zigzagging, light brown buzz cut that looked as if it had not seen shampoo in several days. A mysterious headache had been lingering from the night before, and he felt he could have used a little more sleep. But he was here in Manhattan, three thousand miles from his office, and had deals to make and parties to attend.

Astephen's compact, silver cell phone rang, as it would many times during the day. He peered at the small screen, recognized the caller—one of his clients, a prominent BMX rider—and decided to answer.

"What's up, buddy? When you gettin' in?" He frowned slightly as a
question, clearly relating to financial matters, was asked of him. "I
don't know. Oh, wait—I think that's the big check that just came in.
I'll have to check . . . Don't worry—that helmet's gonna *sell,* baby . . .
T-Mobile—it's a done deal. I just talked to them. That's the biggest
deal, now . . . Your MTV *Cribs* was on again on TV—did you see
it?" In a few short minutes, they had covered all the important
ground: the money rolling in from one deal, the product with his
client's name that was about to roll out, the new endorsement deal in
the works, the mainstream media exposure everyone craved for their
athletes. Astephen and his crew had done their job, and he hung up
feeling satisfied with himself and a bit more awake.

The new era and the new generation called for alternative sports,
and the sports called for an alternative kind of executive. Astephen's
business card read JANITOR/FOUNDER, but that was merely an in-joke.
The firm he had founded, the Familie, was one of the country's
leading action-sports management agencies, and Astephen was the
head manager, helping guide the careers of twenty-three skateboarders, snowboarders, surfers, BMXers, wakeboarders, and motocross
riders. Yet for all his appearance—he always seemed to dress like the
people he represented—he was as serious about his clients and their
abilities to generate cash as they were about their talents; it was just as
easy to imagine him arranging deals with hoop or baseball-diamond
talent. "No one's doing corporate deals like I'm doing," he said in a
roughneck, streetwise voice that reflected his upbringing in a work-
ing-class Boston family. "We don't wait for the phone to ring. We're
goin'. We're sellin.' We're travelin'. There had been agents before, but
they never knew how to sell this world. It's a different world to sell.
It's a different pitch. Kids look up to these guys as heroes; they're
ambassadors, and if they associate themselves with a brand, a kid
instantly thinks, 'Cool.' Kobe Bryant can't go on the court with a
Kellogg's Crunch or Mountain Dew logo on his helmet. But if it's

done right with the right person, the kids sit there and think, 'Okay, I'm gonna drink Mountain Dew! Everyone *else* is drinking Mountain Dew. *I'm* gonna drink Mountain Dew.'" He snickered a bit. "That stuff was collecting dust on the *shelf.*

"The other thing," he continued, describing his typical sales pitch to a business, "is that these athletes are tangible. You can *touch* 'em. You can go to a local skatepark and skate with Bob Burnquist. And whatever they're wearing, that kid wants to wear. There's a reason we sell so many fuckin' shoes in this industry. Kids buy whatever they look up to. You saw the sales go up when Bagel Bites signed Tony Hawk. When Dave Mirra was in the AT&T commercials, you saw the radar movement. It showed an instant return on their investment."

Although he was only thirty years old, Astephen had been involved in this world nearly half his life. He had wanted to ski for a living, but injuries to his knee and back forced him to reconsider, and in 1989, he moved to Vail, Colorado, to see what came next. Sensing a market in the growing snowboarding scene, he and a friend opened a board shop. After a few years, he moved to Lamar snowboards, where he signed up riders for its team; a few years after that, he left to work for a sunglass manufacturer targeting the core market. The product of divorced parents—a father who worked for a water company and a mother who was a nurse—he was always hustling: "I always had more in mind. I never wanted to be poor. I never wanted to be back where I was, so I was going to work as hard as I could." During his tenure at Lamar, he had begun scanning the snowboarders' contracts, pointing out an odd-looking clause here or there, and realized a new calling beckoned. "I was on the other side and I saw how much companies were making," he said. "And even though the athletes were making a *good* living, they weren't making a *great* living. They didn't have audit clauses in their contracts. Anybody can play basketball or football and play it okay. These sports, it's a different world. When you sit and watch someone do a jump on a motorcycle?

Think about that. Anybody can throw a football after a few lessons. You can't just get on a motorcycle and ride it. Can't do it. To me they're the most talented athletes in the world."

Most of them, it turned out, were not being managed; if they were, it was by agents accustomed to working with team sports. Despite having a wife and two-year-old son, Astephen decided to take a leap into the unknown. In October 1998, he moved a few couches and a carpet into the garage of his Carlsbad, California, home and started what became the Familie, "because I wanted to do something good for my family, and all these athletes were like my family." At first, he had only one coworker, four clients (all snowboarders), and hardly any money, but rescue of a sorts soon arrived in the form of Austin Hearst, the grandson of publishing magnate William Randolph Hearst. A Hearst Entertainment executive whose personal fortune was estimated by *Forbes* at $900 million, Hearst had long been interested in the alternative-sports community: He co-owned a wakeboard company and a firm that produced television programming from ESPN and Vans events. For 80 percent ownership and the CEO title, Hearst came aboard, helping Astephen secure office space and ensuring him a line of credit. With that, Astephen was ready to make outside corporations bow down before him. He knew Tom Cruise's sports-agent film *Jerry Maguire* well—"Yeah, yeah, seen it plenty of times," he said, smiling—and was ready to be a Maguire of his own, for *his* world.

Soon he was hammering out contracts, including action-figure deals with two toy firms for his BMX clients Dave Mirra and Ryan Nyquist that netted each man a half million dollars, he said. Astephen began hustling, calling Chevy and telling them they had erred by running an ad with a snowboarder who dared to wear very uncore spandex. "I remember getting on the phone and going, 'You guys are blowing it—you may never like me again, but you guys did the worst thing you could have done by doing that ad,'" he recalled. At first, most of the athletes he approached were suspicious; they kept asking him if corporate sponsorships would ruin their rebel image. Once he convinced them such deals wouldn't, he still had to learn to adapt to their quirks. BMX riders, he said, were "very receptive to corporate America," as were motocrossers, since the high cost of their motorcycles made any financial contributions welcome. Skateboarders were tougher, particularly street riders: "Very finicky," he said. Lately, though, he had begun to make headway: "They're like, 'Electronics, that's cool, we'll do it. MP3 player? We're in.' A few years ago, they wouldn't even do that."

Astephen became a ubiquitous presence at events, panel discussions, and industry conventions. At any X Games, he could be seen hovering around one client or another, backslapping and talking on his cell phone; given his basketball-player height, he also acted as a de facto bodyguard. One of his most celebrated clients was Carey Hart, the motocross rider who invented the Hart Attack trick and became an even bigger star when he began dating pop star Pink. (The two made out, in full view of the public, by the side of one X Games moto event.) At 2002's summer X Games, after Hart successfully completed his first run since breaking his back the year before while attempting a backflip, the cameramen and reporters all headed Hart's way at the bottom of the dirt track. Before they got there, though, Astephen had rushed over, given Hart a congratulatory hug and smile, then peeled the T-shirt off Hart's back and replaced it with a new, clean one sporting the logo of one of his sponsors. The cameras arrived just in time.

The manager could rattle off the names of aging snowboarders he had known a decade before and who had not benefited from the sport: One had been reduced to judging events, another had a small house but not much else. Astephen did not want himself or his people to end up that way, and he knew the dangers associated with these sports made his deal-making all the more urgent. Start with Travis Pastrana, the freestyle-motocross rider who was a Familie client.

"Travis to me—it's sad to say, he's so passionate about what he does, but when he's thirty, I don't know that he'll be able to . . ." Astephen paused. "We're gonna have to do some serious stuff to get him not to have arthritis. Nineteen surgeries in nineteen years, and he just had another one on Friday. But you can't *stop* him right now. He's doing what he loves." Pastrana was just one case. Astephen was, by his own admission, "having a bad year." All of his riders who were supposed to compete in the U.S. Open Snowboarding Championships were on the injured list; one had compound-fractured his knee while riding a rail at a high school. Incidents like those were reminders that the best, most lucrative deals had to be hammered out as soon as possible, since the future and physical well-being of his clients was something that could not be guaranteed by any piece of paper. "I didn't like the agents when they came in," said Danielle Bostick, director of World Cup Skateboarding, which had long been organizing competitions and pro tours. "But now I think they're doing well. They get more money for skaters, which is not a bad thing. The skaters are older and have families now, and they're saying, 'Hey, I like this lifestyle.' "

In the long run, Astephen was not worried. Pastrana, he said, "had millions and millions of dollars" and would likely race cars when he couldn't ride anymore. "He doesn't have to work. He can live off the interest alone. Mirra, Nyquist, same thing. The majority of these guys will be just fine." Some were already talking about opening skate shops or restaurants as ways to invest their income. Naturally, Astephen, too, benefited, thanks to his 10 percent cut; the Familie reported first-year revenue of $1.2 million, and Astephen now had nearly twenty people working under him. As aware as he was of the benefits of working within this world, he also knew the price he had paid for playing hardball. "We're hated outside," he said. "I don't have a lot of *fans* out there. Which is fine with me. There's a lot of jealousy—other agencies, other companies. A lot of companies can't stand me because I look out for the athletes, not for *them*. I could give a *shit* about them."

Since the day the Familie had begun, there were many more people not to give a crap about. The industry was ripe with opportunities for the athletes, who tended to get most excited about deals with makers of cars, soda, and video games, in that order. For some, the bulk of the money came from corporate sponsorship deals with companies like AT&T or Gillette. For others, particularly skateboarders, shoes were the leading revenue generator; for motorcross riders, it was cycle companies. This was the world Mountain Dew had begot, and Astephen was more than happy to benefit from it while the getting was good. There had been crashes in the action-sports industry before, and everyone knew another could come again; as far as his own future, Astephen envisioned starting a clothing company and perhaps buying an event-production business. After all these years, he remained the underprivileged, underdog Boston kid trying to prove to the more entitled types of the world—the noncore, non-action-sports outsiders—that he could make it with or without them, just as the sports he represented had staked their own claim against Major League Baseball and the National Football League. "I grew up hard-nosed and I do business that way," he said. "College to me does nothing for kids. I have more college masters working *for* me and I *still* wonder what the heck they learned."

In the meantime, there were more deals to chase, more contacts to make, more exposure to gain for his athletes and the sports they represented. He was in town in part to firm up deals with a cell-phone company. It was not a stretch to imagine that some of those who had attended the 8th Annual Sports Business Marketing and Sponsorship Forum would soon be calling on him, or he on them. "I have agents from this industry calling *me* to ask *me* what they should charge," he said with a satisfied smile. " 'What should I charge Reese's?' 'What should I charge Hershey's?' Now I know what all their athletes are making. It's a good feeling."

8. CONTEST AS METAPHOR
braving the pipe, the rail, and the mainstreaming of snowboarding at the u.s. open

S ometimes it did not seem like a sport but an untamed beast, especially when one of its hallmark boards was screaming down a mountain beneath slate-gray skies, leaving behind a trail of zigzag-ging gashes in crystalline white powder. When the boards and their metal edges dug into the snow, even the accompanying sound was a little beastly, like wolves ripping their way out of cardboard boxes. It was a noise unlike any other in the world of action sports. In terms of sheer ferocity, neither the *plump-plumping* of BMX tires on ramps, the abrasive scrape of skateboard wheels on concrete, nor the flatulent belching of a dirt-bike engine approached the sonic assault of a snowboard jettisoning down a virginal patch of ski trail or backcountry vista.

At Mount Stratton, the forty-two-year-old resort in the southern terrain of Vermont that had been hosting the U.S. Open Snowboard-ing Championships for nearly two decades, they knew well the sound of the beast. In the early days, it had scared the piping hot cider out of the clans of skiing families that had made Stratton a second home. They had never heard anything quite like it—it was heavy metal to skiing's folk music—and even though most of them had grown accustomed to the noise, hints of resentment lingered. Some could still not believe how popular the beast had become, how it had transformed from what they saw as a misfit diversion into a hugely popular snow-season activity.

The beast was already making itself known on the first day of the Open. Stratton was a speck of a town, snaky two-way roads connecting the mountains with the cluster of hotels and inns known as Stratton Village. Each day, vans shuttled back and forth from the Village up to the Sun Bowl Lodge, the headquarters and congregating place for the hundreds of snowboarders and industry figures who were a part of the sport's longest-lasting competition. This morning, one of those vans was painstakingly maneuvering its way through a snowstorm that had arrived as expected but was growing in intensity by the hour. The driver, a young, dark-haired man who worked part-time at one of the hotels, was a skier, and he was less than thrilled to witness the annual invasion of snowboarders. In his spare time, he also worked at the resort, where he stood at the base of the mountain checking lift tickets. The boarders, he said, would frequently try to avoid paying by whizzing past him and the other employees; even when they had tickets, he said, they would cut in line. "I don't want to say 'punk kids' "—he frowned—"but that's what they're like." He pointed out three police cars in front of a hotel in the Village. Boarders again, he said. Drinking and partying? "Use your imagination," he replied wryly. With some irony, he noted that a few of the snowboarders he had driven up to the mountain were complaining about the extra security in place this year.

Yet even as the beast raged, part of it had been tempered. Like the other action sports, snowboarding was an industry, its imagery exploited in commercials for cars, sodas, Campbell's soup, and Barbie dolls. But it was something more now: an Olympic-sanctioned sport practiced by third-graders, their grandparents, and everyone in between. As much as skateboarders complained about the numbers of dilettantes infiltrating their world and parks, their concerns were minor compared to those of snowboarders, who had seen their discipline attain a crossover success unlike anything else in action sports. By the time of the Open, the National Sporting Goods Association had put annual participants at over five million. Other studies estimated the number of boards purchased at nearly half a million a year, up from 143,000 a decade before, in the early nineties. The slim majority of riders were between the ages of twelve and seventeen, but 1.3 percent of them—or a good 60,000-plus—were said to be seventy-five and older. Not since in-line skating had become a family-unit-friendly recreational activity had one of these sports reached such a wide audience—a thought that, depending on the boarder, was either gratifying or the bearer of dread and suspicion. The days when the sport was the domain of rugged, unkempt young men who snuck onto ski-resort trails in order to strap themselves onto a board and then spin, twist, and hurdle themselves down a slope were a quaint memory, one for the snowboarding history books.

Each action sport was grappling with the opposing forces of hard-core credibility and mass acceptance. Snowboarding, however, was the most extreme in its duality. A combination of its steadily growing prominence, the wide age range of its riders, and its inclusion in two Winter Olympics had made it the most inviting (and arguably accessible) of all the nontraditional sports. Yet it was also the most reviled by those who continued to view it as the breeding ground for troublesome renegades. At times, snowboarding seemed to consist of two completely different sports; it was its own evil twin. Not long before, most ski resorts had banned it; now, all but four were allowing boarders to enter and use the slopes (and were witnessing significant increases in business as a result). But at one of the last holdouts—Mad River Glen, a Vermont ski spot farther upstate than Stratton—seventeen hundred shareholders had voted to maintain a snowboarding ban instituted by its founder. During a later meeting of the cooperative, one shareholder inquired about reopening the discussion. "Get the rope," came a voice from the back of the room.

The shuttle van arrived at the Sun Bowl Lodge, a yellow-hued structure with a mud-soaked parking lot and picture-window views of the trails and hills (and 3,900-foot summit) that soared up behind it. Save for the bare trees that jutted through the snow like beard stubs, everything was so white that sunglasses were mandatory. Earlier that day, parents and their children in the lodge's second-floor cafeteria sat near pro snowboarders, a battalion of young men and women encased in puffy jackets and waterproof pants; goggles were still strapped atop their heads. Now, later the same day, the cafeteria was empty, the kitchenette closed, save for the riders who had assembled for one of the team meetings that took place throughout the Open. The snowboarders, still in their riding clothes with droopy-flap wool hats, wet snow dripping off their boots, slumped in front of the round tables as a ruddy-faced man ran through schedules and rules. He told the women in attendance they would have an hour for practice the next day and told everyone there were two rail judges at the top and four at the bottom. He went through the point system and the setup. If one had not known a snowboarding event was taking place, it would have been easy to mistake the sight for a football team huddling before a game.

Once they hit the mountain, of course, the comparisons evaporated. Whether bulleting down a trail freestyle, or dropping into an imposing half-pipe, or zipping around trees and brush, the riders made the impossible seem easy. The impossible amounted to stepping onto a board (made of a sandwich-style layering of plastic, fiberglass, and wood or foam, and which looked warped when laid on the ground), attaching one's booted feet to it by way of bindings, standing sideways, and then whipping one's self and the whole contraption into the air. The act only grew more implausible from there. Tricks like a backside rotation (rotating body and board clockwise and then counterclockwise) or an inverted 720 (riding up a half-pipe wall forward, rotating twice in the air while doing a front flip, then landing backward), to name two of the hundreds in snowboarding, simply did not seem possible without serious spinal-cord injury. Yet what could have been astonishingly awkward ended up resembling aerial ballet—surfing in the sky but with snow dust rather than water spitting into the air after each twist. The appeal of the sport was not difficult to see. Riding on powder—the preferred base as opposed to harder, crunchier snow—made the rider feel as if he or she were floating on air. Problems were left behind in the gouged snow; the seeming miles of whiteness that lay ahead were what mattered.

"We all good?" the team coach said after fifteen minutes. He was greeted by nods. As the meeting broke, riders huddled around and peered at the list of heats to check their standings, like college students examining just-posted grades. Everyone wanted to be sure he or she was on track and had moved up accordingly in the rankings on the way to possible first place in the various Open contests. Afterward, talk turned to parties—which ones were worth attending and which weren't, and which bars were the most hospitable (the answer: all of them). One of the rites of the Open was watching girls gathering around the riders at the local bars and flirting with the strapping rowdies of the mountain. The promise of sex, alcohol, and limitless good times hung in the air, just as the riders and their boards always seemed to. But first, they had to compete; the beast had to be tamed, at least temporarily.

On their way down the stairs to the exit, the riders passed a sign on the stairs: RESISTANCE THRIVES IN SMALL POCKETS.

Like the ancient wonder in many ways it was, the relic was encased in glass and displayed inside a promotional truck parked at the base of Mount Stratton. Compared to its modern equivalents, the Snurfer—the forerunner of the modern snowboard—resembled one long brown ski, but wider and with small white buttons on the top where the feet were positioned; a white rope, for balance and turns, extended from the tip. Snowboarders and spectators alike popped into the trailer and gave the Snurfer a quick once-over; few seemed to have any idea what it was or what role it had played in the events they were about to witness.

The origins of the beast were straight out of folklore, a tale of old-fangled American ingenuity. Although each of the action sports was unique, they shared one significant ingredient in terms of their creation: Each was the result of someone without access to a corporate lab or design firm who looked at the gear of another sport and decided it would not do; that it needed to be adjusted, modified, tweaked, and sometimes mangled to suit his thrill-seeking needs. The skateboard was the product of grown men staring at scooters and surfboards and making something new out of their fundamentals; the BMX bicycle was, in its way, a mutation of an ordinary bike and a motorcycle. For the most part, these were the fancies of one man and one seemingly off-center idea.

So it was with snowboarding. The first sightings of the beast were hard to pinpoint; based on unearthed film footage and old, snowboard-style sleds later discovered, the sport may have dated back as far as the twenties. But most trace a significant part of its beginnings to an ex-navy man named Sherman Poppen. Born and raised in Muskegon, on the shores of Lake Michigan, Poppen had, after the navy, gone to work for Linde, a Union Carbide subsidiary that specialized in industrial gases and cryogenic fluids, which Poppen would sell to other companies. After three and a half years, he quit— "I decided there was no way I could take corporate culture," he recalled—and in 1958 returned to Muskegon, where he bought into a distributorship for the same products. By December 1965, he and his wife, Nancy, were living in a one-story, wood-frame house with floors so slanted that marbles could roll downhill on their own. The couple already had two young daughters, Wendy and Laurie; a third, to be named Julie, was on the way. When doctors determined that the new baby was of a different Rh factor from her mother, the Poppens were told they couldn't afford to wait full term; the child would have to arrive earlier, on December 28. "So you can imagine the mood *she* was in," Poppen recalled of his wife's temperament three days before, Christmas Day. That afternoon, their presents already opened, nine-year-old Wendy and four-year-old Laurie were inside the house, and the agitated Nancy made what her husband would later call "that famous remark": "Sherm, you gotta get these kids out of the house. I've gotta have some quiet time. I'm just so uptight."

Out into the yard—or what there was of it, since it was all sand—went Poppen and his daughters. The family didn't own any sleds (which didn't work on sand dunes), but Poppen flashed on the pair of wooden kids' skis in his garage that had once belonged to Wendy. "We were outside playing and it suddenly dawned on me that a hill was a permanent wave," Poppen remembered. "Don't know how those thoughts run together, but my mind doesn't work like most people's does." A few of those thoughts actually derived from his love of skiing and his longtime desire to find someplace nearby to surf (the placid Lake Michigan would not suffice). Trudging over to the garage, Poppen dragged out the two skis, cut off the foot straps, laid the skis side by side, and added wooden cross-braces to keep them together (and give his daughter a brace). He then gave the odd-looking invention to Wendy, who began using it to surf the hill, riding perpendicular to the direction of travel. "It was just a ball," he said. "The kids had a good time, and the neighborhood kids wanted to use it, so all of a sudden we stayed out all day."

Poppen's mission—to exhaust his children—had been accomplished; afterward, the kids were asleep in no time. Later, as he recalled, his wife said, "I really think you got something—that was absolutely fun just watching all of you." Over martinis once the kids had gone to bed, Nancy asked, "Well, what are you gonna call this thing?"

"I don't know," Poppen replied, "we'll dream something up."

"Well, you know, you *were* surfing," she replied. Putting snow and surf together, the Poppens derived a name for his new invention—the Snurfer. The next week, Poppen dropped into every Goodwill store he could find in western Michigan, snatched up every water ski for sale, and made a bunch of his new thingamabobs. By the following spring of 1966, he hooked up with a manufacturer, Brunswick (he had met a few of its engineers while sailboat racing), and applied for a patent. Brunswick then went and built the first official Snurfer, a yellow-and-black model made of seven-ply plywood and priced at $5.77. It had been modified slightly since that Christmas afternoon: A rope now extended from its front that the rider could pull on and more or less steer the thing. The rope also allowed the rider to keep holding on if he or she fell off. "Back then, everyone was in galoshes," Poppen said. "You just stood on it and went for it. It wasn't exactly a safe sport." In the marketplace, though, such concerns seemed to matter little. The Snurfer became the winter equivalent of a Hula-Hoop and netted Poppen enough money (about $68,000, by his estimate) to build a new house; a sign over the garage read THE HOUSE THE SNURFER BUILT.

One of many kids who picked up on the new toy was Jake Burton Carpenter, a teenager from Long Island's south shore. Like many of his friends in the late sixties, Carpenter, born in 1954, had a Snurfer of his own, although he couldn't recall when and where he had received it. "Oh, it was so much fun," he recalled over thirty years later. "It was sledding with a purpose. It was almost like a rodeo, staying on the board." Carpenter and his friends went riding on a local golf course, usually wearing sneakers instead of ski boots; living up to Poppen's warning about the safety hazards involved, Carpenter crushed his pinkie when he ran into a tree. As with a small core of

Snurfer fans, Carpenter outgrew the toy but not the idea behind it. "I felt there was a sport there," he said. "I always felt there was an opportunity. It was, the product should be better, and the sport should be real, not like a toy."

Burnt out on skiing, his other favorite winter pastime, Carpenter modified the Snurfer while at high school in Cornwall, New York. Very much a product of his freewheeling time, the shoulder-length-haired Carpenter ambled around, attending the University of Colorado, moving back East to work with racehorses, and then returning to school—this time, New York University—to study economics. Despite landing a job in a business-brokerage-deal company, Carpenter never lost track of his beloved Snurfer. After a falling-out at work, he quit his job and, in his apartment on East Eighty-ninth Street in Manhattan, began planning the prototype for a new snow-riding device that would expand on the Snurfer. Within a few weeks, he moved to Vermont, found a local woodworking shop where he could refine his idea, and contacted a company that could steam-bend wood. His first prototype, a thick, stiff, heavy board of solid ash with a binding akin to those on water skis, was conceived in late 1977. As the designated test driver, he tried riding the device himself on nearby highway embankments. "I remember going down over the hills on the powder," he recalled, "and thinking, 'Yeah, this works.' "

In 1978, Carpenter and some friends went to a Snurfer contest at Muskegon Community College in Poppen's hometown. At first, the organizers—the company that had by then succeeded Brunswick in manufacturing the toy—frowned on the shaggy-haired Vermonter with his large, ropeless board derived from the Snurfer. Eventually, though, they allowed Carpenter and his friends to compete in a newly conceived open portion of the event. "In the Snurfer division," Carpenter said, "those guys were running full speed and jumping on the board and going straight down this hill. And I was putting on my bindings and riding right down the hill—pretty mellow, pretty easy." There were still kinks to be worked out, but the contest marked the public debut of a fledgling new product and sport. Poppen, who attended, didn't mind but was concerned about the name: "I wrote him a little note and said, 'Hey, Jake, you can make all the snurf-boards you want, but that's my word. I own that name. If you wanna make 'em, go ahead—but I wanna be paid.' And what did the smart aleck do? He dreamed up the word *snowboard*."

In fact, Carpenter was just one of several innovators investigating the concept of a new type of snow-sport experience. The Dogtown skateboarders had remade their sport with rock-and-roll excite-ment: Why couldn't others do the same by melding two skis into one larger board and then attempting skateboard-style tricks on it? At the end of the sixties, Dimitrije Milovich, a Cornell University student, had already made an early type of snowboard and started a company, Winterstick, the following decade. Further progress was left to the likes of Carpenter and a Jersey-born skateboard maker named Tom Sims, who, along with designer Chuck Barfoot, began making what Sims called "ski boards" in the late seventies. Back in Vermont, Carpenter took all the cash he'd made from landscaping jobs, along with inheritance money he'd received when his mother had passed away when he was a teenager, and began cranking out sample boards for his newly formed company, named Burton after his middle name. ("I needed to name the company, and it was probably like naming a *dog* or something," he said. "It just seemed to make sense at the time.") He tried plastic, fiberglass over a foam board, and vertically and horizontally laminated wood before settling on a style close to skateboards—horizontal laminated ply-wood, with thinner plys (five rather than seven) and harder, more resilient wood. The nose was curved, but not the tail. By himself, Carpenter would drill holes for the fins and bindings, assemble and finish the wood, and paint and silk-screen each one. "It was like making seven hundred napkin holders," he said. "It was kinda like shop class."

Carpenter—who would soon drop his last name and simply be known throughout the industry as Jake Burton—ended up making almost a thousand boards, thinking he would sell fifty a day, but his hopes turned out to be overly optimistic. He would load up his station wagon, drive as far away as Ohio, and drop into skateboard and ski shops. If he heard a snowstorm had hit his former stomping grounds of Long Island, he'd haul boards down there for a demonstration. But no one knew what to make of his device or how to use it. "It was hell," he said, not relishing the memory. "I'd usually get shunted." For all his work, he only sold three hundred boards that first winter and wound up $100,000 in the hole; to make ends meet, he taught tennis and tended bar.

Yet little by little, the sport began to catch on with a small, devoted clan who sensed its potential and had grown disenchanted, for one reason or another, with skiing. The seventies might have been a time for invention, but by the early eighties, snowboarding had arrived as a cult sport. "We'd sleep under our cars before a contest because we didn't have a hotel that night," recalled championship rider and pioneer Tina Basich of the eighties. "Back then, we'd do anything to snowboard." The tricks grew more complex each year, especially once a group of riders in Lake Tahoe, California, discovered a natural formation in 1981—"more of a ditch, really," according to Kurt Hoy in *Transworld Snowboarding*—and began riding it. With that discovery and an influx of West Coast skaters like Sims, the half-pipe was born, bringing with it a new brand of freestyle snowboarding that differed from downhill racing. "Every contest we went to and every trip we went on, there was so much new stuff happening, new tricks being invented," recalled Basich. "It was so unpredictable. It's become a little more predictable now. They have the circuit, and the half-pipes are this shape made by this machine, and these people are doing these tricks. But it was progressing so fast back then." The community was small, cliquish, and more than happy to challenge the formality of the skiing world. Everything about snowboarding—the freedom of movement, the comparative lack of gear, the thought of doing the sport anywhere, anytime, and without paying for an expensive lift ticket—was diametrically opposed to the skiing community, and immensely appealing as a result. That individuality extended to clothing—brightly colored neon outfits in particular—and to its rowdy lifestyle. "The first snowboard event I ever went to, the people at the start area were passing around a bong," recalled Peter Foley, head coach of the U.S. Olympic snowboarding team and a onetime ski racer. "So that was a bit of a difference."

For that reason, many resorts initially banned snowboarders, fearing the boards would destroy the snow and the boisterous riders would clash with packs of skiing relatives. The jagged lines of snowboarders threw them off as well. But by the late eighties, the sport, the beast, could not be stopped. According to author Susanna Howe in *(Sick)*, her history of snowboarding, Burton and Sims began selling tens of thousands of boards and the media took notice, especially once official contests like the Breckenridge World Championships in Colorado were instituted. Simultaneously, the business end was on the rise. In 1989, *Ski* magazine noted that "snowboarding has become a 'sport,' complete with all the big-time trappings," and estimated the industry was raking in $10 million annually, what it called "a phenomenal growth rate." Due to a downturn in the popularity of skiing, an increasing number of winter resorts had practically no choice but to allow snowboarders to enter their grounds. By the dawn of the nineties, nearly three fourths of all ski resorts were allowing riders on their trails. Dozens of companies sprang up, including snowboard pioneer Mike Olson's Gnu, some of them making boards flashier than those of Burton. Pro riders began receiving large checks in the mail and attracting outside attention;

early stars like Shaun Palmer, with his drunken-rebel image, rose to the fore. Soon enough, it was possible to attend a snowboard event in the hills of New Jersey at which riders catapulted into the air in frigid cold while alternative-rock bands blew white puffs of smoke as they sang on a nearby stage. Adding to the rock-star chic of the atmosphere, Noel Gallagher of the then popular Oasis sang a few songs at one 1996 snowboarding contest before being whisked away by helicopter.

In 1997, ESPN presented snowboarding as part of its first Winter X Games, and there, with television cameras and large audiences at the ready, the sport received some of its most prominent general-public exposure. At one later X Games, Danny Kass, the sardonic, New Jersey-born rider dubbed the "hellion of the half-pipe" by *Sports Illustrated,* roared down the pipe and was greeted with celebrity-level screams and cheers as he skidded to a stop at the bottom. Tearing off the numbered card that dangled around his neck, he hurled it into the mob; a half dozen kids desperate for a souvenir turned the crowd into a mini-mosh-pit. Then four hulking young men yelled out his name. When Kass turned toward them, they tore off their coats and shirts in spite of the ten-degree weather. Each had painted one letter on his back, and upon turning around, their shirtless torsos spelled out *K-A-S-S.* It was a sight straight out of a hockey game, and all the more telling for it. Snowboarding had arrived.

To watch any of the contests at the U.S. Open Snowboarding Championships, spectators first had to be subjected to something many regulars had not seen before: a bag check. At the entry point, stern, ruddy-faced officers from the local Winhall township police department (the town of Stratton, which had a population of 140, did not have its own unit) sifted through backpacks, purses, and bags. Until just three years before, the Open had not required such inspections, but in light of past problems with riders and the crowd, the time to enforce rules had arrived. "You have to take precautions," said Stratton spokeswoman Myra Foster. "This is a huge event and there are more people. These are world-class athletes and *they* certainly don't want to be hit in the head with a bottle. They want to showcase the sport in the best possible light. Those times, though they're limited, don't help the event in any way."

Without intending to, the U.S. Open Snowboarding Championships had become a microcosm of snowboarding's dual nature. As laid out in Howe's *(Sick)*, the eighties gave rise to the competition circuit, which included a rivalry between the East Coast Burton riders and the West Coast Sims riders. The U.S. Open began life as the National Snowboarding Championships, held at the aptly named Suicide Six resort in Woodstock, Vermont, in 1982. "I remember all of us being really scared at the starting gate, a sort of nervous energy," Carpenter recalled. "You hit the finish line, and you just sort of dragged your body to stop." About fifty riders on snowboards or still prevalent Snurfers, some wearing wool pants and sneakers since snowboard garb did not yet exist, attended; one of them, Doug Bouton, was clocked going over sixty miles an hour down the steep hill. Three years later, the name of the event was changed to the more professional-sounding U.S. Open Snowboarding Championships— since it was open to anyone who signed up and paid the entry fee, which was now $65—and the locale moved to Stratton. Carpenter knew the area well: He had been living nearby, tending bar at night and hiking up Suntanner, one of the resort's trails, to test out his boards. Stratton, which had opened in December 1961, had begun allowing snowboarders onto its trails starting in 1983, when Carpenter had asked the mountain's operations director for permission. Sensing the connection with skiing, the resort went along with the idea. Within a few years, the number of U.S. Open competitors had quadrupled, and among the early winners were Sims and a young, charismatic Washington State rider named Craig Kelly.

Everybody had fond memories of the early years of the Open. Tina Basich recalled helping dig the half-pipe by hand in 1989, her first year at the contest; after a day of practice, she and others would grab shovels to fix it back up. Others remembered the days when inverted aerials (which involved the rider being upside down in the air) were banned due to insurance restrictions. As the sport grew in popularity, so did the Open. There were now 550 riders competing, more than double that of a decade before, and they arrived from the world over. To the surprise (and slight dismay) of several Burton employees, the event had a title sponsor for the first time—it was now the Philips U.S. Open Snowboarding Championships, thanks to a major cash infusion from the electronics company.

The Open had grown up; it had had to. During its first fifteen-odd years, it was known as much for its hard partying as its hard riding; as the season-ending competition, it was the place to let off as much steam as possible. The Open attracted a notoriously raucous and devoted group of spectators, who, according to Winhall township chief of police Jeffrey Whitesell, engaged in "assault, vandalism of hotel rooms, thefts, and drinking and alcohol violations." Some in the crowd would chuck Mountain Dew bottles at each other across the half-pipe. Rappers and rock bands booked to play at the event were required to sign contracts specifying they wouldn't swear onstage (and thus incite the crowd), but that didn't stop at least one hip-hop act, the Pharcyde, from doing it anyway. "Do we see a rise in drugs and alcohol during the U.S. Open?" Whitesell asked himself. "Yes, we do—no question about that. Some of these riders, you can talk to them one-on-one and it's okay. But get them with a group and it's a different story."

The 1999 Open was, in the words of one Burton employee, a "turning point." At one of the lodges, a group of European alpine (downhill-style) riders wound up in a fight with each other and, eventually, police. A performance by rappers Fat Joe and Big Punisher nearly resulted in a riot when someone in the audience threw a snowball onstage; a bouncer leapt into the crowd in pursuit of the chucker. "It was all about how much booze you could sneak up on the hill and how drunk you could get during the finals," recalled one employee. "It was way more core. Parents would stay *away*. After that, things got clamped down." Recalled one rider, "Before, it was party all night and if you make your start time, good. Everyone had a cabin and you could see the parties. Now it's more controlled. They took away from it as far as the stories go."

Not everyone minded the change, especially the younger riders who were looking ahead to a possible career of contests and prize money. For them, the U.S. Open Snowboarding Championships remained a prime destination and a major showcase for their talent. Despite a cold front accentuated by the cloud-heavy skies above, the male riders began warming up in the half-pipe on the second day of the event. Dropping in, they rode back and forth between the two walls to gain momentum, then scraped up the sides, launched themselves above the lip, and took a shot at tricks like the 360—a full spin with a forward landing. A new rider dropped in before the preceding one was finished, making for a striking sight: a nonstop loop of riders that resembled a choreographed show. Like the sport itself, the demonstration was infused with both a gonzo sensibility and a goal-oriented sobriety. The latter aspect was also apparent in the choice of headgear. In past U.S. Opens, riders wore wool hats or baseball caps. These days, everyone wore helmets— even though they were not required—and every rider sported a large blue bib prominently displaying his or her number and the Philips logo.

"The athletes take it more seriously," said Burton promotions and events coordinator Liam Griffin. "They're training heavier. No one is chugging a beer before dropping in." The liquor would come later; now, it was time to figure out how to best execute their tricks without wiping out, and how to decimate the competition and nab the $20,000 first-place prize.

Stuffed into waterproof pants and down jackets, the women were huddled at the base of the hill inside a tent that had been specially set up for the riders. Kelly Clark, who was eighteen, was swaddled in a huge coat; her small, bespectacled face poked out from beneath a wool hat and hood. Sitting nearby was her friend and sometime road roommate Gretchen Bleiler, three years her senior, whose waterfall of blond hair was also tucked beneath a hat and hood. There was time to kill before the start of the women's half-pipe semifinals, and conversation turned to the other, even larger competitive event now linked to the sport.

"They have a lot of rules," Clark said dryly of the Olympics and the governing body of the snowboarding events.

"Like when you drop in without your bib, you get a fine," Bleiler said.

"That's not snowboarding," Clark added sharply.

Clark knew of what she spoke. The previous year, she had competed in the 2002 Winter Games in Salt Lake City. A resident of West Dover, Vermont, and the daughter of a couple who owned a restaurant in the area, she seemed disconcertingly small and unassuming, almost bookish. Yet on February 10, 2002, she had dropped into the 426-foot-long snow pipe and, despite having fallen on her back during practice a few days before, executed a dazzling, lightning-fast routine that included one of snowboarding's most demanding tricks. The McTwist was an inverted aerial in which the rider spun around one and a half times and, at the same time, did a front flip before landing frontward. Watching it, it was easy to imagine the body being pulled apart by such conflicting contortions, but Clark not only kept it together but nailed it and took the gold medal. The next day, her goggled, helmeted face was plastered on the front pages of newspapers worldwide. Clark and the other members of the U.S. snowboarding team were proud to represent their country, but it was no secret that for every rider who dreamed of being part of the Olympics, another had little use for its rules, uniforms, and judging standards. As Clark admitted, "You do take hits for being with them." After the games, she left the team and headed to Costa Rica for several weeks to surf. "I wanted to take time off," she said, "to enjoy snowboarding again."

During the first half of the nineties, the International Olympic Committee introduced nineteen new sports into the games—a gesture intended to both add more women and bolster sagging television ratings. The generation dubbed X, it was turning out, was not as enthralled with figure skating and gymnastics as past viewers had been. In December 1995, after a year and a half of discussion and debate, IOC president Juan Antonio Samaranch announced that snowboarding, along with curling and women's ice hockey, would join the lineup starting with the 1998 games in Nagano, Japan. (Curiously, one of the sticking points was not culture clash but money: Organizers in Nagano were concerned about the additional costs of presenting snowboarding until the IOC agreed to help foot the bill.) With its youthful demographic and growing number of female competitors, snowboarding would meet both of the IOC's initial requirements.

Immediately, the boarding community cocked its collective eyebrow at the news, and not simply at the thought of having to wear official Olympic uniforms. The IOC handed over the supervision of snowboarding to the Fédération Internationale de Ski (FIS), the Switzerland-based organization that dated back to 1924, and not to the rider-organized International Snowboarding Federation (ISF). ("Snowboarding is a sport, not a discipline," went the latter's motto.) The FIS—which everyone pronounced "fiss"—was known for running ski events like World Cup Alpine races. The idea that snowboarders would be in the hands of a ski racing organization did not sit well with most riders, especially when it was learned that one Olympic event would be slalom, or racing, and that riders would have to submit to FIS's own schedule of competitive events and drug tests. Like skateboarders and BMXers, snowboarders did not like to see themselves as jockish competitors. Also, FIS judged snowboarding on the basis of, among other things, standard maneuvers and amplitude (the height a rider reached above the pipe)—the same criteria that applied to figure skating. Many riders felt such restrictions would result in less satisfying runs and limit their creativity. "Right off the bat we were like, 'Whoa, this is way different than anything we've experienced before,'" recalled Tina Basich. "This was very organized and by the book, and snowboarding had never been like that before. With the ISF, every year we were changing the formats: 'Okay, let's do two out of three runs, let's do a five-run jam format.' Nothing was set in stone until the Olympics. Then, it was all mapped out and planned and organized."

Before the first snowboarding Olympic competition had even taken place, several prominent names, including the brilliant Norwegian rider Terje Haakonsen, boycotted the event. The snowboard team of the U.S. Ski and Snowboard Association (USSA) encountered resistance of its own when some riders contacted by the organization declined an invitation to sign up. "Every year we have a selection criteria and we send letters to everybody that makes that, and some people choose to be a part of the team and some people don't," said coach Foley. "Which is the way it should be." Still, plenty of riders from around the world signed up for the Nagano games, which proved to be a learning experience for all involved. Many officials didn't know what to make of the riders and their less-than-subdued culture; the American team did not do particularly well thanks to rain and bad visibility (Ross Powers and Shannon Dunn did, however, score bronze in the half-pipe). To some, the most memorable incident was the news of Canadian rider Ross Rebagliati testing positive for marijuana and surrendering his gold medal for slalom. In arbitration, he would retrieve the award when it was determined he had been the recipient of secondhand smoke in Canada not long before, but the damage to snowboarding's image had, for some, been done.

Privately, no one was shocked that a rider had been accused of toking up. Drugs and alcohol were not rampant in the world of action sports, but neither were they invisible. "I usually smoke a little joint before I go out," one professional skateboarder said. "I can concentrate more when I'm high. It makes me relax. It helps me get into the zone. Sometimes I skate better when I'm stoned. If I'm having a bad run in a contest, I'll go out, have a little smoke, come back, and do the run. It zaps everyone out and makes you focus on your board." As with team athletes following a big football game, it wasn't uncommon to visit a local bar after a skateboard or BMX demo and find the participants getting gleefully hammered before cramming in only a few hours of sleep. Given the pressure from sponsors, teammates, crowds, and video makers—pressure that, granted, they had brought on themselves—a release valve was called for. Asked if he had yelled at any of his riders, one coach chuckled, "Yeah, probably, but it was probably not about anything to do with riding. More like, 'Why did you crash the van into that?' "

Even so, many professional riders were embarrassed by the Rebagliati incident and were made even more suspicious of the media when the story received such prominent coverage. Their distress was perhaps the first sign that snowboarding had entered a new, even more accomplished era. Four years later, when the Olympics came to Salt Lake City, the attitude toward the riders was markedly different. "They aren't cut from the traditional Olympian mold, but in the increasingly modern day, there's a place, too, for athletes of a new generation," said one of the television announcers at the start of the snowboarding segments. The day after Clark's victory, another impressive display took place when the American male riders—led by a heart-stopping routine by Ross Powers that included his own McTwist—nabbed all three half-pipe medals in a surprising sweep. Afterward, *Newsweek* reported that seven journalists tried to follow bronze medalist Danny Kass into a men's room. Then came the offers: Minutes after the sweep, agents for the riders began receiving phone calls from potential sponsors. (After much negotiation, Nestea took the honors and soon after presented all three men in a television ad.)

Although snowboarding's bond with the general populace had been building for two decades, the Olympics left no doubt that the sport had completed its transition from nonconformist enclave to respectable athletic event, complete with the frenzied press coverage normally accorded traditional Olympic contests. Coming so soon after the September 11 attacks, the American riders' victories also became swept up in the pursuit of anything remotely patriotic. Ironically, the same sport that had been barred by ski spots for its fringe-element connection became a symbol of American derring-do. The Nielsen ratings, too, were impacted; the IOC's goal of using snowboarding to attract younger viewers worked, as NBC pulled in 30 percent more eighteen-to-thirty-four-year-olds than at the 1998 Nagano games. It hardly came as a shock when the Committee announced it would be including BMX racing in 2008, an obvious way to lure the same under-thirty demographic to future summer games.

By the time the American riders dominated the Olympics, wariness of the games had dissipated. Jake Burton Carpenter and his company still had qualms, which were included in the business's media kit: "Burton supports Olympic athletes," read the statement. "Burton does not necessarily support the concept of the Olympics as a snowboard competition. Snowboarders didn't ask for the Olympics." Yet one sports agent noticed an increase in the number of riders who participated in the Grand Prix, one of the qualifying events for the winter games. When asked about the games, many semipro and amateur riders said they were well aware of the hindrances but were nonetheless stoked at the thought of competing in such a worldwide arena. "Younger riders aren't so much against it," said nineteen-year-old James Brumfield, a Massachusetts native who had by that age participated in two U.S. Opens. "No one likes the way they judge it. But it's the Olympics. The fact that the sport is recognized on that scale—we're into it. And to see Danny Kass pumped makes you want to go."

Another rider trudged into the tent, shaking off huge snowflakes. "The first couple of years, everyone would ask, 'How do you feel doing a guy sport?' " She snorted; a glint of anger flashed in her bright blue eyes but quickly melted away. "And it's *not* a guy sport. It's a *sport*."

Only two years shy of thirty, Tricia Byrnes was preparing to partake in her thirteenth U.S. Open. Although she had been born and raised in Greenwich, Connecticut, the arc of her career was similar to that of many in snowboarding. Like other riders, she had first taken up skiing—at Stratton, where her parents had a nearby winter home—but didn't stick with it long. Much to her father's disapproval, she found herself playing video games in ski lodges during family outings. ("But I was *good* at them," she remembered.) Also like many of her generation, she drifted into snowboarding, in her case during high school, after sensing a potential for movement and freedom rarely found in skiing. She had then gone on to win the women's half-pipe finals at the 1992 Open, followed by fourteen World Cup titles; in 2002, she secured a slot on the Olympic team alongside Kelly Clark and ten-year-plus veteran Shannon Dunn. Talk to any number of snowboarders, especially women, and one heard similar stories about deserting skiing and team sports for snowboarding; only the towns and states were different. Gretchen Bleiler moved

from Dayton, Ohio, to Aspen when her parents divorced and took her
first snowboarding lesson at age twelve. Her initial day on the slopes,
she learned how to turn and sensed right away a world far removed
from the skiing regimen.

As Byrnes settled into a folding chair near the entrance to the tent,
riders and spectators clomped by. The weather was growing defiantly
uncooperative. More snow was coming down than anyone had
expected—the inches seemed to be piling on by the minute—and
the temperature was plummeting toward twenty degrees, far colder
than it should have been in the middle of March. Tractor plows were
pushing their way through the snow accumulating along the serpentine highways between Stratton Village and the mountain, and the
visibility on the slopes began deteriorating, especially in the half-pipe.
It was one thing to stand at the top of an intimidating pipe and realize
one had to plunge into it and up its walls and pull off complex
maneuvers; it was another to have to do all that when the air was
frigid and one could barely see to the end of the pipe. (To their relief,
West Coast riders did not have to worry about such considerations.)
For many of the riders, especially the women, the day ahead felt as if it
would be more work than usual.

Few complained openly, however. Women had long been in the
minority in the world of action sports, but each year, their number
inched upward. More female skateboarders seemed to be popping up
at demos and contests; at least two, maybe three professional women's freestyle motocross riders were revving their engines alongside
the boys. (BMX, by comparison, appeared to be exclusively male.) "It
seems like there's a whole 'nobody wants to see a girl get hurt' deal
going," commented Heidi Henry, a freestyle motocrosser who had
made it as far as an X Games demo. "It's hard to be accepted until
you've really, really proved yourself. A guy can come out of nowhere
and say, 'I'm gonna go bust that ramp.' If a girl does it, they go,
'Ohhh, I don't know if she can do it.' A girl's got to prove herself.

You've got to see it with your own eyes for you to believe she can handle it." None of those preconceptions, though, seemed to apply to snowboarding. According to the research firm Board-Trac, women now accounted for one quarter of the snowboard market (other studies put that figure at 32 percent), which was easily double the number of female skateboarders. Byrnes was asked why more females participated in her sport than in the others. "Easier?" she cracked. "It's not as painful when you fall." To many women, the sport was simply less daunting, and it played up their gracefulness in ways the other disciplines rarely did.

Among the earliest to take the plunge was a Sacramento-area teenager named Tina Basich, who began hanging out at a local core shop to watch the skater boys and attempt a few moves on her own. Soon after, in 1986, she, her brother, and their mother found themselves hiking up Soda Springs, near Lake Tahoe, to try their hand at a new activity called snowboarding. Basich hadn't taken lessons beforehand—there *were* no such things at the time—and wore ill-fitting moon boots and corduroy pants. Affecting a skateboard stance on the board, she kept trying and falling, often finding herself in the snow with only her socks. "But," she recalled, "there was something special about snowboarding."

There was also something special, for better and worse, about the role of women in this world. From the dominant number of male participants to the punk rock that became its soundtrack, the action-sports world was actually more testosterone-jacked than its image would lead anyone to believe. To repeatedly suffer injuries and bruises with few complaints—indeed, to *expect* such beatings and proudly point to the resulting scars—was considered nothing short of heroic; to gripe about it was nothing less than emasculating. One consequence of such a mind-set was an unsettling strain of homophobia that lurked within segments of the action-sports community. It would be wrong to say such a belief was prevalent, but a conspicuous strain of intolerance among these athletes manifested itself by way of typical adolescent mockery. It was not uncommon to hear the word *gay* used as a kneejerk catchall for anything unpalatable, from corporate involvement in contests ("a fucking *gay* fest," in the words of one) to a slur against in-line skaters. It didn't help that the number of alternative-lifestyle athletes on the scene was small; one of the few prominent ones, downhill mountain biker Missy Giove, came out in the mid-nineties with few, if any, corporate consequences. Overall, though, action sports was an unspoken boys' club, and a straight boys' club at that.

Like gays (and in-line skaters), women suffered from the dominant machismo of the community. That world, especially in its formative days, appeared to be less receptive to female riders than the more conservative land of team and traditional sports. During Basich's early years, the more accomplished male riders were supportive, yet she still recalled—with a semifond laugh—contests where women were not allowed to jump and had to push their way in. One comment in particular—that she was "pretty good, for a girl"—began popping up with increasing frequency. "At first I took it as a compliment, like, '*Yeah*, they think I'm pretty good,'" she said. "Then that changed to me thinking, 'What are they *really* saying?' That comment motivated me to be better, and to be better than some of the guys." Years later, she would title her autobiography after the semi-offending phrase.

Even when women began being included on snowboard teams, they would often find themselves the only female among a slew of men; in Basich's case, she would have to act as the designated driver after a raging party. "At some photo shoots," she also recalled, "we'd roll up and they'd say, 'Okay, we're gonna do this. Tina, you can do that small cliff over there.' In my mind, I would quickly think, 'Can I do this or not?' Sometimes I'd do it, sometimes I wouldn't. But once you step up and rise to the challenge a couple of times, people stop saying things like that." With the exception of the Open, men's prize money was higher than the women's. Even relatively simple concerns like clothing proved to be an obstacle. In snowboarding's early years, there simply *weren't* specific riding clothes for females, who were forced to wear men's bulky, overlarge garb. "It was always, 'Oh, there's no need—you can always wear the guys' stuff,'" Basich remembered. "We were *way* swimming in our clothes." To have riding jackets and pants that were trimmer, more stylish, and more feminine, the women had to do it themselves. In 1994, Basich and Dunn formed Prom, the first clothing line designed specifically for female snowboarders.

The respect of the industry and male riders alike grew slowly and steadily. By the mid-nineties, women snowboarders could choose from six apparel companies that catered to them. Although male competitors in a few past U.S. Opens had griped to organizers about the equal cash prizes (fewer women than men were competing, they argued), it was not unusual to hear some of those same riders referring to the women—especially literal trailblazers like Basich and Dunn—as rad. "It used to be, like, all the guys were pretty good and the girls were like watching paint dry," said USSA coach Foley. Now, he and many other male observers and participants admitted the women had stepped up in a major way, attempting tricks on par with those of men. After members of the U.S. snowboarding team were tipped to a young Kelly Clark, they ventured to contests and saw her nail a McTwist like no other women was doing, going six feet into the air just like some men.

During the first few years of the Open, no women participated at all; later, the number amounted to a mere handful. Now there could be over a hundred, each with a very different image. "We're not like the figure skaters with their attitudes and entourages," said Byrnes. "Now you have tomboy girls and girls who get off the hill and are all girly. Not every girl is butch or a pussy." The range of presentations and sensibilities was on full display at the Open. With her glasses and small (albeit buff) frame, Clark had the look of the most studious girl in the class. Bleiler was an apple-cheeked quasi-Southern-belle who wore red fingernail polish when she rode. Sixteen-year-old Australian rider Torah Bright, now relocated to Utah, had the delicate features of a figure skater and the bright-eyed, fresh-faced-ingenue air of a young Olivia Newton-John. Byrnes, aptly described by *People* magazine as "a Gen-X Pippi Longstocking," had a clear-eyed ebullience and a distinctly tomboyish persona.

At noon the following day, the female riders congregated at the top of the halfpipe for the women's preliminaries. Twenty-three contestants would start out; only six would make it to the finals. As a Beastie Boys song pounded away, the sun finally emerged, lifting the temperature ten degrees higher and dramatically improving visibility in the pipe. Yet even beneath sunnier skies, the half-pipe was a massive, intimidating creation. Comprising 225 million gallons of frozen water, it was much bigger than those in the early days of the Open: Its walls now rose up nineteen feet (compared to six in the old days) and were separated by fifty-two feet. Given its length—460 feet, longer than a standard football field—it was far more daunting than the vert ramps used in skateboarding and BMX. Up close, the pipe, called a superpipe, looked like nothing else on the planet; it had the spooky air of an alien spacecraft that had been submerged in ice for thousands of years and had just been excavated.

The female riders were accustomed to it, though, and one at a time they smoothly glided down the slope and up onto the lip. Then they dropped in, and their runs officially began. Later, one male rider commented that he sometimes couldn't distinguish male from female riders, and it was easy to see why. Even if the female riders weren't going as high as the men, their multiple-trick runs demonstrated how far women's snowboarding had come in two decades. It was particularly evident in Bleiler's run, which included a huge Crippler—a backflip with a 540-degree spin. At the end of each run, the riders glided to the bottom of the pipe, and then the real work began. Plopping down in the snow, they unbuckled their bindings and made their way back up the side of the pipe, their boards behind their backs as they trudged through the crunchy snow and up the steep incline of the pipe walls. As Byrnes remarked, it was a good way to warm up or keep warm.

Some of the riders, like Clark, did not immediately slog back up the pipe to the starting point. After her run, she sat down in the snow alongside two other riders, as if they were not competitors but college friends sticking together at a boisterous party. The camaraderie continued when one rider fell; the others immediately rushed over to see if she had been injured. Seeing action-sports athletes congratulating each other during a contest was not unusual, but it was striking—and intimate—to see women relaxing together on a board that lay on the snow like a flattened bench. For their part, the riders denied any sense of bloodthirsty rivalries. Said Byrnes, "After someone finishes a run, I say, 'I want to do that, too'—not, 'I want to beat that person.' It kicks me in the butt." Others, including Basich, who did not compete in the Open that year, pondered how such an easygoing, noncompetitive atmosphere would endure in light of highly competitive events, professional jealousies, and bigger stakes. "With the pressure of the Olympics," she said, "I thought, 'I wonder what it's like at the top of that half-pipe right now.'"

The competition heated up in the second runs. Bleiler did another huge Crippler, a frontside 540, a backside 540, and then back-to-back 540s. Clark pulled off a frontside 720 but was having an off day. Both women finished behind the first-place semifinalist, fifteen-year-old Vermonter Hannah Teter. During the finals the following day, where they were given only two runs to get it right, Bleiler was, as they said, dialed in, ending her routine with a Crippler 720 and snaring the $20,000 first-place purse. Everyone watching was impressed, but the big news was that the sight of a woman pulling any of these huge-air tricks *was* no longer big news. (The same could be said of women in alternative rock during the same period.) Although male riders still dominated the contest and the sport, snowboarding was now as much a woman's discipline as a man's.

A few months later, the male-dominated Burton team, which included Clark, embarked on a promotional tour of America and Europe. Not long after the riders arrived in New York, they conducted an autograph-signing session at a board-sports store. Most of the acne-scarred boys and giggling girls who lined up were there to snag the male boarders' autographs or have their photos taken with them. Clark sat quietly, signing her posters while conceding all the attention to the boys. Later that day, the team made its way into a loud, overpacked midtown club, where a DJ cranked hip-hop to backward-hat-wearing throngs. In a side area surrounded by guards, the male riders hoisted beers and schmoozed with invited *Playboy* bunnies. Again, Clark sat quietly to the side, sipping a beer. She almost looked as if she had accidentally stumbled into the wrong party, yet no one doubted she belonged there.

By and large, the regulars at Stratton had grown accustomed to the snowboarders, their gear, and their attitudes, but they had not yet seen it all. As snowflakes continued to pelt the mountain, skiers on nearby lifts glanced down and saw something deeply, weirdly incongruous at the midpoint between the half-pipe and the base: a set of stairs and a handrail.

Although the steps looked like the type one would see leading up to the door of the local courthouse, they were not, in fact, stairs in the traditional sense: They were made of wood that had been painted concrete gray. The yellow-lined, wrought-iron rail that ran down the middle was real, though. A half dozen riders braved the cold and began practicing for the newest addition to the Open, the Rail Jam.

The organizers had decided to drop a quarter-pipe contest (which they felt was not progressing and was inflicting too many bruises on riders) and replace it with a rail event, which attracted a different, more hard-core crowd of riders and fans. Two dozen spectators stood alongside the steps and watched, with whoops muted by the cold, as each rider came gliding down the hill, vaulted into the air, and peeled down the handrail. Although the wood steps would not inflict as much damage as concrete should the snowboarders fall, there was still something nail-biting about the experience. Sometimes the riders jumped on and slid down fakie, or backward. The whole time, a video creeper filmed the action, shouting "Oh, shit!" with each near-fall. Every run was accompanied by the sound of a new and different kind of beast: a scraping cacophony more akin to street skateboarding than half-pipe runs or slope-style riding.

Although the beast was more legitimate than ever, it still needed to test its limits. The backlash to big-time snowboarding had actually been in the works for over a decade. Snowboarders opposed to contests and competitions took to free riding, or venturing out into backcountry hills and mountains in search of virgin powder; if a video crew accompanied them, the trip could lead to a prominent part in a video and a degree of fame and cash. The other response to corporate America's interest in the sport was the rise of rail riding, truly the equivalent of street skating—raw, punkish, and unpretty, and practiced on city and suburban streets. It was more accessible and even cheaper: Riders didn't need a pricey lift ticket to do it. In ways such as these, snowboarders sought to take on nature one-on-one and, just as important, push the boundaries of their sport by separating the weekenders from the hard-core.

Everyone knew multiple risks were involved, and several horrific, jolting reminders had arrived shortly before the Open. The rising California-based star Jeff Anderson had attempted to slide down the spiral staircase (without his board) of a hotel in Japan, where he had traveled for an event. Shortly after three in the morning, according to reports, he somehow slipped and plunged fifty feet to his death. His passing came a month after that of Craig Kelly, the talented and highly regarded snowboarder who had abandoned competitions to focus on backcountry free riding and its offshoot, avalanche riding. While attempting the latter in British Columbia, Kelly, along with six others, had been overwhelmed by a wall of snow estimated to be three hundred feet long and one hundred feet wide. He was thirty-six. The same month, French rider Tristan Picot was also killed in an avalanche. "It was a really bad year," said Basich. "With Craig's death, you just realized it could happen to anybody. Craig knew everything." In a fitting tribute, the Open's rail had been designed with direct feedback from Anderson, who had sent in the first round of drawings.

By the time of the Rail Jam finals the following evening, the barely attended afternoon practice was just a memory and everything had been amped up. Thousands of spectators lined the barricades alongside the setup, which since practice had been expanded to include two sets of wooden stairs and a double-kink handrail for extra trick challenges. Spotlights swept the area; a large, miniature-drive-in screen broadcast the event live to those who chose to stay inside the Sun Bowl Lodge, sip hot chocolate, and avoid subjecting themselves to the single-digit temperatures. Banners for corporate sponsors like Right Guard and Jeep were erected. Punk-rock anthems courtesy of Minor Threat and Pennywise pummeled the speakers and the crowd alike, as a DJ exhorted everyone to "Give it up!" for snowboarding.

The goal of the Rail Jam was to pull the sickest trick, and the tricks did not only seem sick but somewhat beyond any notion of safety and well-being. Tearing into fresh powder or plunging into a half-pipe was undeniably daring and physically demanding. Strapping one's self onto a snowboard and then attempting skateboard-style tricks on a handrail with kinks that stretched out as far as thirty-four feet seemed to be an act crying out for a stretcher. When it came to witnessing spectacular crashes, action-sports aficionados generally opted for freestyle motocross over snowboarding. The Rail Jam changed that perception: The possibility that a rider could lose his balance during a run and smash into metal or wood was very real, especially since the Open allowed riders to take as many runs as they liked over the hour.

But down the hill the competitors came, ollie-ing onto the rail on the first set of stairs, scraping down it, then vaulting onto the next. There were boardslides and 50/50 backsides and Cab 270s and backside 270s and nollies (an ollie but done with the nose of the board rather than the tail); one rider collided with a movie camera that had been attached to the rail, destroying it and igniting the crowd. Through it all, those huddled on either side of the stairs emitted frosty breaths and watched silently during the runs, applauding and oohing at the end of each. Before their eyes, the beast was running wild, and all they could do was try to stay out of its way.

9. THEY GOT GAME
espn, the x games, and
the quest for the gold

"**I** still remember that night in February 1964," Ron Semiao said between drags on his cigar. The vice president of programming and managing director of the X Games, a division of ESPN, which in turn was a division of the Walt Disney Company, leaned against a rail in a backstage loading dock at Philadelphia's Spectrum Arena. As usual, he was speaking in a voice—jocular, raspy, and above all loud—that sounded as if a megaphone had surgically been implanted in his throat. "We were watching the Beatles on *Ed Sullivan* and my parents didn't get it," he continued. "They were like, 'What is *this*?' The next day at school, we were all talking about how great it was. The teacher asked us what our parents thought, and we all said, 'Oh, they thought they were a bunch of jerks and had hair like girls.' It was so clear-cut that it was generational. It's the same thing now. People think these aren't real sports and that the people who do them aren't real athletes."

A bulldog of a man with a thatch of thick, dark hair and graying wisps of sideburns, Semiao was one of the creators of the X Games and was now its genial, unofficial mayor; he never failed to insert *pal* or *big guy* into his sentences. Just beyond the dock was the bustling, hyperactive event he had helped develop for his network a decade before. Now in their eighth year, the X Games had become, to the pride of some and the distress of others, the public face of action sports. Every summer, they brought together celebrated and rising skateboarders, BMX riders, in-line skaters, wakeboarders, freestyle motorcyclists, and wall climbers to compete for medals and cash prizes; the same event also took place each winter with snowboarders and snowmobile racers. This week in Philadelphia, the Spectrum parking lot had been converted into a vast and frenetic sea of booths and tents dubbed the Interactive Village, with each corporate hut boasting one variation or another on *extreme*, as in 7-Eleven's Extreme Slurpee. The crowd, which grazed from one free-sample booth to the next, encompassed teenagers, their parents, and young-ish couples clutching small children or pushing strollers. An all-ages, family-oriented playground, the Village was part state fair, part outdoor mall, and 100 percent X Games.

Tossing away his half-finished cigar—there was simply no time to smoke the whole thing given his jammed schedule—Semiao made his way back into the arena, past the framed photos of basketball and hockey players and the attendees streaming toward their seats while balancing trays of hot dogs and cheese-soaked nachos. Here was the America Semiao had hoped to reach—not simply the kids who participated in or related to the sports but the part of the country that once looked upon these activities with skepticism.

Eventually, Semiao marched his way up an escalator to the VIP area, where sponsors who forked over one of the six- or seven-figure advertising packages were given hospitality suites. Semiao sat down at a small table to relax. Overhead, in yet another manifestation of his vision, a television set blared commercials for AT&T and Adidas that featured two leading BMX riders. X Games VIII, that odd mix of the corporate and the kamikaze, was up and running.

They had laughed at the idea of entire cable networks devoted to news and weather. They had laughed even harder—or, at least, smirked—

when, in 1978, a former Westinghouse ad executive and Hartford
Whalers radio personality named Bill Rasmussen had announced, at a
sparsely attended press conference, that he was launching a network
devoted exclusively to sporting events in Connecticut. Rasmussen
originally called it ESP, for Entertainment and Sports Programming;
the *N* for "network" was tacked on later. Someone had probably
laughed at the name, too, but just as the chuckles eventually ceased
for CNN and the Weather Channel, so, too, did they for ESPN.
Slowly and steadily, the network had become a major player in sports
and the television industry. By the nineties, ESPN, based as always in
Bristol, Connecticut, had won Emmys, broadcast NFL and Major
League Baseball games, and reached sixty million eyeballs. Equally
important, it affirmed the power of niche marketing in an industry
just getting a taste of such a concept.

Success on that scale, though, was not enough. Like many in the
television industry, ESPN executives were intrigued by talk of new
cable systems that promised hundreds of channels—five hundred, by
some estimates—and by the promise of branding, turning the network into a franchise complete with spin-off sibling networks. Given
the variety of different sports that existed—locally, nationally, and
internationally—the concept seemed a natural for ESPN, and company president and CEO Steve Bornstein was instantly intrigued. By
1992, the idea of launching other ESPNs was put in motion. However, there was an immediate hitch: After ESPN employees spoke
with cable distributors and viewers, it became apparent that neither
group wanted another ESPN with the same traditional-sports programming. If the network was to branch out and create new offshoots, each one would need its own identity and focus—a niche
within a niche.

It didn't take long to determine what that zone should be. Bornstein
had already hired John Lack, a veteran cable executive who, as CEO
of Warner-Amex Satellite Entertainment, had overseen the creation of

MTV. Lack's background came into play soon enough. ESPN had already begun seeing portions of its younger audience lured away by the music-television channel, in particular the extreme-steeped series *MTV Sports*. ESPN already had a daily afternoon series, *Max Out*, that set footage of extreme skiing and other activities to music, but the ratings were minuscule. In the context of ESPN proper, the series didn't fit in—but perhaps a network featuring such programming could pull in the Generation Xers who increasingly seemed to have little patience for stick-and-ball sports. "We felt that sports and music and younger sports that weren't on ESPN were a way to get that audience back," remembered Lack, the network's then vice president of programming and marketing. Lack (and, according to Bornstein, the company's marketing department) pondered the idea of making one of the new networks appeal to viewers over twelve and just into their thirties.

Lack pitched the idea to Bornstein at what was, accidentally or not, the optimal moment. Just as Pepsi would discover during the same period with its relaunch of Mountain Dew, so did ESPN realize that Madison Avenue and its corporate clients were desperate to connect with an audience younger than ESPN's twenty-five-to-fifty-four de-mographic—the thriving Lollapalooza generation. ESPN, in turn, was more than ready to serve their advertisers. "Revisionists might think we knew what we were doing, but we didn't," said Bornstein. "We were trying to respond to the advertising community with differentiated product. We knew we wouldn't get distribution from our cable partners if we just put more of the same stuff on there. It became pretty smart to differentiate it by calling it hipper and younger and cooler." Bornstein gave the go-ahead to spend $12 million launching what Lack dubbed a "young-adults sports brand" net-work.

The spin-off, announced at a San Francisco press conference on June 7, 1993, was called ESPN2 and given a launch date of November of that year. (It ultimately debuted a month earlier, on October 1.) In addition to being in sync with the revised target audience and marketplace, the nascent network benefited from another timely break. As part of the retransmission-consent portion of the 1992 Cable Act passed by Congress—a tangle of deals between broadcast and cable stations—conglomerates like ABC and Fox were able to start up new networks and elbow them into many cable systems. One of those beneficiaries was ESPN2 (at the time ESPN was owned by ABC/Cap Cities), which, upon launch, found itself installed in twenty-five million households. Initial viewership was small—about two million viewers—but despite its unimaginative name, ESPN2 immediately distinguished itself from its older sibling. The talk shows, like *SportsNight*, featured fast-talking types like Keith Olbermann (later a news anchor at MSNBC) and a garrulous, loose-tie atmosphere; MC Hammer, then a major, big-panted star, appeared in its commercials. National Hockey League games, which attracted younger viewers, were initially part of ESPN2's programming, but so were motorcycle racing, skiing, Dutch soccer, go-kart racing, and sumo wrestling.

Alternative sports were more problematic: Few people were filming such contests, so ESPN2 crews had to go out into the field and do it themselves. Eventually, though, snowboarding, skysurfing, and volleyball joined the programming lineup, and the power of television immediately left an impression on all involved. Attending an extreme-skiing event in Aspen, Lack recalled a skier approaching him and telling him that, thanks to the network, three times as many people had attended the event as had six months before. "We knew immediately we had something here that the appropriate audience really wanted," Lack said. "We also knew it would take time to grow it into a mainstream audience. But the early signals were very good. The advertisers were sensing that the drums were beating. They just needed an outlet to support, and we gave them that."

As Lack remembered, not everyone at ESPN, especially in the upper echelons, was so taken with the new sports or had confidence in their popularity and appeal. "My biggest fights inside ESPN," he said, "were with the traditionalists, who said, 'This is tarnishing our image as a sports broadcaster. We're ESPN! We're the *New York Times* of sports!' And I kept saying, 'Well, we *are*, and we're not changing that. But this is the *New York Post* of sports, and this audience *wants* it that way.' These were antisports even though they were sports, and these were antiheroes as opposed to heroes." (As late as 1999, the network still didn't seem to know what to make of action sports: That year's edition of its *Information Please Sports Almanac* listed X Games results on page 945, in an appendix, "Miscellaneous Sports," that also included soap box derby, pro rodeo, and chess.) Bornstein remembered the clashes differently: "The issue wasn't how real extreme sports were, the question was how big they were going to be." At the same time, he worried the new approach would alienate ESPN's older viewers. "Frankly," Bornstein admitted, "we got pushed into positioning a little younger than I wanted to. We were kind of backed into the positioning of making it younger and hipper by our marketing people more than anything else." Still, no one could deny that ESPN2 was developing its own style and identity; more important, it was expanding the definition of televised sports.

Along with Lack, another newcomer to ESPN2's programming department was Ron Semiao (pronounced "*sem*-ee-oh"), a thirty-seven-year-old former accountant for Capitol Records and onetime production auditor at NBC. Semiao, who had longed to become a major-league pitcher during high school and college, had moved from his native Connecticut to Los Angeles to work for Capitol and NBC, but in 1984 returned East to join ESPN as a program finance analyst, responsible for overseeing show budgets. In August 1993, Semiao transferred to what he described as an "infantry" position in programming at ESPN2. Ambitious, gregarious, and a longtime fan of the wackier portions of ABC's *Wide World of Sports*, Semiao began paying particular attention to the fledgling world of action sports. "There was no recipe book for 'here's what an action sport is,'" he said. "You had small groups of people inventing things like street luge." On a trip to a Barnes & Noble near the company's offices, he scanned the magazine racks, saw the numerous individual core titles, and realized there was no all-encompassing outlet for them all. With that, he began to formulate an idea for what he called "the Super Bowl of these sports, a big competition."

With his background in financial affairs and accounting, Semiao laid out a multipronged pitch to his bosses that stressed the monetary rewards of such an undertaking. First, he detailed the advantages of creating an event the network would own, thereby saving ESPN the vast amount of money it spent renting rights to baseball or car-racing competitions—rights that could range from a half million to several billion dollars a year. Not only would the network *not* have to pay anyone for these extreme-sport games, but it could also, Semiao said, "build the brand" and branch out into ancillary businesses. Owning the event also meant the network could court advertisers with promises of on-site signage as well as commercial airtime. Additionally, Semiao proposed, the games would provide the network with a library of programming that would help fill airtime on ESPN2.

In 1993, Semiao proposed the idea to David Zucker, then an ESPN vice president, who brought it to Bornstein. Bornstein thought the initial costs of such an event, over $10 million, to be a bit high but in general considered it a "brilliant idea"; in particular, he felt sole ownership was critical. Discussions moved fast. On October 20, 1993, Zucker sent an e-mail to Lack and another ESPN executive, Loren Matthews, saying, "Our goal would be to start with a Summer Olympics in 1995 . . . If we wait too long to make an announcement, we might find CAA/Nike announcing an 'Extreme Olympics' on MTV . . . It'll be expensive to execute but it could become *the* ESPN2 franchise property." Bornstein agreed. When Semiao returned to the

office from lunch a few months later, on February 24, 1994, he
received the verbal orders: the "Olympics" for the new sports were a
go. It was now his job to find out exactly what those sports were and
how to transform a loose, ad hoc community into something close to
a group of professional, trained athletes. "Did you ever see *The Dirty
Dozen?*" Semiao said, referring to the film classic about army prison-
ers recruited for an elite World War II squadron. "I felt like Lee
Marvin picking out the troops."

The name came fast because it had to. Still worried that a rival
network could swipe their idea and steal their thunder, ESPN decided
the games had to be called *something,* quickly, and that the name
should be registered. At Bornstein's suggestion, the games would use
an Olympics-inspired system of gold, silver, and bronze medals to
make the event more accessible to non-action-sports viewers. For
legal reasons, though, the use of the word *Olympics* was instantly
abandoned. After much discussion, an executive in programming
planning blurted out, "Why don't we just call it the Extreme Games?"
The moniker sounded fine to everyone, and Extreme Games it would
be. "That shows how uninformed *we* were," Semiao recalled. At the
time, no one had any idea how distasteful the word *extreme* would be
to the very people they would want to participate in it.

The problematic name would be the first of many lessons learned in
planning a large-scale event never before attempted in the world of
action sports. Semiao and his coworkers (including executive director
Jack Weinert, another leading architect of the games) went to work
lining up potential advertisers and sponsors and found that a handful
of corporations—Miller Lite, Taco Bell, Mountain Dew, Nike, Chevy, and AT&T—were willing to fork over a little more than a million
dollars each to have their commercials aired during the telecast or to
have signs with their logos prominently displayed at the venues. The
"official pain reliever" was Advil. "We heard about the Extreme

Games through our agency," said Pepsi vice president Dave Burwick, "and we thought, 'This is perfect, a perfect big entry.'" By contrast, reaction within the action-sports community was, Semiao remembered, "mixed." Even before the official go-ahead from Bornstein, Semiao had started contacting athletes and sanctioning bodies and was, not surprisingly, greeted with everything from cautious interest to outright skepticism. "Some people were very excited," he recalled. "Some people were, 'Wow, sounds kinda corporate.' There was certainly a wariness, like, 'What's this gonna be—like a circus?'" BMX riders in particular were miffed when Semiao contacted the National Bicycle League, which specialized in racing rather than freestyle. Some leading skateboarders considered steering clear of the festivities until Tony Hawk, always keen on expanding skating's audience and profile, argued otherwise: "I'm like, 'If we *don't* go there, someone *else* is going to go, some random dude, and everybody's going to know *that* guy's name and not know who the best skaters are.'" As Semiao said, "Some people had the astuteness of recognizing the opportunities that could come from this."

By the time the first Extreme Games were held, between June 24 and July 1, 1995, both Semiao and the anti-ESPN faction could claim to have been correct in their intuitions. Interested in boosting the state's tourism income, the Rhode Island Sports Council had lobbied hard to get the games (although the city council of Newport came close to voting it down, suspicious of the audience it would attract). Nearly two hundred thousand showed up in and around Newport, Providence, and Middletown to watch 350 athletes compete in a bumpy quilt of activities that included everything from serious sports like skateboarding, mountain biking, luge, freestyle BMX, and aggressive in-line to more dubious activities like kite-skiing, barefoot jumping, and most notoriously, bungee jumping (with contestants sitting in kayaks or on bikes) over the Woonasquatucket River.

For spectators and television viewers alike, the Extreme Games amounted to an introduction to a new world sports order they had heard about but rarely seen. During the games, they caught Tony Hawk win the vert skateboarding match and BMX leader Mat Hoffman conquer the vert bike stunt contest; helmet cams on the athletes made viewers feel as if they were participating themselves, adding an up-close-and-personal twist. The world was also a new one for the athletes. BMXer Rick Thorne said he and his friends laughed when they first heard the name of the event, but deep down, Thorne said, "We just wanted the exposure. I was *waiting* for it to be televised." Upon arriving in Rhode Island, "there was an athlete tent with food in it, even bananas. That wasn't common. Now, people complain, 'Oh, these bananas are hard.' But back in '95, we were like, 'You mean, this soda and bananas are for *us*? Sick! No *way!*'" The lifestyle differences were immediately evident to Bornstein, who walked into the athletes' tent and was surprised to see "a hell of a lot more cigarette smoking" than anything he'd seen in the world of traditional sports.

Not everyone was impressed: "ESPN reaches a new low," opined the *Boston Herald,* slamming the network for "shameless self-promotion by putting people in danger of being mangled." But in Rhode Island, the impact was felt immediately: the first two X Games, both held in the state, mainlined a reported $30 million into the local economy. Within the sports community, the games also left their mark. After the first telecast, some of the major medal winners found themselves recognized on the street for the first time in their careers. Although ESPN initially planned to stage the event every two years, the ratings were respectable enough—and advertiser interest keen enough—that it was decided to put on the games annually instead and, shortly thereafter, to institute a winter edition.

Yet every victory was met with an equal number of gripes and grievances. The BMX riders were bugged that the games included dirt jumping but not street or flatland and weren't happy with the ramps they were forced to use. Semiao found in-line skaters to be "immature, arrogant, and brash, but that's what happens when a sport gets very big and the athletes are very young." Skater Mike Vallely recalled a last-minute meeting at which the invited skateboarders planned to boycott after ESPN required they wear numbers on their shirts as if they were marathon racers. (Semiao did not recollect such an incident but did add, "Maybe we asked them to pin a number on their T-shirt for ID purposes.") Many were irked by the inclusion of bungee jumping—done, in one case, by an Elvis impersonator in a kayak. In the discerning eyes of the skaters and riders, bungee jumps were a stunt, not a skilled activity, and they resented being lumped in with what they viewed as freak-show acts who exhibited no true athletic skill. "It was very experimental, all over the place," said Hawk dismissively of the first Extreme Games. "It was 'wacky sports'!" After the first year, Bornstein suggested the event name be shortened to the X Games, which he felt was "cooler" and provided for better branding opportunities. That most of the attending athletes cringed at the E word also played a factor.

Over the next few years, as the summer games shifted to San Diego and then San Francisco, the culture clash between the action-sports community and ESPN continued, followed inevitably by a series of discussions and compromises. "There was plenty wrong with it," said BMX rider Dennis McCoy of the early years. "I remember getting a group of riders together and saying, 'We're marching over there and telling them we can't do this!' We weren't used to outsiders running our event." In particular, BMX riders were irked at starting times much earlier than normal. "Suddenly we're having an eight A.M. prelim inside an arena at Disneyland in Orlando, and I'm like, 'How the hell did *this* happen?'" recalled McCoy. "We all thought TV was going to be a positive thing, and in many ways it was. But it got to the point that they were running these events with scheduling quirks and union workers and I thought, 'This is insane.'" The riders confronted

Semiao to move practice back to one P.M., and he agreed. "We needed to learn to listen to the athletes," Semiao said amusedly. "They weren't used to taking orders and abiding by rules, so it was an interesting situation." ESPN initially hired announcers with backgrounds in televised events like car racing, and much to the athletes' irritation, words like *amplitude*—another groaner, right down there with *extreme*—entered the ESPN lexicon. Years later, skater Bob Burnquist would still roll his eyes when he remembered the decidedly unsubtle way in which he was introduced to the audience before an early X Games contest: "Bob Burnquist has a rocket in his pocket and who knows when it'll go off!" It didn't help that an advertising campaign dubbed the games "sheer unadulterated athletic lunacy."

"You'd watch the X Games to see your friends, but you'd turn the volume off," recalled future ESPN on-air personality Sal Masekela. "You spent most of the time thoroughly embarrassed." Several years into the X Games, the network hired Masekela on the basis of his telegenic air, his background in various aspects of the action-sports world, and his camaraderie with skaters and boarders. But his hiring also proved a jolt to old-school ESPN journalists and producers unaccustomed to the unabashedly tight relationship that existed between the athletes and the action-sports media. Masekela felt it firsthand—or, rather, heard it—thanks to earpieces he wore during tapings that allowed him to communicate with his producers. "I'm in the middle of an interview and I hear, 'We'd like it if you weren't so chummy with the athletes because it doesn't look right,'" he said. "ESPN had *no* relationship with the athletes past 'Come to our contests and please don't freak out.' I spoke the same slang I speak when I talk, and these people would stop me during interviews and say, '*What* was that last phrase you said?'"

Eventually, with the aid of executives like Semiao, many of the early wrinkles were smoothed over, and the games grew into increasingly earnest affairs. At the 1999 games, the White House Office of

National Drug Control Policy installed a booth prominently displaying the slogan "Get Vertical. Not High." Borderline sports were
dropped or pared down. After the second X Games, Bornstein
ordered the producers to ditch the bungee jumps, feeling they cheap-
ened the event. Semiao agreed: "That was just a pure mistake from
the beginning." (The jumpers didn't help their cause when they
demanded a fixed amount of cash for their prize money—but without
informing Semiao that they had never *had* a tournament before.)
Shovel racing, which was neither a sport nor much of a skill, also
lasted just two years. Semiao had seen photographs of kite-skiing in a
magazine article and immediately signed it up, but didn't realize until
later that only two people in the country participated in it.

Perhaps the biggest wrinkle between ESPN and the athletes, one that
would refuse to be ironed away, involved money. The total purse for
the first X Games was roughly $370,000. In subsequent years, the
amounts would increase; by 2002, the purse topped $1 million, with
the leading contests—motocross freestyle, skateboard park, and BMX
park, vert, and dirt—each doling out a total of roughly $70,000. But
publicized reports of the network's advertising income and revenue
from recurring sponsors like Pepsi and AT&T grated on the athletes
even as ESPN claimed it had lost money on the first X Games and only
made six-figure profits in the years to come. BMXers were annoyed
that their purse wasn't equivalent to that of skateboarding and in-line.
Some athletes griped about traveling to their event on their own dimes
and leaving with nothing for their trouble. "This is a capitalist society,"
responded Semiao. "Have you ever heard anyone say they don't make
enough money? We're comfortable with the purse. We pay what we
can." The cash-prize issue would cast a pall over the X Games for years
to come but did not come anywhere close to shutting them down.

Even before the first skate session had taken place at X Games VIII, it
had been a good week for nontraditional sports. A few days earlier,

XXX, a clumsy, big-budget action film in which beefy-slab actor Vin
Diesel portrayed a new-generation spy who applied snowboarding,
skateboarding, and motocross skills to his line of duty, had opened at
the top of the box-office charts. For additional authenticity with the
audience it hoped to attract, Hawk, Thorne, and Vallely, among
others, made cameos. The same weekend, the *New York Times* ran a
left-field editorial that praised the virtues of skateboarding. In "Skateboarding: A National Pastime?" the *Times* opined that "this quality
of being an individual and yet still belonging is classic Americana."
Talk of a possible baseball strike was in the air, and thanks to the
overwhelming media coverage it received, more people than ever
knew that the average salary of major-league ballplayers was a
million and a half dollars a year. (Basketball players made, on
average, almost double that amount.) No one was under any delusion
that skateboarding or its companion sports would replace baseball
(or basketball or football or even soccer), but any chink in the armor,
any disparaging of traditional sports, was welcome.

Although each of those events was noteworthy, the center of the
action-sports universe that week was the X Games. The State of
Pennsylvania had shelled out a reported $1.2 million for the privilege
of hosting the event and, it hoped, generating additional tourism
dollars along with it. Over nine humidity-soaked days, roughly two
hundred thousand spectators would push their way through the
Spectrum's turnstiles to catch motorcycles, skateboards, and bicycles
give a middle finger to the limits of gravity. There and on special
courses set up outside, between thirty and sixty athletes in each of the
disciplines would be partaking, accompanied by an army of four
hundred ESPN technicians, producers, executives, and publicists.
Everyone in the action-sports community, from sneaker manufacturers to soft-drink companies to agents, seemed to be there, and
everyone seemed to know everyone else. At any moment, fans could
watch BMXers warm up on a vert ramp inside the arena, fixate on in-

line skaters competing in a semifinal at the other end, or wander outside to an adjoining parking lot to watch a session of skateboard park tricks. (Street luge had been discarded because, in the eyes of ESPN, it hadn't grown as a sport. Multiple gold medalist Biker Sherlock, for one, reluctantly agreed: "In a sense, it's true—it wasn't progressing.") Edited tapes of the competitions would be broadcast not only on ESPN and ESPN2 but also on ABC, in prime time at that.

In the air-conditioned arena, the audience watched in-line skaters from Japan outdo every other competitor on the ramp. The crowd looked on with anticipation as helmeted freestyle motocross riders attempted to do backflips, or as grown men pedaling on bikes half their size whooshed down vert ramps. Had they arrived a few days early, the spectators would have witnessed wakeboarders—men on snowboard-style boards who executed flips and spins while being towed by a boat—competing on the nearby Schuykill River. Some may have witnessed a vert skateboarding doubles competition in which the eventual winners, Hawk and the similarly long-standing pro Andy Macdonald, did not one but two board switches in one routine to the accompaniment of an Eminem song. After skating over and around each other on the ramp, Hawk stopped on the deck as Macdonald flew up toward him, pulled the board out from under his feet, and snatched the one from Hawk's hands and replaced it with his own. Such an adept, choreographed maneuver, strikingly close to Olympic-style acrobatics, embodied the X Games' most crowd-pleasing aspect and its most radical concept: making sports rarely played in arenas seem as if they were meant to be there, cheered on by insiders and newcomers alike.

All through the week, video cameras continued to roll, and the tapes would eventually be turned into a multinight television show. The X Games were not televised live (until the Winter X Games in 2004) for a specific reason: As ESPN executives readily admitted, raw footage would not have made for good television. Gen X and Y viewers, accustomed to the quick cuts of music videos and Hollywood movies, wanted as little downtime and as much action as possible. A live broadcast would be much too slow and dragged out for their sensibilities, so warm-ups and practices were left on the editing-room floor, and different, punchier music was dubbed in. A certain number of crashes were retained since they, too, were audience favorites. Complete with MTV-style graphics, countless shots of fanatical fans waving at the cameras, and bracing punk and heavy metal, the X Games telecasts were as showy as anything on ESPN2 or in sports programming overall.

They were nowhere near as huge in the ratings as World Series or Super Bowl games, nor, for that matter, close to the biggest sport events on ESPN proper. The first few years, the X Games only averaged a 1 rating, or about 750,000 homes. Even when the competitions were aired on ABC on a Saturday afternoon in 2000, ratings still hovered around the same point. But the games helped improve ESPN2's overall Nielsen standing, and equally important, the network could boast that those three quarters of a million people were precisely the demographic it had told advertisers it would reach: according to a report in *Variety,* substantial numbers of viewers between the ages of twelve to twenty-four and twenty-five to thirty-four. The U.S. Marines, which set up booths in which skateboards were given to those who did the most chin-ups, bragged of reaching two thousand would-be recruits one year.

By then, Bornstein's and Semiao's dreams of branding had also come true. The X Games logo was splattered across CDs, skateparks, and PlayStation games as well as an IMAX movie, *Ultimate X,* which featured major stars of the genre. (This, too, had caused controversy when the athletes were asked to sign waivers that suggested footage of their performances could be used in the movie without payment. According to a report in the *Village Voice,* the athletes, led by Andy Macdonald, threatened to stage a walkout until ESPN capitulated and removed the clause.) The games were so successful in reaching their target demo that a copycat was inevitable. It arrived in 1998 with the Gravity Games, a like-minded action-sports competition held each summer and broadcast on NBC. Asked how they felt, ESPN executives said they felt flattered by the imitation; behind closed doors, they cut deals—like one with Hawk in 2000 that prohibited him from appearing at the Gravity Games. Skateboarding and BMX were fun, but the X Games were, after all, a serious endeavor.

After prequalifying by way of early invitational rounds in other cities and countries ranging from Japan, Brazil, and Spain to Thailand, the athletes had arrived in Philadelphia from the world over. Befitting an event of its magnitude, X Games VIII was rigidly scheduled. On one given day, for instance, vert-skateboard preliminary practice began at ten A.M., followed by BMX and motocross practice each from eleven A.M. to two P.M., vert-skateboard prelims at noon, BMX dirt practice at three, women's in-line finals at four, and a BMX preliminary at six. On the last day of the X Games, practice for the skatepark session began at ten in the morning, and many skaters—especially the Brazilians—arrived promptly for warm-ups at the outdoor street course that had been erected in one of the Spectrum's parking lots. "They live and breathe this stuff," said an ESPN skate overseer watching as young South Americans began grinding rails on the course in front of him. "Americans roll in whenever."

The American skaters eventually arrived, two hours late, but show up they did to practice and prepare for the finals later that day. "Back in the early years," Semiao said, "some people showed up for practice, some didn't. Now, everybody's there." For the generation that had emerged since the dawn of the X Games, professionalism ruled; the sports were both calling and avocation, not simply guerrilla street theater. "Hopefully, after this X Games, I won't be just a girl wanting to jump somebody's ramp," said Heidi Henry, one of two female motocross riders participating that weekend. "It'll be, 'Oh, you're Heidi from the X Games.'"

Even after nearly a decade, finding someone who had a beef with ESPN or the X Games was never difficult. There was the manager who felt the company used his promotional ideas without credit, the TV personality who sensed he'd been blackballed for not playing by ESPN's rules, the riders and agents who saw spectators hoisting signs that hailed specific athletes that, they charged, were made backstage by ESPN staffers (to promote certain athletes over others). "I *know* it's ESPN making the signs," said luger Sherlock. "There were Biker signs at my race, and *I* didn't make them. They were handing them out." (An ESPN spokesman confirmed the rumors but added that managers and athletes also partook in the practice.) As in any sport, some of the athletes looked warily at the judges sitting above them, jotting down notes and point impressions. The way in which all the sports were lumped together as one, despite their divergent styles and gear, also frustrated some participants. "It *is* weird," said Hawk, "because people now say, 'Oh, you skate? You're into extreme sports.' No, I *skate*. They just automatically make that assumption, that generalization. You ask them if they play baseball and then say, 'Oh, you're into baseball? You must be into *ball* sports—billiards and golf and jai alai.'"

However, the loudest voices of criticism were far away, in the parks, concrete plazas, streets, and drained pools and reservoirs where the hard-core fringes converged and practiced. A mere percentage of those who skated, in-lined, rode BMX or motocross, and wakeboarded attended the X Games (according to Danielle Bostick of World Cup Skateboarding, there were an estimated twelve hundred pro skaters, only about forty of whom qualified to be in Philadelphia). The number of participants was roughly equal to those who did not want anything to do with the event. The reasons weren't simply ESPN's avid pursuit of corporate sponsors, its Disney connection, or

the network's fixation on taking the sports into the cultural mainstream. "It's the same old shit," said *Thrasher* editor Jake Phelps,
whose magazine routinely tweaked the games. "Corporate monkeys
trying to bite on something that's cool. And then they'll be *gone* in
two years, on to 'aggressive stamp collecting.' We make fun of it. We
laugh at it."

The matter of competition itself was perhaps the largest quibble.
Thanks to the X Games, outsiders were left with the impression that
board and bike sports were about contests and medals—good old-
fashioned Americana but housed in low-slung jeans and exceptionally
thick sneakers. At this thought, many skaters, bikers, and snowboarders blanched. To them, their sports were a matter of expression and
boundary-pushing, not competition; part of the reason they had
deserted team sports for these activities was to avoid the duels of
ball sports and what they felt was their repressive community. They
particularly resented the way ESPN's X Games broadcasts strove to
create rivalries between skateboarders or bikers that didn't exist,
simply for the sake of dramatic television. "It isn't like a Tonya
Harding thing, like a skater sabotaging another skater's board," said
Zoo York team manager Jeff Pang. "Everyone stands behind each
other. Even if there's a rivalry between skaters, they still want to see
the skater do as good as they can."

As a result, numerous esteemed athletes in each of the areas—
British skateboarder Geoff Rowley or California cult hero Chad
Muska, among them—refused to participate, at least for a while.
"Skateboarding is not a contest to see who is the best," wrote Muska
in an e-mail. "It's about having fun and bringing people of all
different kinds together. The state of skateboarding now on TV is
all based around competition. Therefore it leads kids to believe that if
you are not good enough to enter a contest, then you shouldn't be
skating. If you can roll down the street and that's all you can do, it's
all good because that's what skating is—riding and having fun." For

the likes of Muska and Rowley, the preferred alternative was devoting time and energy to video parts, an alternate route to recognition and status that did not involve dealing with ESPN rules and regulations and had an inherent credibility the games could never attain.

For better or worse, the X Games represented an inevitable juncture for the world of action sports: the moment when it became a trade. In that regard, it paralleled the rock and roll with which it had long been linked. Originally a mongrel art form that grew out of much older genres like blues, country, and R&B, rock upset many applecarts during its early days before gradually, unavoidably, becoming a global business. The rebels and the underground remained in place and always would, in the form of independent labels, experimental and hard-core bands, and file sharing, but something about the music had been curbed and lost over a half century. Action sports had not been around as long, but the advent of the X Games meant the sports had to face a similar struggle for their souls. Should skating, biking, and the rest become the domain of the rigidly skilled and trained? Should they follow snowboarding into the Olympics? Or should the participants of the sports hold on to their individualistic, anti-team-spirit sensibility? The X Games were like a stern parent informing an unruly child that it was time to grow up and get serious, and many didn't want to hear the lecture. Even Muska eventually acquiesced; a year after denouncing the concept of contests, he, too, participated in the X Games, even winning a gold medal in street skating.

For all the concerns, it appeared that the lure of ESPN was proving to be too strong, too powerful. The X Games had become an institution and a profitable enterprise, and the best everyone could do was adjust and go along for the ride, or not be part of it at all. Back inside the arena, Semiao prepared for a midday press conference at which he would announce the launch of a new offshoot—the Global X Games, at which skaters, boarders, and BMXers would be grouped together by country to compete with teams from other nations. Even more so than the basic X Games, the new offshoot would truly be inspired by the Olympics.

"They were taking liberties with and changing the sports," admitted luger Sherlock. "But the sports needed help. At the end of the day, I'm sure all the athletes say that without the X Games, we'd be nowhere."

10. MOTO RISING
freestyle motocross and the two-wheeled sky kiss

H e h a r d l y t o l d anyone he was going to try it. Why should he? As he knew all too well from experience, there was little to be gained by raising expectations. He had done that before, and the plan had always backfired in his small, triangular-shaped face, not to mention other areas of his anatomy. It was better just to do it without any grand pronouncements. That way, once it was over and all his limbs, organs, and vertebrae had been accounted for, he could kick back, flash that loony-redneck grin of his, and take in the dazed expressions on the faces of all who had written him off. Whether they believed in him or not, he would show them what a motorcycle catapulted into the air could do.

Shortly before the competition was to begin, he *had* clued a few of the television announcers into his plans, and they responded in such a way that made him think they doubted him or didn't completely believe in his ability. Maybe it was his looks: With his modest, bony frame, thinning hair, scruffy goatee, slightly upturned nose, and pointy chin, he looked more like a scrawny, undernourished Mephistopheles than a freestyle motocross rider. In a drawl that managed to be both cavalier and cocky, he'd patiently explained to them that if he *didn't* do it, he would just be cheating himself. They still hadn't completely swallowed it, he thought, but by then, he didn't mind. It bugged him much more when he'd learned that another rider, that young gun with the self-assured attitude and upstanding-youthful-citizen looks, had supposedly bet fifty bucks that he, Mike Metzger, wouldn't make it.

Sucker.

His manager, who had started working in the parts department of a cycle dealership and knew more than a thing or two about motorcycle racing and jumping, sensed something big was about to happen as soon as he learned his client had arrived in Philadelphia a week earlier. With time at his disposal, Metzger could carefully inspect the launch ramps and landings. Another sign arrived the day before the contest: The manager watched as Metzger straddled his Honda, twisted his right wrist to rev its 250cc engine, zipped onto the dirt field outside the Spectrum Arena that would serve as the freestyle course, and rode up onto one of the dune-style mounds of dirt on the large, oval-shaped track. There, he stopped and looked around, gauging the distance to the next hill. The last time he'd tried a move similar to the one he was pondering, the gap had been seventy-four feet. This time it was eighty, and those seemingly insignificant seventy-two inches could mean the difference between a trip to the trophy stand or to the nearest emergency room. At that moment, he turned for advice to his manager, who told him he should try it only if he felt he could do it safely. The manager could have attempted to talk his star client out of such a trick, but he knew that tactic would do nothing but feed into Metzger's apprehension that yet another person did not believe in him. It was best to let the kid ultimately decide for himself.

Metzger could not deny that his chosen sport was far wilder than the motorcycle racing world from which he had emerged, and that one of freestyle's holiest grails, a backflip, was not the province of a sane mind. When the flip had initially come up at an ESPN meeting six years earlier, everyone in the conference room had laughed; no one thought it was even remotely possible. But those days were over. Metzger had first practiced a flip on a BMX bicycle, repeatedly jumping into a foam pit until he nailed it. Still, a world of technology, machinery, and peril existed between trying the move on a pedaling machine and on a motorized one. One time, he'd come up short, flipped forward, and been knocked out with a concussion; another day, he'd been pitched off the back of the bike. Even though he had successfully pulled a flip in public a few months before, he knew the odds of succeeding each time were fifty-fifty at best. He could only imagine what his parents would say; they would have preferred if their son had stuck to racing. That other freestyle rider, the one dating the rock star and nabbing all the endorsements despite having barely won any contests, had tried a flip, and look what happened to him: a broken back, a year out of commission, a year's worth of lost income.

The X Games at which Metzger was competing were intended as a culmination of a year's worth of big-time action sports, which now included freestyle motocross, the sports' newest and, to some, craziest offshoot. On the morning of the contest, though, nature was not cutting him any slack. The mercury was zooming toward one hundred degrees, which felt even more sizzling inside the jumpsuits he and his fellow riders had to wear for their protection. Then the wind had picked up, from five miles an hour to fifteen, resulting in miniature hurricanes that whipped around the course and posed additional dangers for the riders once they were in the air. The conditions were yet another reminder that as practiced and professional as they were, the riders never had complete control over what they did; too many variables loomed. Traction was crucial. They had to approach the launch ramp at a certain speed and then, just as the tires grabbed on to it, accelerate up the ramp. Yet they could easily stall on it or think they were in second gear when they were actually in third. If they went up too fast, they could fly right over the handlebars; if they didn't go fast *enough*, they could land short, with equally dire results. The bikes themselves were not as burly as prototypical Harley-Davidson road hogs; with their raised front fenders (to ward off flying dirt debris) and rear frames that jutted out like wings, they could be mistaken for giant metallic hornets. What looked like a defect—irregular, V-shaped slots cut into the plastic side plates on either side of the seat—were, in fact, homemade alterations by the riders: the easier for them to grab on to the subframe and hold on for dear life when the cycle was aloft.

"Has anyone done a backflip yet?" someone in the VIP area alongside the course asked before the event began.

"No," replied a colleague, "but I doubt they'd do it until the finals."

"Yeah," said the first, with a grim nod. "If you're gonna die, you might as well do it during the finals."

The contest, it turned out, would be shorter than first anticipated, since a half dozen riders had injured themselves before arriving in Philadelphia and would not be able to compete; one of them, the star Travis Pastrana, was hobbling around on crutches. Beneath a tent set up by the side of the course, those who were physically able to compete sat, with grim determination, in the protective armor of their profession: logo-strewn jumpsuits, chest protectors, helmets with face shields, and thick, scuffed, knee-high boots that looked like leftovers from moon-landing expeditions. At the start of the event, their names were announced, their motorcycles sprang to life with a sound not unlike that of a chain saw ripping into action, and they rode out onto the field to meet the fans. Seeing the packed rows of bleachers before them, not to mention the television cameras, neither Metzger nor his competitors could resist a few flashy, crowd-pleasing moves during their introductions. They rode to the top of a mound, revved their motors, shook their hips, and thrust their arms into the air. They knew a few displays of machismo weren't merely good showmanship but distinguished them from the comparatively self-effacing skateboarders and bicyclists. They were *men*, and they wanted everyone to know it.

Finally, it was contest time. One by one, they tore toward the ramps and hit them hard, at which moment the most remarkable spectacle took place: Their bikes and bodies, all three to four hundred combined pounds of them, seemed to be swept up into the air as if by the hands of an invisible giant. During the five or so seconds when they were aloft with nothing below them but dirt, they pulled a trick as fast as possible. They might throw their legs back horizontally while keeping one hand on the seat, known as a Superman Seat Grab, or essentially do a handstand on the handlebars, legs spread apart (the Hart Attack), or, if they were especially daring, lean over to smooch the front bumper with their helmet, aptly known as the Kiss of Death. They rounded the bend of the course and came back, doing several more tricks along the way, as many as they could during their allotted time.

Near the end, the announcer called Metzger's name, along with his nickname, The Godfather, and he knew his moment had arrived. The night before, chowing down on Chinese food in the athletes' tent, his manager had grabbed a few fortune cookies. Before one run, he had shown Metzger the first, which read, "The prospect of an exciting time lies ahead of you." Metzger had laughed at that. Then, right before he decided to go for the big one, he asked the manager to crack open the other cookie. This time, the little white sliver of paper read, "Miracles happen to those who believe in them." Again he smiled at the timeliness of the message, as much of a sign as anything he'd witnessed in his life.

Metzger started out impressively enough. Doing a Cliffhanger, he threw his arms straight up, touchdown-style, while only his feet, wrapped around the handlebar, held him to the bike. Then came a Rock Solid, in which he extended his body parallel with the bike, removed his legs and then arms, and for the briefest, most intense moment had no physical connection to the bike whatsoever. He'd pulled each of these maneuvers many times before, and his experience showed. Then he returned to the starting point. Everybody in the bleachers seemed to sense what was coming and could hardly contain themselves, knowing they were about to witness a flip—or, at least, an attempt at one. Metzger gave the engine some gas and headed straight for the metal, quarter-pipe-shaped ramp. Within seconds he was in the air and, before anyone knew what happened, had jerked his bike over his head. For a moment, when he was in the clear gap with nothing underneath him, he couldn't see a thing; the ground vanished, and it was just him and the bike, upside down, in the air. But he had that sense of where he was, and soon enough, he and the bike were right side up and back on the ground in the proper position, so smoothly that it looked impossibly easy when later seen on videotape.

The crowd was cheering, but he couldn't hear them, nor was he done yet. Others had beaten him to the backflip earlier that year, so he had no choice but to make his mark the best way he could. In those few seconds while he had been upside down in the sky, he had shifted into second gear, an impossible move in and of itself given that his concentration had to be on his balance and landing. But in doing so, he was able to get right on the gas once the bike landed in the transition, at which time he could gun it for the second hill without losing any momentum. As the commentators, spectators, and other riders watched and as the cheers went silent for a moment, he raced up the second mound, jettisoned into the air again, and did *another* backflip. No one had seen anything like it: One flip was hard enough, but two in a row? He landed and, more importantly, stayed on the bike after it touched down. And with that, he was done.

Since he was still wearing his helmet, no one could see his face when he landed, but inside, he was smiling to himself. All the doubters would now be kissing his ass; that kid had just lost his fifty-buck bet.

One of the dubious television announcers was going ballistic, breathlessly rasping to the standing, screaming audience that they had been witnesses to history—*history!*—and that freestyle motocross had a new champion and a new era. And Metzger, of all people, had been one of the people to take it there.

Suckers.

It took a different type of person to become involved with action sports, and it took an especially singular sort to partake in freestyle motocross. Unlike skateboarding and snowboarding, moto was the realm of men with oak-tree necks, thick, stocky torsos, and tattoos of their own names carved into their limbs. Sporting monikers like Cowboy and Mad Mike, they carried themselves with the hard-living swagger of Apollo astronauts. But theirs was a different kind of right stuff. They had deeper scars, more boisterous laughs, and bigger guts, literally and figuratively. In skateboard videos, the footage between tricks generally amounted to goofy skits, shots of the athletes at home or on the road, or montages of crashes. Moto videos would have none of such slacker mirth. In *Total Chaos*, coproduced by rider Brian Deegan and featuring members of his goth-moto posse the Metal Mulisha, riders engaged in slap fights with outsiders, lunged at women in bars, punched each other for the seeming hell of it, leapt off hotel roofs and into the pools below, and emceed breast-baring contests during breaks at contests. In the movie's credits, the names of the bikers were scribbled on the butt cheeks, legs, crotches, and stomachs of G-string-clad women. The names of the tricks they mastered—the Dead Sailor, the Corpse, the Mandatory Suicide, the Suicide No-Hander Lander, the Dead Body—said everything about their world and its hazards. "These guys, they don't like doctors and EMTs," said Greg Thomas, promotion manager of Clear Channel, the multimedia monster that put on its own traveling freestyle tour each year. "They're like, 'I'm fine, leave me alone.' If they're not fine, they know it."

They had been different from the start. While other children their age were playing in the dirt, they were racing in it. They were the products of the American working class, sons of construction workers and auto mechanics and part-time cyclists who found themselves sitting atop dirt bikes at absurdly young ages and were immediately addicted to the power and speed. Rather than discouraging their interest, their fathers worked hard at their blue-collar jobs to buy their sons bikes, gear, and equipment, and the dads would watch and coach dutifully as their offspring raced around their backyards or nearby fields. Soon enough, the parents were driving their children to weekend races, where the kids would gun their engines and compete on dirt courses against other neighborhood tykes on small 125cc bikes. The kids always knew they would have to face the wrath and disappointment of their fathers if they lost, and that fear also came to set them apart from skateboarders and BMXers. They were far more competitive; they wanted to *win*.

From there, it was only a matter of time before they progressed to bigger bikes and the next, natural steps: motocross (outdoor races on rocky, bumpy natural terrain) and supercross (contests on man-made dirt tracks held in indoor arenas and stadiums). The sport had its roots in European racing, but by the eighties, motocross had become as indigenous in the United States as the World Wrestling Federation, complete with riders swathed in corporate logos courtesy of the leading motorcycle manufacturers. The money was minimal, but on those bikes, the kids were no longer the poorest ones in the most wrecked homes but champions.

Yet it was not enough, and the most maverick riders began veering off in the same direction. They still loved to race—the velocity and rivalry would always be appealing—but the sport began feeling routine. Neither motocross nor supercross paid that well, and both were fairly dangerous: If a racer made a wrong turn on a track, he could easily wipe out and be run over by one of the five or six bikes flanking him. Racing was also growing a little too corporate for some of their tastes. One rule in a Clear Channel supercross manual read, "All riders and mechanics must present a clean and neat appearance." If anyone had bothered to ask, some riders would have remarked that *clean* and *neat* were hardly part of their own private dictionaries and never would be. As freestyle-moto event producer Tes Sewell recalled, "At supercross, all the guys in the mechanics pit have their shirts tucked in. Ours don't."

To get stoked on a motorcycle, there had to be other, more creative ways beyond tournaments, and they found them in the mountains, the deserts, and the dunes. When they weren't competing or working day jobs, the young motocross racers would push their bikes into the back of pickup trucks and head for the hills, where they would let loose and completely ignore everything they'd been taught. Around this time, 1993, a fledgling young filmmaker named Jon Freeman began hearing about them. Freeman, a native Californian with a filmmaking degree from Malibu's Pepperdine University, was working in the small enclave of action-sports videos, producing snowboard and surf films as well as a video for championship surfer Kelly Slater. Freeman had grown accustomed to making illegal trips up ski-resort back trails to film illicit snowboarders tearing down mountains, or visiting Hawaii to videotape surfers having their backs ripped off by sharp reefs.

Then his partner, a snowboarder named Dana Nicholson, told him about a group of motocross racers who were doing insane things with their bikes out at the Dumont Dunes, way out in the far reaches of southeastern California. The Dunes amounted to 8,150 parched acres of sand hills, the gaps between them stretching to 110 feet. One day, Freeman tagged along, and there they were: guys on dirt bikes flying into the air and throwing their legs over to the other side in midflight

or barreling up the sides of brush-sprinkled cliffs. Just as skateboarding had derived from surfing, this new activity derived from BMX
stunt biking, and it turned motorcycle riding into a new, breakneck
art form. "They were just *flying* off these dunes," Freeman recalled,
"and I just couldn't believe it. Flying through the air, that far, and
smashing into your face—that's unique."

Freeman filmed the riders and stuck a few of the clips into his
snowboard videos until friends and fans began suggesting he make an
entire tape of the motorcycle daredevils. Before long, Freeman was
driving his video camera out to the dunes and other, similar wide-
open areas in California like Glamis and Pismo Beach. After several
years of on-again, off-again filming, he finally completed the thirty-
minute video in 1996. "I remember being out there with the wind-
storms," he remembered, "and waking up in the morning, you have
sand in your nose and eyes and ears. You're basically a ball of crust.
And the guys were speed demons, air demons." Thus inspired, he
called the movie *Crusty Demons of Dirt.* The participants included
Jeremy McGrath, a supercross champion (and former BMXer) who
invented the nac-nac, swinging a leg from one side of the bike to the
other by way of the rear fender; Mike Metzger, an increasingly
disillusioned racer from the area who was seen dropping in off a
cliff; Brian Deegan, a teenager from Omaha, Nebraska; and Brian
Manley, another successful motocross racer from California. *Crusty
Demons of Dirt* amounted to shot after shot of these and other riders
catapulting their dirt bikes skyward; nothing else like it existed at the
time. The film didn't flinch from the occasionally ugly end results:
One rider, Seth Enslow, was seen not only overshooting a landing and
falling on his face but lying on the ground flashing that very same face
caked with blood. Viewers also saw another of his injuries that went,
literally, to the bone of his leg. (For evident reasons, Freeman,
Nicholson, and their other partner, Freeman's wife, Cami, named
their company Fleshwound Films.) But the mood was of exhilaration

and adventure, not morbidity. In between the tricks, viewers were able to see what the riders did in their spare time: dressing up like johns for an uninhibited "pimps and hos" party, dancing with girls who were more than happy to unzip their tops, and entertaining themselves during those dark, lonely desert nights by whipping out AK-47s and shooting up old, rusty bikes they had already set on fire. Mysterious, menacing, and out of control, the tape was a peek into a community that was equal parts sports team and motorcycle gang.

The words *freestyle motocross* were nowhere to be found on the packaging. Perhaps they should have been, since motorcycle shops were initially reluctant to carry Freeman and Nicholson's film. "We'd call them and they'd say, 'Well, we don't really sell tapes like that,'" recalled Freeman, "because they didn't exist." But word of mouth spread and *Crusty* became a cult hit, selling out its initial run of several thousand copies and becoming one of the most lucrative action-sports videos of all time; over the years, it led to nine increasingly grim-reaper-defying sequels. More importantly, the tapes spread word of the new sport around the country and the world. Clifford Adoptante, a half-white, half-Hawaiian-Filipino son of an air force officer whose family eventually settled in Oklahoma City, was one of many affected by it. Racing his dirt bike around the trails of Lake Draper, Adoptante turned racing pro at eighteen, winning numerous competitions and establishing a reputation as a sullen, braided loner. "I was thirteen when I started racing," he said. "You're at the age when you're interested in *girls*, you know what I mean? I could ride my motorcycle over to the chick's house instead of a bicycle, and I'd take 'em for a *ride*." Then he saw the first *Crusty* and its footage of a heel clicker, in which the rider would extend his feet over the handlebars and, while holding on to them, smack his feet together. "I was like, 'Man, check that out! That's crazy looking!'" he said. "Then I said, 'I wonder if I could do that.'" A month later, home during the racing off-season, he practiced, and nailed, the trick

in the freezing Oklahoma City cold. Shortly thereafter, he debuted it
in front of a crowd at a half-time freestyle show at a motocross race in
Fort Worth, Texas.

"People were just like, 'What the *hell*? What the hell did that kid
just do?' " he recalled with a smile. "They were kind of shocked. They
came there for racing. They were completely amazed by something
they'd never seen before. It was a whole different aspect of it."
Adoptante had always had mixed feelings about racing, partly from
a bad leg break he'd experienced years before. But freestyle—with its
increasing media attention and prize earnings in the thousands of
dollars—motivated him to quit racing altogether in 1998. He went on
to immortalize several signature moves. In one, he would land with
his legs lying atop the handlebars; it was dubbed the Sterilizer, since
anyone who didn't get it right risked the possibility of never having
children. Adoptante was one of many former motocross racers who
headed to Las Vegas in 1998 for the first freestyle championships, co-
organized by *Crusty* auteurs Freeman and Nicholson.

With each passing year, the sport took another giant leap in
prominence. At one major snowboarding event, boarders brought
copies of *Crusty* tapes to a bar where the athletes were meeting and
greeting fans. When the *Crusty* video started, recalled Tes Sewell,
"Everyone shut up and watched. We saw there was something
happening." In 1999, ESPN introduced the first freestyle moto event
at the X Games, where it made a literal big splash when Pastrana, the
teenage moto champion from Maryland, ended his second run by
taking himself and his bike into San Francisco Bay (resulting in a
$10,000 fine due to local environmental laws). ESPN never aired the
footage in compliance with the city, but thanks to Pastrana, moto
proved such a crowd-pleaser and formidable ratings-getter that two
other events, Step Up and Big Air, were eventually added to the games
in 2000 and 2001, respectively. The International Freestyle Motocross Association (IFMA), which held contests and events around the

country, was purchased by Clear Channel. Etnies began making cotton twill baggy-fit shorts and jeans especially for the riders. The crowds who parked themselves in arena seats to witness these exhibitions and contests—where freestylers competed for a purse that could, if they were lucky, bring them a $50,000 annual income, ten times more than their racing salaries—saw the sport quickly explode. Basic moves like the nac-nac were important, but only in combination with other moves; what also mattered was how smoothly and quickly they could be done before motorcycle and rider plunged back down into the hard, unforgiving dirt below.

Technically, the riders were part of the action-sports community, yet they seemed to exist on a separate plane. A few hours after Metzger pulled his historic backflip to backflip, one of many invitation-only X Game parties was occurring at a small theater in the heart of Philadelphia. By midnight, the upstairs bar was standing schmooze only, BMXers and skateboarders jostling for free drinks alongside managers, marketing executives, and representatives from sneaker companies. Everyone was there—except for the moto riders, who took over an empty balcony adjacent to the bar. Displaying virtually no interest in anything outside their circle, they threw back drinks and enjoyed the company of women in tight T-shirts and hip-hugging jeans who eagerly sat on their laps. The moto riders rarely ventured into the VIP lounge, and no one from the lounge wandered onto the balcony. One manager, who represented a prominent skateboarder and BMX rider, said he had no interest in signing up any freestylers: He described them as "lugheads" who were "too dark" for him. The invisible curtain between the two worlds remained up for several more hours until everyone had downed enough free drinks and the time came to seize a few hours' sleep before trying to kiss the sky once more.

The tattoos originated on one arm, spread to the other, then snaked down to his ankles, and together they told the story of the innumerable highs and lows he had experienced on the job. He pointed to the METZGER logo burned into his muscular upper right limb and then began running his finger down the arm, stopping at each tattoo along the way. A spark plug represented his father ("my best friend and fan growing up," he said), followed by a woman on a cycle in flames that symbolized his mother, "representing her pain of having to deal with me suffering throughout the years," he added somberly. Below them was a burning eyeball and a chaos symbol, "representing all my friends and our chaotic life," followed by a rocket ship, "meaning I wish I had a way sometimes to get the hell outta here, you know," he chuckled. Then came a tattoo of the enduring children's toy Mr. Potato Head—"because," he said, "I feel like I'm the Mr. Potato Head of motocross. Throw me up against the wall and you can put my arms back on." Signaling his impending baldness, a pompadour was falling off Mr. Potato Head's skull. Finally, on his ankle, was his admitted favorite: a tattoo of a man with a gun to his head, dollar bills bursting from his pocket. Over the image were the words MY CON-FUSED LIFE. He was only twenty-six.

For one moment at least, the confusion and chaos had subsided. The day after he had made freestyle motocross history, the man who had remade the record books with two consecutive backflips, a move he dubbed the Double Fritz, was relishing his glory. Metzger was doing so in the large white motor home one of his sponsors had rented for his cross-country drive to Philadelphia, a vehicle that sported a pale green carpet and a framed photo of a barely clad Britney Spears. "I feel I *am* the best right now in the world on a 250cc dirt bike," he said, sitting at a table and clad in a sleeveless T-shirt and shorts. "I can make it do whatever I want. And pretty much all the riders, the judges, the fans, right now, everyone knows I'm the best."

The point was debatable—ask any of the insiders who disparaged the idea of a backflip and saw its practitioners as motorized one-trick metal ponies—but for all he cared, they could go to hell. A California native, born and raised in Huntington Beach and later nearby Corona, he was the son of a general contractor and a part-time motocross racer, Ted Metzger. By the age of three, Mike had already been set atop a dirt bike; by six, he was racing around on a track his father had built behind the house. He had joined sports teams at his elementary and high schools, but the experience had been less than positive. "Tried soccer," he said. "Until I busted my nose wide open at the first game I played. Wrote soccer off. Figured I liked wearing a helmet better. Tried football. Played tackle football in like eighth or ninth grade. Broke my arm really bad. My dad was like, 'Okay, well, you're either gonna get hurt riding your dirt bike or you get hurt doing this—choose one or the other.'" He chose racing because, he said, it was "lot funner, I gather. Once you're healed up and you can walk around and get back on your bike, there's nothin' funner."

He would spend an inordinate amount of time both riding and healing over the next two decades. Metzger would arrive home from school every day and immediately jump on his bike ("Wasn't interested in having any friend at school because my main friend was my dad"), and his father took him racing every weekend at a nearby track. Like many of his fellow riders, he wanted more out of his bike, so he began doing what everyone else did at first: taking one palm off his handlebars, then the other, and finally both. Soon, he was doing jumps during halftime shows at races. At first, he was worried he'd injure himself and not be able to compete, thereby angering Ted, but he couldn't help himself. By the early nineties, he was perfecting moves like the heel clicker and no-hander, and he fell in with the Dumont Dunes crowd. Out in the desert, he distinguished himself for being "always willing to try anything," recalled Freeman. "He would jump off anything, *over* anything. He would do a heel clicker and people would freak out. Nobody'd ever seen someone go over the bars like that."

The life was a freewheeling, unrestrained one, and Metzger was

happy to go along with it. "A lot wilder, a lot more erratic," was how
Russell Stratton, his manager of several years, described him during
that time. "He was a crazy kid. He was into tattoos and partying. The
motorcycle world, some of these kids, you can be eighteen years old
and be doing fairly well moneywise, and it's not an experience most
eighteen-year-olds are prepared for." In the first *Crusty Demons of
Dirt*, there Metzger was, wearing a pimp outfit, downing drinks, and
flashing his trademark look—eyes rolling and tongue stuck out the
side of his mouth, like the town loon who'd just busted out of county
jail. In between tricks in the *Total Chaos* video, he could be seen
throwing up in a sink.

He still loved to race, loved that the winners were more unequi-
vocal than at freestyle events, where the judging felt more subjective.
But two aspects of racing led to his disenchantment with it. First were
the wounds. In a particularly bad accident in 1998, he was coming
around a turn and was rammed in the back by an opponent's bike;
falling off, he got sucked into the rear wheel of the other motorcycle.
"I was wedged in there," he said. "It took three people to get me out
of the rear wheel." When he emerged, he also had third-degree burns
on his body. "That's what you gotta deal with in racing," he said with
the most arid of chuckles. "Racing's way gnarlier. You're out on a
course with twenty guys and you can't trust any of 'em 'cause they're
out there to beat ya."

The low income he made at supercross and motocross contests
didn't make them more attractive either. "You don't make squat
racing," he said. He turned to a friend reclining on the floor of his
trailer. "How much money you make racing?"

"*Minus* several hundred grand," the friend cracked.

"Yeah." Metzger nodded. "You work your ass off, you train, you
run every day, you go to the track, you do the race, and if you don't
finish top three or top five, you're going home with a couple of
hundred bucks if *that*. For me, I'm six figures right now. Right now,

for the last year, I pulled in over three hundred and fifty grand." He let out one of his drawl-chuckles. "And this year I'll probably almost double that."

Still, the road between racing and this point in his career had been bumpier than most. The years leading up to his double backflip had been full of hopes and dreams left for dead in the soil. He developed a habit of not always warming up before contests, with increasingly predictable results: an injury during practice at the 1999 X Games, two broken vertebrae in his back and two broken heels a year later at the Gravity Games when he overjumped and dropped thirty feet straight down. Attempting a backflip at a later Gravity Games, he overrotated and crashed. That, Stratton said, had been a low point, and afterward, Metzger announced he was giving up freestyle altogether and returning to the racing circuit. Immediately his paycheck shrank when one of his freestyle sponsors offered him only a portion of his previous salary. Between injuries he worked at a tattoo shop.

Along the way he had also broken both arms, his back (three times), his collarbone, his lower legs, and his ankles. The injuries did not end when he began racing again. At a supercross event, he came up short in practice and smashed his chin on the front number plate, breaking five teeth on each side of his mouth (he would eventually replace them with gold fangs). "That kind of took the wind out of his sails for supercross," Stratton said with a laugh. Then, one night soon after, Stratton received a voice mail from his client, who declared he was heading back to the Dumont Dunes with his ramps to learn the backflip and travel the world over doing it. A combination of money, kicks, and self-respect—a need to erase the humiliation he had suffered in front of his peers at all those high-profile events—had pulled Metzger back in.

By early 2002, freestyle motocross had become home to an array of tricks that did not seem the domain of right-thinking minds, but the backflip stood apart from them as the unattainable goddess, the trick everyone fantasized about but no one could master. The riders had been inspired by the sight of BMX bicyclists doing flips and assumed that the same could be done on a motorcycle. Everyone knew the flip could prove harmful to one's health and gear, but it was so alluring in its danger—it was motocross heroin.

Thus began the crusade that had left numerous bodies in its wake. The first person to come the closest was Carey Hart, the affable, movie-star-handsome rider from Las Vegas, who, at the Gravity Games in July 2000, became the first to pull one on a 250cc dirt bike. Technically, he hadn't succeeded, since he fell off his bike while landing, but the excitement and awe emanating from the stands and the other riders made everyone forget he hadn't ridden it out. Trying again a year later at the 2001 X Games—this time with a month-old shoulder injury along for the ride—Hart fared much worse: He ditched early from thirty-five feet up and landed hard, breaking his tailbone, crushing his right foot, and silencing the crowd in the packed Philadelphia arena who had come to cheer him on. Sidelined for a year, Hart was forced to cough up $20,000 for $500,000 in disability insurance in case the worst happened again. Then, in April 2002, Caleb Wyatt, a rider from Oregon with a profile far lower than that of Hart or most of the major freestyle riders, pulled off a flip on a dirt ramp, riding it out and owning the videotape to prove it. Debate raged over who nailed the trick first: Was it Hart, despite his faulty landing, or Wyatt? Then, everyone shut up, at least temporarily, when both Pastrana and Metzger each executed perfect flips a few months later at the Gravity Games. Suddenly, the maneuver was not a fluke but a genuine trick.

Having proven himself to his peers, Metzger was a changed man. No longer the out-of-control party animal of his youth, he was now married—to Mandi, a small, brown-haired woman with a heavily tattooed right arm—and together they had a daughter, Michaela Rose, and another about to pop out. In their three-thousand-square-foot home in Menifee, California, he was also growing more serious every day about his artistic aspirations. A fledgling illustrator, he was forever looking through books on Picasso and van Gogh as well as contemporary comic books; painting, especially spray-can art, eased his mind during the months he spent recuperating from injuries.

The difficult trick he now had to pull off was balancing family life with his line of work. One moment he was chasing after his daughter in his motor home; the next he was talking with friends about his next move. He was pondering a 360 (combining a backflip with a full horizontal rotation); in his mind, he would move his body to one side or the other, using himself as a pivot. He also wanted to combine the backflip with other moves; in one of them, a Disco Inferno, he would point one finger in the air and the other toward the ground, similar to John Travolta's dance-floor stance in *Saturday Night Fever*. Sometimes, talking about possible future tricks, he had to catch himself at how loopy it all sounded. "Any way you look at it, it's not sane," Metzger chuckled. "Because every one of us knows we could end up in the hospital at any given moment. And we know that." But for the moment, at least, he was king of his world.

Several months and hundreds of miles away, at another freestyle competition in another dank, cavernous arena, Jake Windham was thinking about the unthinkable. A dough-faced, peach-fuzz-headed twenty-seven-year-old, Windham had joined the ranks of those who had made the switch from racing to freestyle. His official T-shirt, on sale at booths in the arena lobby, bore his helmeted likeness along with his moniker JAKE THE JAILER and the phrase PARDON DENIED. The nicknames derived from his $21-an-hour job as a dusk-to-dawn-shift guard at the El Dorado County Jail in Placerville, California, just outside of Sacramento, the last stop for convicted felons before they were exiled to prison. There, he said with a grin, he had seen everything from "guys who committed measly crimes to a guy who chopped up a family." By comparison, riding the ramps and risking his limbs was a fun distraction.

Windham was hunched on his yellow-framed motorcycle in the middle of Long Island's Nassau Coliseum. His fellow bikers, all part of the IFMA's annual winter series tour, whizzed by within inches of him as they warmed up. For the occasion, the main floor of the Coliseum had been converted into a massive field of soft, spongy dirt. As technicians continually wet it down to ward off the cold, dry February air seeping into the venue, the riders zipped up twelve-foot-high chain-link ramps and flew seventy feet to the landing across the arena; if the venue had been set up for a concert, they would have jumped from the stage to the back-hall floor seats. Later in the day, they would be competing for all of $2,000; the grand tour purse was $30,000. Some freestyle riders scoffed at such low prize money, but many others were happy to send in homemade videotapes of their riding and vie for the chance to be part of a national tour. Over and over, they practiced their nac-nacs, lazy boys (leaning back on the seat, legs crossed underneath the front handlebars), extensions, and seat grabs; in what amounted to a form of shotgun motivation, a point would be deducted from their score if they *didn't* do a trick while in the air. Little by little, exhaust fumes became the reigning aroma, lingering like a pungent fragrance. Hitting a landing, one of the riders fell, and Greg Thomas, the production manager, yelled, "Stay back!" to everyone around as he raced over to the hill, but the rider was fine, to everybody's relief.

Taped to the front of Windham's bike, in such a way that he could glance down at it from his seat, was a yellow piece of paper scrawled with two handwritten columns of abbreviations and acronyms: OHIA (a one-handed Indian air, or crossing one's legs during a Superman seat grab while keeping just one hand on the bars), KOD (the kiss of death), OHSG (a one-handed seat grab). Along with more familiar words like *nac* and *lazy*, these tricks would be the ones he would attempt during his run, and they constituted a list of the basic and advanced playbook for freestyle motocross, the moves every rider had to know, learn, and combine.

The only missing abbreviation was one for the backflip. Windham was asked about it, and for a moment his amiable grin vanished, replaced by a shrug and a grimace. "I'll have to do it someday," he said. "I guess. Hopefully it'll be easy. I don't know how it'll go. I'm not looking forward to it, that's for damn sure."

Ordinarily, little seemed to rattle the likes of Windham. Free-stylers were known for riding with cracked ribs or partly healed broken legs. Everyone had heard the tale of the rider who, at the X Games only a few years before, had hit the ground headfirst during a jump; to expedite the healing, doctors had had to induce a coma. But thanks to men like Metzger, the flip had finally been tamed, which meant everyone else had to master it or be left behind. For months afterward, the very thought sent a rare shiver down the spine of men whose own backs had been battered and broken but still functioned. On the one hand, the financial ramifications were considerable. Once the media had spread the word that riders had conquered the flip, the public wanted to see one for itself—or, at least, see what would happen when someone tried it—and the riders and their managers were taking full advantage of the curiosity factor. If promoters wanted Metzger do a flip at one of their events, they now had to fork over anywhere from $50,000 to $100,000, nearly ten times what he had received before, and calls from potential sponsors were making Stratton's cell phone light up incessantly. "It was amusing for him because a lot of those people had turned him down in the past, said he was over with or washed-up," the manager said. "So it's fun for him to get those calls where they'd be like, 'You're the man again.' Nothing has been the same since that first backflip."

Thanks to the flip, riders had the opportunity to earn in one or two afternoons what they made in a year of hauling their bikes from dirt course to dirt course, from large city to backwater town. And yet they knew it was the closest to a deal with the devil they had ever encountered. If they screwed up and a 250-pound cycle fell atop them, their careers, and possibly their lives, could end. For that reason, the flip had been banned from competition in Australia. "If *we* fall, we know we're going to get up and try again," said Tony Hawk of himself and his fellow skateboarders. "Try to learn a trick on a motorcycle and mess up, it's a *tragedy*." If the riders were lucky, they might be able to push the bike out of the way in time to avoid a more serious pulverizing. Either way, the odds were considerable that they would sustain one injury or another, which made even the most hardened motocrosser flinch a little. "Seeing Carey [Hart] get hurt doesn't put a good positive vibe on it, to see what can happen, you know what I mean?" said Adoptante, emitting a nervous chuckle and glancing downward. Not surprisingly, the backflip brought with it a bevy of controversies. Some discounted it as a boneheaded stunt or an invitation to a fatality; others saw it as a new learning block, just as the nac-nac had been a decade before. What no one could deny was that it had taken the sport to a different level and that, to be competitive, riders would have to attempt it, sooner much rather than later.

Nothing quite like the backflip existed in skateboarding, BMX, or the other action sports; a BMX flip, for instance, was considered a comparatively standard trick that lacked the ominous ramifications of its motocross namesake. Yet no matter the sport, the people who immersed themselves in them were inextricably linked; something about them was not normal, although that wasn't the same as not being quite *right*, either. It took a certain breed to straddle a motorcycle or stunt bike or step aboard a snowboard or skateboard—or, for that matter, climb atop a cliff or building with only a parachute and then take the next step, be it plunging down or shooting toward the clouds. To some, that next step was masochism. But after spending any amount of time with the skaters, the boarders, and the bikers, it became clear that their attraction to this world was deeply ingrained, rooted in an inborn fearlessness as well as being profoundly linked to environment and upbringing.

Those who gravitated toward these sports were not upper-middle class, not the captains of the sailing team nor the honor-society students. Most were the products of the working class, with parents who had little interest in holding them back; if anything, their guardians actively encouraged them to take on whatever sport or hobby appealed to them, no matter the risks. As luck (some of it bad) would have it, those parents did not always stay together; in the family histories of action-sports athletes, divorces and separations ran rampant, and the absence of one custodian or another only fed the children's desires to escape into their own worlds. The young men and women who emerged from these combined circumstances all were, as the *New York Times* had put it in its pro-skateboarding editorial, "classic Americana," part of an ongoing lineage of pioneers, explorers, eccentrics, and nonconformists. In a sense, the most shocking element about the rise of action sports was that it hadn't happened sooner.

Though the athletes preferred not to think or speak about their psyches and motivations, the medical establishment did. Still, surprisingly few had devised a scientific, medically sound reason—even after years of study—as to why anyone would willingly do such things without a shred of apprehension. Everyone seemed to agree that those who boarded and rode were born to do so; theirs were not skills and attributes learned in school. That determination aside, the medical theories were wide and varied. Was the motivation, for instance, purely biological and linked to dopamine? A compound secreted by the brain, dopamine was a common enough internal chemical (and neurotransmitter) responsible for, among other matters, muscle motions; it was used to treat Parkinson's disease. Unleashed during heightened experiences, dopamine told the brain that sensations from sex to shooting a basketball through a hoop to taking a potent drug were immensely pleasurable. No one had tested it on humans, but mice bred without the dopamine gene grew lethargic; those injected with it avidly explored different areas of a cage. One particular gene, the dopamine D4 receptor, responded to dopamine unusually well and sensed its presence; according to Dr. Dean Hamer of the National Institutes of Health, studies indicated "a correlation between that gene and people's extent of novelty seeking." In other words, certain people might need more dopamine to reach normal levels and therefore partook in riskier or thrill-seeking activities to generate the necessary extra compound. The need for speed, then, might be an innate, unstoppable necessity—an internal addiction over which the athletes had little control.

The academic theories ran rampant as well. Temple University professor Frank Farley, studying risk-taking in the eighties, also felt thrill-seeking was "biologically based" but avoided the dopamine connections. Instead, he concentrated on separating people into two distinct types: big Ts and little Ts (both for "thrills"). Farley described the former category as those who preferred "high risk," "novelty," "high intensity," "high conflict," and "uncertainty"; small Ts drifted toward the dreary-sounding opposites of "certainty," "predictability," "low risk," and "familiarity." Again, such traits were instinctive; according to Farley, people were born either a small or big T, with no choice in the matter. Even wider in scope was a study by University of Delaware professor Marvin Zuckerman, who broke down the new study of "sensation seeking" into four factors: heredity, "psycho-physiological phenomena," neurotransmitters in the brain receptive to such sensations, and a rush of estrogen and testosterone.

Then again, perhaps the roots of the phenomenon weren't altogether biological; maybe the culture was equally responsible. Action sports had come to mainstream fruition in the nineties, a time of peace and low risk, at least in the United States. Little in the way existed for those in all age groups to prove themselves—no wars to fight, for instance, an obsolete notion post–September 11—and the world had become a rigidly scheduled place, ruled by Palm Pilots, its days arranged to the last microsecond. Jeopardy was downplayed; everything felt more regimented. (Accordingly, work stress increased, accounting for a *Wall Street Journal* report in 2000 about tech-sector and stock-market types partaking in parachuting, white-water rafting, and mountain climbing as a form of release.) The sports— whether skateboarding, snowboarding, motocross, freestyle BMX, or tangential activities from wakeboarding to hang gliding—may not have been merely a generational trait or an indication of a hereditary gene. They may simply have been a sign of the contented times themselves.

Now it was just a matter of where it went from there and who would have enough teeth left the following morning to talk about it. The freestyle contest that had led to Metzger's double flip was merely one of three free-riding events at the X Games. Two more competitions were on the schedule, and most of the riders were expected to participate in them. Although Metzger had already won a gold medal for the Double Fritz, he knew he had to conclude with a different kind of bang. In his motor home, he mulled over his options—there seemed to be so many now that his sport was incorporating so many different tricks—until he finally made his way back into the arena, holding his daughter in one arm and a bottle of water in the other. As always, he hung with his fellow riders—and their bikes, and a bevy of chesty, midriff-bearing women—in the pit by the side of the main floor of the Spectrum Arena; there, he joked with and offered tips to the other riders, all while considering his own options.

In the second event, Step Up, riders attempted to clear a horizontal bar over thirty feet above the ground. The competition, which motocross organizers had quickly thought up as a way to entertain crowds during halftime at the new freestyle events, caught on faster than anyone had imagined. "We thought it was a goofy idea," recalled Sewell of Step Up's introduction at a freestyle demo in 1998; some riders initially resisted it as well, since the landing was hard on their legs and ankles. As simple as the trick looked, it could be hard on the body. But the audience loved the elementary thrill of watching bike and rider do a pole vault, so Step Up became part of the regimen. At the X Games, bikes began barreling toward a dirt mound fifteen feet high and shooting straight up its side. The suspense lay in the moment when the bike and rider reached the crossbar, whose first placement was twenty-six feet up. For a second, the bike seemed to freeze in the air, then both bike and rider grunted, shifted, and squirmed until, if they had calculated the jump correctly, they *just* . . . *about* . . . *cleared* the pole, sometimes by less than an inch. Those who knocked the bar down were eliminated; if they didn't already know, the sound of the emcee growling "Hit the showers!" served as a reminder. Then the bar was raised, foot by foot, until only three riders remained. Metzger was knocked out next, at thirty-three feet, and the winner, once again, was Step Up king Tommy Clowers, a quiet, stocky, baby-faced man who beat Metzger by a foot.

Then, finally, came the Big Air portion of the motocross contests. Tellingly, it was the closing event of the entire X Games. In just three short years, freestyle motocross, the sport no one had seen coming, was dominating the entire action-sports Olympics. Part of the reason lay in its theatrical tricks, which suited the large scale of an arena far better than the other sports. The other reason was crowd bloodlust; as Hart had unfortunately demonstrated the year before, no one knew when a run would end successfully and when it would be a pulse-stopping disaster.

By the six P.M. showtime, people continued to stream into the arena even though most of the seats were filled. Entering the venue, those fans might have thought for a split second they had taken a wrong turn in the parking lot and wound up at a death-metal concert. To initiate the proceedings, the lights were killed and a foghorn blew loudly; spotlights began crisscrossing the venue, and a death-march bell started clanking slowly, ominously. The throaty belch of the announcer welcomed everyone as careening speed metal engulfed the building. The sun-blanketed, late-afternoon summer day outside was nowhere to be seen or felt. Inside the darkened arena, the mood was that of doomsday, albeit one with hot-dog vendors roaming the aisles and fans holding aloft signs that read THROW ME YOUR GLOVES AND GOGGLES. The names of each of the seventeen participating riders were announced, and individually they roared up one of the dirt hills that covered the main floor. In their red, white, or yellow jumpsuits and helmets, they looked like nothing less than metallic knights. (As one ESPN employee pointed out, the fact that the bikers tattooed their own names onto their backs, necks, or arms was helpful, since their outfits made them look interchangeable.) The thousands in the arena cheered, and the riders saluted back by gunning their engines and shooting bunny-tail puffs of white smoke out of their exhaust pipes.

Big Air differed from the freestyle portion of a few days earlier in that it required just one major trick, which riders would have three attempts to nail. In some ways, it was merely a way to show how well a freestyler could do a Sterilizer or Kiss of Death, but drama lingered in the air. Pacing around the rider area was Carey Hart, preparing for his first public appearance since having broken his back the year before. He and manager Steve Astephen could be seen huddling by the side; later Astephen would admit that Hart was so scared that they almost bailed and left the arena. Then there was Metzger: Would he, or could he, top himself—and with what?

As the contest officially began, the riders screamed down the track, flew into space, and threw what they considered their flashiest trick.

Metzger (introduced as "the man who started it all!") did a backflip,
Adoptante a Sidewinder. The latter, an example of the sport's
progression, started as a can-can (in which a rider threw his leg over
the gas tank and back again), then became a Cat Walk when the rider
took his feet off and "walked" in the air, then transformed into a
Sidewinder when the rider removed his *hands*. The tricks were
completed so fast that it was difficult to appreciate their difficulty:
Only in slow motion, on television, could one ascertain what had
taken place and how monumentally difficult it must have been to,
say, take one's feet off the pedals of a motorcycle and throw one's
legs behind. When they removed their legs or arms from the vehicle,
some riders appeared to be flailing about in midair, but all managed
to get back on the bike within the seconds necessary to avoid a tragic
finale. When the bikes landed, chunks of earth blew upward, and the
soil clouds slowly settled down like dusty rain. "Let me tell you about
this guy—he's absolutely *nuts*!" barked the announcer more than
once.

Hart opted out of his first two runs, leaving some with the
impression he would bail out altogether. Finally, during the third
and final runs, he emerged, stoic and firm, and rode to the top of the
ramp. Knowing his story, the crowd hushed as much as tens of
thousands could. He adjusted his helmet, revved his engine, and
plowed down. Rumor had it that he might be gunning for a 360, but
instead, he went for a backflip, the same move that had once
debilitated him. As the crowd watched, Hart hurtled into the air,
threw his bike over his head, and this time, rode it out. While landing,
he dropped one foot from his peg, injuring himself slightly and
requiring a pair of last-minute crutches, but that pain was nothing
compared to what he had experienced before. The place erupted as
much out of relief as congratulations.

After the judges tallied their numbers, Hart moved into second
place with 94.67 points, and the pressure was on Metzger, who was

barely holding on to first with 95. Down the ramp Metzger went, his bike grunting beneath him, and once more, he went into a backflip. But as he was upside down, he and the bike quickly descending, he did something only a few would have predicted: He took both hands off the handlebars. For another few heart-killing moments, he had no control over his motorcycle as it lay atop him forty feet in the air. The move was over in seconds, long enough to miss if one looked away, but few did. "That's insane," exhaled an ESPN employee on the sidelines. It was another first; freestyle's own Comeback Kid had managed to squeak by yet again, winning his second gold medal of the games along with his large share of the $68,000 in prize money.

For the trophy ceremony, Metzger, as well as Clowers and Hart, scrambled to the top of the dirt hill he had landed on moments before. Wearing pressed blue jeans and a dress shirt, Russell Stratton stood to the side, beaming with fatherly pride as Metzger accepted his second-place Step Up medal. He'd shown the doubters, twice over. Stratton said he felt overwhelmed. "I learned to never try to stop him from doing anything," he said. "He used to do things as a reaction to something else. I made him stop and think. He learned to do something first before he tries it out." With the ceremony, the annual X Games—and what amounted to a full season for most of the sports—crashed to an end. The time to unwind was finally at hand, at least until the athletes' cell phones began tweeting with the lure of future contests, photo shoots, and video tapings, and the time to get stoked would again be at hand.

When that time arrived, at least one freestyle moto rider would opt out. Within a year of Metzger's Double Fritz, an X Games qualifying contest outside New York City found at least a half dozen riders completing backflips; only one was injured, with a sprained shoulder. By then, the flip was such old news that runs that included the maneuver elicited only brief suspense. The major innovation became the 360, wherein riders twisted and turned the bike on its side while in the midst of a backflip. With each contest, the riders sought to top themselves and each other in a particularly audacious game of truth or dare; moto injuries at the following year's X Games increased. Metzger sensed what was happening, and he decided he wanted no more part of it. Just six months after his double flip, he surprised many by declaring he would once again return to racing and reduce his freestyle appearances; an injury during a jump not long after his announcement only reinforced his decision. "It's not enjoyable when you continue to beat your body up," he said later. "Gettin' hurt's not that fun. There comes a certain time where you gotta say enough's enough and that going out and jumping bikes really isn't that fun. Getting concussions, getting knocked out—I've had enough in my lifetime. The level of doing tricks, where it is now, you're gonna get hurt, no matter what. You're gonna get knocked out and get broken bones. I still gotta do demos. It's not like I can say, 'No, I don't ever do it.' Sometimes I wish I could. But it's not realistic. I have other people in my life and business that tend to persuade me to do things I don't wanna do sometimes." He would be missed, but not for long. Ready to take his place was a gaggle of new-generation, clean-cut riders who, despite the sport's image, had procured sponsorships with the Target chain, a symbolic indication of how far the sport had come. In another sign of the mainstreaming of freestyle motocross, a moto-world insider admitted these new riders "don't want any scandal, nothing rocking the boat." Too much was at risk, and not simply body parts.

Inside the Spectrum, those events were still months in the future; it was time to concentrate on victory. On the dirt mound, Metzger grabbed a guitar-shaped trophy from ESPN's Ron Semiao and began hamming it up for the cameras, using the award to play air guitar along with the heavy metal lacerating the PA system. Once again, his tongue jutted out the side of his mouth, and his eyes bugged out; the family man was gone, and the madman was back in the house.

"He used to feel under a lot of pressure," Stratton was saying. "But he has responsibilities and a family now. He's matured."

11. EPILOGUE
the awards show, the day after

The boards were everywhere, hung side by side, one row atop the next, until they swarmed up the walls from floor to ceiling like a frenzied but disciplined horde of wooden lizards. Some, chewed up and beaten down, survived from decades past and had the roller-skate wheels and logos of defunct companies to prove it; those of more recent vintage had kicktails jutting up from each end at forty-five-degree angles. Across the room, new boards were streaking across the floors of the king-size shoebox of a building an hour north of Los Angeles. The sound the decks made was immediately recognizable and had a cadence all its own: the scrape of polyurethane wheels, followed by the *clack-clack* of a nose or tail slamming down onto the surface, then the inevitable silence as the ride came to an end, with or without the rider on board. The sound could be heard all the way out in the parking lot, and it only grew louder inside.

The ESPN Action Sports and Music Awards had wrapped up twelve hours earlier: The camera crews had departed, the lime-green carpet had been rolled up, and the seatfillers had returned to their college classes and day jobs. And yet the sports themselves did not come to a halt. They carried on in vacant parking lots, on back-country bluffs, and at places like this, a world removed from the catered postawards party that had continued into the early-morning hours of the same day. The building had once belonged to companies that made plastic trash cans and cinematic special effects, but it was now an indoor skatepark, and home to what its owners trumpeted as "the world's biggest skateboard museum." Beyond the foyer, which housed the army of old decks, were three large, open areas—totaling nearly twenty thousand square feet—of miniramps, quarter-pipes, bowls, miniature pyramids, adjustable rails, and other tools of the skate trade. Located in Simi Valley, a sprawling suburb best known as the residence of the Ronald Reagan Presidential Library and Museum, the building was neither glamorous nor easy to locate. One had to first drive past the city's expanse of ranch homes, strip malls, gas stations, and fastfood joints, then make a quick right-hand turn just before the railroad tracks and onto a slender street. There, across the street from a colorless office complex and down the road from a mobile-home park, was Skatelab.

Every week, nearly a thousand locals made the pilgrimage to the site they had heard about or seen pictured in skate magazines. These were not the professionals, the stars seen in the pages of *Transworld Skateboarding* or *Slap*, nor the ones raging the night before at the ESPN affair. These were kids like David, a fifteen-year-old from Moorpark who loved punk rock and both street and vert skating and who came to Skatelab because, as he said, the police would harass him if he tried grinding in his school's parking lot or in front of churches. Nearby was Garrett, a sixteen-year-old from Simi Valley who had been coming to Skatelab twice a week for over a year. Garrett had been introduced to skateboarding by his friends and, when asked why he enjoyed it, fell into a recitation of the no-coaches-no-practice mantra. "When I first learned to stand up on a skateboard, when I was five, it was the greatest thing," he said, taking a break on a bench, his voice a shy monotone, his brown mop of hair smushed under a scuffed helmet. His father was an auto mechanic and his mother toiled in a car dealership, yet they had both skated when they were younger; his mother had even held on to her vintage signature board of Dogtown rider Tony Alva, which Garrett had ridden a few times. His father was so supportive of Garrett's skating that he had built his son a small wooden ramp for their yard.

Garrett went through a new board every two to three months; his current model sported a Nixon sticker even though the watches were too expensive for him to afford. He liked his shoes simple and his skaters hard-core, although he said he respected the likes of Tony Hawk ("for skating that long") and had a passing interest in the X Games ("skaters need money, and it's a good way to make money"). As an extracurricular activity, he made his own skateboard videos. He was thinking about learning how to snowboard; unlike the team sports in which some of his friends participated, snowboarding felt like the next logical step.

"At first I was scared to come here," he said as the *clack-clacking* around him grew louder with each new arrival. "But the people were really nice and would say 'Go ahead' and we'd take turns. No matter what kind of skater you are, everyone's nice to each other. It's not like, 'You suck because you're different.'"

Skatelab, conceived and run by a stocky, no-nonsense type named Todd Huber, was the result of one dependency replacing another. At the dawn of the nineties, Huber, who had grown up in Simi Valley and worked in a surf shop, quit smoking. As part of his therapy, he was told to calculate how much he would have spent in a year on cigarettes and then to write down what he would have purchased had the money been in his pocket. He jotted down an early Schwinn Cruiser bicycle, but upon realizing how expensive vintage bikes were—in the thousands of dollars—he reconsidered his choice. Co-incidentally, a friend in Florida asked him to keep an eye out for old skateboards; the friend was collecting them and was always on the lookout for new additions. As a favor, Huber went to a flea market and found one, for what seemed like an outrageous sum of $20.

Instead of giving it to his friend, though, he became fascinated with the board, its shape and feel, its unknowable history. "I found that once I got it, I couldn't get rid of it," he said as he replaced the tape grip on a customer's board, a pencil behind his ear. "It was too cool. And it started from there. My friend got mad, but he understood." And unlike bikes, he said, "You can fit a *lot* of skateboards in a one-car garage."

So began Huber's obsession. On more Saturdays and Sundays than he cared to remember, he found himself awakening at four in the morning and heading for yet another street fair while his wife stayed in bed and slept. "Collecting skateboards is like fishing," he said. "You get up, pack a lunch, drive all the way to the lake, spend a lot of time looking for the stuff, and you might catch the big one, or you might get skunked." He learned how to ask "Do you have any skateboards?" in Spanish in order to get first dibs in certain neighborhoods. For his trouble, he had made a number of impressive scores, such as the time he came across an original Dogtown board for twenty bucks. "I guarantee you I can get twenty-five hundred for it," he said proudly.

Eventually, Huber amassed so many boards that he hit upon the idea of starting a museum, with an attached skatepark, in his hometown. At first he received no response from the city council, but after lobbying further and recruiting friends of friends who knew people who knew other people in the local government (as well as enlisting a high-profile partner, Scott Radinsky, then a pitcher with the Los Angeles Dodgers), Huber put his concept before the city's planning commission in October 1997. The members voted unanimously in favor of allowing Huber to build a park in an industrial area like the one he was targeting, and Huber was granted a special-use zoning permit. Two weeks later, the city council approved the project. Timing also helped: With the passage of Assembly Bill 1296 a month earlier, skateboarding had been officially declared a "hazardous recreational activity" in California. Once the law went into effect, any public park that promoted "stunt or trick" riding, as the law put it, would not be held liable in the event of injuries. Skatelab, then about 15,400 square feet, opened its doors in December 1997 and became so well regarded that the Old School Skate Jam, an annual reunion of hundreds of veterans from the sixties on, was held there.

In many other ways, history loomed large at Skatelab, especially in the museum tucked away on the second floor. There, behind glass, were over a thousand rare, collectible boards as well as some of the rotting wooden scooters that had first inspired skateboard manufacturers; two-decades-old issues of *Thrasher* were wrapped in plastic. Around the bend was another glass-protected collection of artifacts documenting skating's decades-long infiltration into pop culture: a skating Goofy on the cover of a comic book, a copy of Jan and Dean's "Sidewalk Surfin'" 45 rpm single, a Bay City Rollers board, lunch boxes and bubblegum packages with skate images, plastic Snoopy and Muppet figures on boards, and posters for every laughably inept skate movie that had been made since the seventies. The display was testament to big business's perpetual fascination with the sport—one that long predated ESPN's—and the corporations' ongoing interest in using the sport to their advantage.

Certain aspects of that tale, though, were conspicuously absent. "We could have had a Mountain Dew logo," said Huber, who was thirty-seven and wore an outfit—blue, short-sleeve shirt over a T-shirt—that made him resemble a feisty bowler. "They came in and wanted to put Dew shit everywhere, and Pepsi wanted to pay for the sign as long as we had this Pepsi ball next to it. We've turned down a lot of crap like that. We can buy our own sign. We don't need a Pepsi logo up there. Leave it for the ice rinks." No one at Pepsi could recall making such an offer, but the company did score a victory of sorts: Cans of Dew were sold in Skatelab's lone soda machine.

*   *   *

As the afternoon surrendered to early evening, the clatter of boards on ramps increased and, thanks to Skatelab's high, vaulted ceilings, made for a cacophony akin to marbles ricocheting around a tin can. One after another, skaters dropped into half-pipes, attempted to grind one of the metal rails, and barreled down ramps streaked with the scuff marks of earlier runs. The sound system pumped out rap one moment, punk the next. "It's amazing," said Phil, who had a shaved head and goatee and was taking turns carving a kidney-shaped wooden bowl. "There was a *six*-year-old shredding up here before."

The age difference intrigued Phil, who had been skating since the seventies and was now thirty-eight; his first heroes were the iconoclasts documented in *Dogtown and Z-Boys*. He also skied and snowboarded, but skating remained his principal sporting passion; it had even filtered into his profession. Phil wrote for television and film—his résumé included a stint on the envelope-pushing comedy series *In Living Color* as well as a cowriting credit on the slasher-film parody *Scary Movie*—and he had no doubt about the extent to which skateboarding had shaped his work. "Guys like Tony Alva and the Dogtown guys, they had a sensibility," he said between drop-ins. "My whole attitude—the fuck-you attitude we had in *Scary Movie* and *In Living Color*—that all came from Tony Alva and Jay Adams [the most rebellious and anticareerist of the Dogtown crew, later jailed on drug charges]. My attitude is totally informed by Tony and Jay. The reason I'm a success is because those were my heroes and their attitude was pushing the extreme and the limits." To this day, he used an Alva signature model, which he dubbed "a *man's* board."

Events like the X Games and the Action Sports and Music Awards were determined to demonstrate how these sports had been fully integrated into mainstream American culture and accepted by authority figures. But a trip to Skatelab and conversations with the likes of Phil served as a reminder that those days had not yet arrived, and that no amount of Walt Disney Company funding could completely dispel the sports' renegade roots. Two months before, Phil had tried skating in the abandoned pool of a deserted Ventura County home and, for his trouble, had been arrested for trespassing after neighbors called the police. "I spent five hours in jail with alleged drug offenders," he spit out. "The cops treated me like garbage, like a criminal. They said there were a lot of teenagers riding here and the neighbors wanted to press charges. And I said, 'Do I look like a teenager to you?' They confiscated my board for two months. They said, 'We're keeping it as evidence.' I said, 'What evidence? I confessed!' They treated me like *crap*." Just as it had been for many years, one man's canvas for expression was another's vandalism. Garrett, too, had frequently been harassed by local law enforcement. "All the time," he said, nodding. "I'll be skating home and just stop and sit down for a break because I'm tired, and they'll come over and say, 'Leave.'" Chances were that the officers had never seen an X Games contest or one of Hollywood's recent attempts to buy into the world, like the pandering comedy *Grind*. To the police, skateboarding was a nuisance, and the sooner the skaters realized it, the better.

Talk of another industrywide crash would soon return like diabolic clockwork. For the first time in a decade, the billion-dollar industry that was action sports was headed for a corrective to the massive growth it had experienced starting in the mid-nineties. At the X Games, insiders exchanged murmured, disconsolate rumors of skate-shop closings and companies on the verge of shuttering thanks to sales declines. The economic aftermath of September 11 was one reason cited; another was the widespread belief that a percentage of teenagers who had been captivated by Tony Hawk video games—and then bought all the necessary equipment to learn for themselves— quickly realized the sport was far more difficult than the games made it appear. As *Thrasher*'s Jake Phelps put it, "Skateboarding is a completely difficult thing. All it takes is one broken leg—'Shit, doesn't feel like I wanna *skate* no mo'.' It's a fuckin' *hard deal*." By requiring that retailers buy entire lines of their products rather than just specific shoes, the footwear companies would soon be left with piles of unsold merchandise. (It was also discovered that skateboard-shoe buyers purchased fewer pair a year than, say, basketball players, since they *wanted* the sneakers to look as scuffed as possible for credibility.) Again missing its goals, Vans would within a few months be forced to shutter a few of its skateparks and would see its stock value plunge. ESPN acquired rights to NBA games and, to accommodate the additional basketball programming, began relegating the bulk of its action-sports coverage to after midnight or before dawn; cheerleading, aerobics, and drag racing ate up quality time on ESPN2.

A glimmer of hope emerged with the arrival of Fuel, a twenty-four-hour cable network devoted exclusively to action sports. In two signs that larger businesses still wanted in, the Familie was purchased in 2003 by the L.A.-based Wasserman Media Group (run by Casey Wasserman, grandson of Hollywood mogul Lew), and in April 2004, Vans would be acquired by the VF Corp., home of Lee Jeans. The collective industry also took comfort in context. Previous crashes had occurred before companies like ESPN had pumped up the sports and inflated their ranks. By the twenty-first century, board and bike activities were so prevalent that, it was hoped, any drop-off in equipment and shoe sales was not likely to have the same damaging impact it had had in the past. The sports were simply too much a part of the culture—in America and, just as importantly, the rest of the world—to die off.

But that was industry talk, little of which mattered this evening. At Skatelab, there were no cameras, no award trophies, no agents scouting for talent, no potential sponsors taking notes. No matter his age, each of the skaters (and a few in-liners, much to the skaters' chagrin) was singularly absorbed in mastering a trick; as was often the case in places like this, conversation was kept to a minimum, amounting to terse, respectful nods and exchanges. "There's nothing like it," Phil said. "You can always get better. It's just you and the board. Like this guy here." He pointed to the man on the next bench, a twenty-nine-year-old male nurse who skated weekly but didn't tell his coworkers for fear they would look askance at the manner in which he put himself in harm's way. "If you have a nine-to-five job," Phil said, "you come here and you're a superstar."

For his part, Garrett said he skated "until it gets too dark or I get hurt." By ten P.M., closing time, the sun was long gone, and he knew it was time to squeeze in a few more runs to make the most of his $49 annual membership. He walked over to a long, narrow ramp, climbed up it, and began attempting a kickflip landing fakie (backward). He missed the first time. And the second time. And the third time. A fellow skater alternating with him tried the same trick and succeeded, and afterward the two slapped palms.

As the kickflips and ollies proceeded, Huber began flicking off the overhead fluorescent lights, which was sometimes the only way to get the kids to leave. One by one, they did, rolling past the front desk and nodding quickly in Huber's direction as he said good-night to each rider by name. Then Skatelab locked its doors for the evening, and Garrett and his fellow riders pushed off into the parking lot and down the asphalt lane until they were engulfed in blotty darkness. With each stride, the *clack-clack-clacking* grew dimmer. But on the way home, there would be curbs to jump, stairs or benches to grind, and other opportunities to prove they truly didn't suck because they were different—that they were good at something, that they mattered. Then they would resume the next day, and the day after, and the day after that.

bibliography

Without question, any exploration of the world of action sports must start with the spunky, invigorating media that cover it full-time. My homework for *Amped* involved spending hundreds of hours sifting through stacks of new and old issues of the core magazines: the *Transworld* empire *(Transworld Skateboarding, Transworld BMX, Transworld Motocross, Transworld Snowboarding)*, *Thrasher, Ride BMX, MX Machine, Slap, Big Brother, Snowboarder, Skateboarder, Eastern Edge, BMX Plus!,* and *Dirt Rider,* among many. Their writers, editors, and photographers chronicle this scene with a devotion, depth of knowledge, and commitment to integrity that never failed to impress me.

Among the many Web sites that cover this community, ESPN's extensive EXPN.com was a valuable source of news and data, along with the collective *Transworld* sites (www.skateboarding.com, www.transworldsnowboarding.com, and www.bmxonline.com) and the following bookmarks:

For skateboarding tricks and commentary: Clubtonyhawk.com; www.geocities.com/acemandave2000/tricks; and Dan's World (www.dansworld.com).

For BMX: Notfreestylin.com; Geoffrey Hudick's Geoff's BMX Freestyle Land (www.geocities.com/Coloseeum/8527/howto.htm); www.bmxtrix.com; BD's Freestyle BMX Zone (www.angelfire.com/

yt/bdbmx/dirt.html); the BMX Riders Organization (bmxriders.org/bro/home.cfm); and Dennis McCoy's www.bikesrule.com. For motocross: www.720ice.com/motocrosstricks.htm; www.pacefmx.com (home page of the IFMA); and freestylemtx.com. For snowboarding: www.snowboardermag.com; www.snowboarding.com, www.snowboarding-online.com, and www.fisski.com, the site of the Fédération Internationale de Ski.

Additional statistical and trick information came from the Mountain Dew collector's site (www.dewcollector.com/articles.shtml); extremewipeouts.com; www.americansportsdata.com; and www.nsga.org, the site of the National Sporting Goods Association.

Additional Source Material

Despite their widespread incorporation into the culture, action sports haven't always infiltrated mainstream media. But Sean O'Heir and Emmett Williams, my two valuable and organized researchers, did a first-rate job of unearthing the sporadic coverage of skateboarding, BMX, et al. in newspapers and magazines around the world. The following books and articles were valuable sources of information and are recommended reading for those who want to plunge deeper into the action-sports community. Of those reporters who have made this field their beat, Sal Ruibal at *USA Today* in particular needs to be singled out for his energy, estimable reporting, and insight.

Books

Baccigaluppi, John, Sonny Mayugba, and Chris Carnel, eds. *Declaration of Independents: Snowboarding, Skateboarding + Music: An Intersection of Cultures.* Chronicle, 2001.

Basich, Tina, with Kathleen Gasperini. *Pretty Good for a Girl.* HarperCollins, 2002.

Blehm, Eric, ed. *Agents of Change: The Story of DC Shoes and Its Athletes.* ReganBooks, 2002.

Brooke, Michael. *The Concrete Wave: The History of Skateboarding.* Warwick Publishing, 1999.

Cuda, Heidi Siegmund. *Warped Book: Tales of Freedom and Psychotic Ambition.* 4 fini inc. Publishing, 2002.

Earl, Robert. *X-treme Cuisine.* HarperEntertainment, 2002.

Freeman, Michael. *ESPN: The Uncensored History.* Taylor Trade Publishing, 2001.

Hart, Lowell. *The Snowboard Book: A Guide for All Boarders.* Norton, 1997.

Hawk, Tony. *Between Boardslides and Burnout: My Notes from the Road.* ReganBooks, 2002.

Hawk, Tony, with Sean Mortimer. *Hawk—Occupation: Skateboarder.* ReganBooks, 2000.

Hoffman, Mat, with Mark Lewman. *The Ride of My Life.* ReganBooks, 2002.

Howe, Neil, and William Strauss. *Millennials Rising: The Next Great Generation.* Vintage, 2000.

Howe, Susanna. *(Sick): A Cultural History of Snowboarding.* St. Martin's Griffin, 1998.

Lipsitt, Lewis P., and Leonard L. Mitnick, eds. *Self-Regulatory Behavior and Risk Taking: Causes and Consequences.* Ablex Publishing Corp., 1991.

Schapp, Dick, ed. *The Best American Sports Writing 2000.* Houghton Mifflin, 2000.

Thrasher (editors). *Insane Terrain.* Universe, 2001.

Weyland, Jocko. *The Answer Is Never: A Skateboarder's History of the World.* Grove, 2002.

Selected Noncore Newspaper and Magazine Articles

Baker, Jim. "ESPN Reaches New Low." *Boston Herald,* June 23, 1995.

Barbieri, Kelly. "Getting 'Warped': Crowds Rise for Tour." *Amusement Business,* Sept. 17, 2001.

Bitz, Karen. "The AP/Deo Market." *Household & Personal Products Industry,* March 2000.

Borden, Mark. "X-Treme Profits." *Fortune,* March 4, 2002.

Bowie, Melia. "This Camp Marks the Spot for X-Sport Enthusiasts." *Philadelphia Inquirer,* August 30, 2000.

Browne, David. "Sports Extremist." *New York Times Magazine,* May 19, 1996.

Carofano, Jennifer, and Sarah Taylor. "Balancing Act." *Footwear News,* September 16, 2002.

Carpenter, Jake Burton. "My Half-Pipe Dream Come True." *Fortune Small Business,* October 2002.

Carr, Debra. "Girl Power: Footwear Companies Are Responding to Women's Growing Participation in Extreme Sports." *Footwear News,* April 24, 2000.

Chamberlain, Tony. "Snowboarding Has Slid Easily into the Olympics." *Boston Globe*, December 7, 1995.

Cleland, Kim. "Action Sports Form Fabric of Generation." *Advertising Age*, April 16, 2001.

Collins, Glenn. "Ya-hooo! A Marketing Coup: At 50, Mountain Dew Manages to Tickle Innards of Young Men." *New York Times*, May 30, 1995.

Craig, Jack. "Brand New on ESPN2: Channel Aimed at Younger Males Will Feature Offbeat Sports." *Boston Globe*, June 8, 1993.

——————. "ESPN Takes a Chance by Going to 'Extremes.'" *Boston Globe*, June 18, 1995.

Dempsey, John. "Low-Cost 'X Games' Hitting ESPN's Target." *Daily Variety*, August 31, 2000.

Dougherty, Conor. "Corporations Seek X-Factor." *San Diego Union-Tribune*, June 27, 2003.

Dreyfuss, Ira. "Team Play Up but Overall Game Participation Down." Associated Press, October 27, 2000.

Elliott, Stuart. "The X Games: Going to Extremes in an Effort to Tap a Growing Segment of Sports." *New York Times*, June 21, 1996.

Ferguson, Tim W. "Grandpa to the Grunges." *Forbes*, February 12, 1996.

Folmar, Kate. "Council Backs Plan for Skateboard Parks." *Los Angeles Times*, October 29, 1997.

Gellene, Denise. "DC Shoes Following Giants' Steps." *Los Angeles Times*, July 26, 2000.

Gilbey, Ryan. "Just Give Me a Board and I'll Do It." *Guardian*, June 14, 2002.

Glionna, John M. "Phat, Dude! Huge Air! An Old Man at 29, Tony Hawk Still Dazzles as He Leads Skateboarding's Second Coming." *Los Angeles Times*, October 5, 1997.

Goldman, Lee. "Going to Xtremes." *Forbes*, April 3, 2000.

Greenfeld, Karl Taro. "Killer Profits in Velcro Valley." *Time*, January 25, 1999.

Heath, Rebecca Piirto. "You Can Buy a Thrill: Chasing the Ultimate Rush." *American Demographics*, June 1997.

Hiestand, Michael. "ESPN Maxes Out on Extreme Games." *USA Today*, March 2, 1995.

Higgins, Matt. "Rolling for Dollars." *Village Voice*, March 6–12, 2002.

Hochman, Paul. "The Brand Killer." *Fortune Small Business*, May 2002.

Hoover's Company Profiles. Hoover's, Inc., Austin, Texas.

Horyn, Cathy. "Snowboarding Style Grows Up and Blends In." *New York Times*, January 2, 2001.

Hymowitz, Carol. "New Economy Chiefs, Seeking Stress at Play, Find Golf Too Stodgy." *Wall Street Journal*, June 27, 2000.

Johnson, Robert. "For Heidi Lemmon, Skateboarding Is a Political Maneuver." *Wall Street Journal*, July 3, 2000.

——————. "Maintaining Rebel Appeal While Building Profit Proves a Tricky Move." *Wall Street Journal*, July 17, 2001.

Keteyian, Armen. "Chairman of the Board." *Sports Illustrated*, November 24, 1986.

Koerner, Brendan I. "Extreme Sports." *U.S. News and World Report,* June 30, 1997.

Kramer, Louise. "Just Dew It: Green Soda Poised to Pass Diet Coke." *Advertising Age,* August 23, 1999.

Kuczynski, Alex. "Hey, Mom and Dad, That's Our Sport!" *New York Times,* January 6, 2002.

Kyle, Susan B., Michael L. Nance, George W. Rutherford Jr., and Flaura K. Winston. "Skateboard-Associated Injuries: Participation-Based Estimates and Injury Characteristics." *Journal of Trauma: Injury, Infection, and Critical Care,* 2002.

Layden, Tim. "What Is This 34-Year-Old Man Doing on a Skateboard? Making Millions." *Sports Illustrated,* July 1, 2002.

Litsky, Frank. "Riding Daredevil Bicycle Ballet to Fame." *New York Times,* September 28, 1986.

Lloyd, Barbara. "Snowboarding Blazes New Trails." *New York Times,* December 14, 1995.

Marin, Rick. "Blading on Thin Ice." *Newsweek,* December 12, 1994.

Mortimer, Sean. "Times, They Are Changin'." Skateboarding.com, September 26, 2002.

"A Motor Sport Takes Off, Leaving a Trail of Broken Bones." *New York Times,* September 2, 2002.

Nelson, John. "ESPN Plans Second Sports Cable Channel." Associated Press, June 7, 1993.

Nelson, Kathleen. "Stunted Growth: St. Louis Bicyclist Is Part of 'X Games' Generation." *St. Louis Post-Dispatch,* June 20, 1997.

Nord, Thomas. "The Next Big Thing in Extreme: FMX Is Riding High." *Courier-Journal* (Louisville, KY), September 27, 2002.

Perry, Susan. "Freestylin': Teenagers Have Wheel Fun 'Tweaking That Undertaker' to the Beat of the Beastie Boys." *Los Angeles Times,* July 30, 1987.

Petrecca, Laura. "Going to Extremes." *Advertising Age,* July 24, 2000.

Price, Wayne T. "In-Line Skating on a Roll." *USA Today,* August 24, 1993.

Raymond, Joan. "Going to Extremes." *American Demographics,* June 2002.

"Recreation Market Report." Sporting Goods Manufacturers Association, May 2002.

Romero, Elena. "The Kings of Zoo York," *Daily News Record,* March 26, 2001.

Rosenberg, Debra. "All Aboard." *Newsweek,* February 9, 1998.

Ruibal, Sal. "Chairman of the Skateboard." *USA Today,* March 9, 2000.

——————————. "X Games Roll from the Edge to the Burbs." *USA Today,* August 17, 2001.

——————————. "X Games vs. Olympics." *USA Today,* January 17, 2002.

Sabedra, Darren. "Stunt Bicyclist Wins Over Tough Critics—His Parents." *San Jose Mercury News,* July 2, 1999.

Seidenberg, Rob. "'Boarding Breaks the Big Time." *Ski,* November 1987.

——————————. "Shreddin' USA." *Ski Buyer's Guide,* 1989.

Sherrill, Stephen. "How to Backflip a Motorcycle." *New York Times,* April 8, 2001.

Sinker, Daniel. "Extreme Exploitation." *Punk Planet*, November/December 1999.

"Skateboarding, a National Pastime." *New York Times*, August 17, 2002.

St. John, Allen. "I'm on the Olympic Team? Bummer!" *New York Times Magazine*, January 27, 2002.

Thomas, Pete. "The X Factor." *Los Angeles Times*, June 19, 1996.

Thompson, Stephanie. "Tony Hawk Gains Clout as Pitchman." *Advertising Age*, February 17, 2003.

Tkacik, Maureen. "As Extreme Goes Mass, Nike Nips at Skate-Shoe Icon." *Wall Street Journal*, April 24, 2002.

——————. "The Worlds of Extreme Sports and Hip-Hop Are Hangin' Together." *Wall Street Journal*, August 9, 2001.

Van Biema, David. "Look, Ma! No Feet, No Fanny, No Road." *People*, May 26, 1986.

Verducci, Tom. "Baseball Beware." *Sports Illustrated*, August 26, 2002.

Walker, Caroline, with Jeanne Gordon. "Boarding's Year of the Woman." *Newsweek*, December 19, 1994.

Wheatley, Tom. "Leading Spokesman." *St. Louis Post-Dispatch*, June 27, 1996.

Whelan, David. "Who's the Child?" *American Demographics*, August 2001.

Wilner, Richard. "Extreme Sports Stocks Deliver Extreme Returns." *New York Post*, April 15, 2001.

Wilson, Stephen. "Snowboarding Approved for 1998 Games." Associated Press, December 5, 1995.

Wong, Edward. "Clark Starts with Pain and Ends Up with Gold." *New York Times*, February 11, 2002.

——————. "Riders Keep Looking for More Air Time." *New York Times*, February 10, 2002.

acknowledgments

This book would not have been possible without the professional and amateur athletes, executives, gear and shoe makers, video directors and producers, store owners, camp managers, marketers, journalists, photographers, skatepark operators, and industry analysts who were interviewed for it and are quoted herein. For taking the time to patiently explain themselves, their motivations, and their community to an outsider, I can't thank them enough; each person enriched my understanding in manifold ways. Thanks to them, I now know the number of spokes on a BMX bike, the nuances of skate-shoe design, and the breakdowns of more tricks than I could have imagined, to name just a few of their contributions.

In addition to those quoted, my thanks for information, pointers, advice, contacts, and transportation to Jerry Badders, Karen Bakos, Peter Bonventre, Michael Brooke, Jennifer Carr, Sonja Marie Catalano, Ray Chelstowski, Chris Conrad, Peggy Cozans, Jenn Davis, Tim Dixon, Sonny Fleming, Josh Friedberg, Brian Gass, Jim Guerinot, Mary Huhn, Albert Kim, Wook Kim, Bob Klein, Michael Klingensmith, David Kushner, Edward Levy and Adventures Northeast, Kevin McAvoy, Dave Morris, Noah Robischon, Liz Ronan, Rob Seidenberg, Phil Shalala, Steve Shure, Taylor Steele, and Larry Stevenson.

The enormity of the action-sports world was often overwhelming. So, for helping to point me in the right directions and easing my transition into it, thanks to Shelby Meade; Sarah Hall and Eda Kalkay at Sarah Hall Productions; Josh Krulewitz, Ian Votteri, Amy Lupo, and Melissa Gullotti at ESPN; Lhotse Merriam; Ryh-Ming Poon at Activision; Leigh Ault and Sandy Yusen at Burton; Caroline Andrew at Missy Farren & Associates; Ivy Balnarine at Chelsea Piers; Sally Murdoch at DC; Joel Silverman at Blades; Connie Coutellier at the American Camping Association; Dora Radwick at the NPD Group; Sara Finmann; Kim Peterson; Scot Burns and Jack Smith at VAS Entertainment; Jeremy Kent and Jamie Redmond at Fuse; Cheryl Lynch; Dave Dececco at Pepsi; Roy Elvove at BBDO; Kristine Ashton at MSO; Christopher Dauer at the Strategic Research Institute; Margo Zinberg at Nickelodeon; Meredith Cammaker at Bragman Nyman Cafarelli; Terry Hardy and Lisa Kidd at SLAM/Rebel Waltz; Heidi Ann-Noel at Girlie Action; Juan Casas at the Mars Group; Kristine Ambrose; Chris Overholser at Vans; Chris Carlance, Joey Ream, and the staff of Woodward Camp; Eric Friedman at Mad River Glen; Zaynab Behzadnia; Juliann Fritz at the U.S. Ski and Snowboard Association; Susan Stanley at Wells Fargo; Heather Gould at HarperCollins; and last but far from least, Ben at the Enterprise Car Rental in Lewistown, Pennsylvania.

As always, my agents, Sarah Chalfant and Jin Auh, and everyone else at the Wylie Agency, had my back from the start. Karen Rinaldi, Colin Dickerman, and Mike Jones at Bloomsbury took on the project enthusiastically and without a moment's hesitation, for which I thank them immensely. Panio Gianopoulos was a sharp, scrupulous editor, and Greg Villepique and Marisa Pagano helped keep everything on track. Thanks to Rick Tetzeli, John McAlley, and Jim Seymore at *Entertainment Weekly* for permission to wander from the front lines. Sonia Chamen helped keep the home in order during the writing. As always, love to Maggie and my family for their support—especially my daughter, Maeve, who always managed to barge into the office at just the right moment with an extreme smile to erase any and all creative frustrations.

A NOTE ON THE AUTHOR

David Browne is the music critic for *Entertainment Weekly* and author of *Dream Brother: The Lives and Music of Jeff and Tim Buckley* (2001), which was a finalist for the Ralph J. Gleason Music Book Awards. A former reporter for the New York *Daily News*, he has also written for the *New York Times, Sports Illustrated, Rolling Stone, New York, Mojo*, and other publications. In 1996, he received a Music Journalism Award for excellence in criticism. He lives in Manhattan, where he can occasionally be spotted kayaking or skateboarding.

A NOTE ON THE TYPE

The text of this book is set in Linotype Sabon, named after the type founder, Jacques Sabon. It was designed by Jan Tschichold and jointly developed by Linotype, Monotype, and Stempel, in response to a need for a typeface to be available in identical form for mechanical hot metal composition and hand composition using foundry type.

Tschichold based his design for Sabon roman on a font engraved by Garamond, and Sabon italic on a font by Granjon. It was first used in 1966 and has proved an enduring modern classic.